Great Spirits

Great Spirits

Portraits of Life-Changing World Music Artists

Randall Grass

UNIVERSITY PRESS OF MISSISSIPPI   JACKSON

www.upress.state.ms.us

The University Press of Mississippi is a member of the Association of American University Presses.

Copyright © 2009 by Randall Grass

All rights reserved

Manufactured in the United States of America

First printing 2009

Library of Congress Cataloging-in-Publication Data

Grass, Randall.
    Great spirits : portraits of life-changing world music artists / Randall Grass.
        p. cm.
    Includes bibliographical references.
    ISBN 978-1-60473-239-9 (cloth : alk. paper) — ISBN 978-1-60473-240-5 (pbk : alk. paper) 1. Musicians—Biography. I. Title.
    ML385.G82 2009
    780.92'2—dc22
    [B]   2008053000

British Library Cataloging-in-Publication Data available

Contents

Acknowledgments

My heartfelt thanks go to the many people who helped make this book a reality: Shirley, the love of my life, for her general wonderfulness as well as her support during the writing process; my parents, for giving me the opportunity to pursue my ambitions; James McBride, who pushed me to finally write this book and who gave generously of his time and advice; David Freeland, for helping me make the connection with the University Press and otherwise advising me; Craig Gill, for seeing a way that my vision for this book might work and giving me the opportunity to refine it; Tim Hayes, for his friendship and insight; Craig Anderson, for his friendship and our many talks about our mutual writing ambitions; Richard Nevins, for sharing his wisdom and knowledge; Phyllis Saretta, without whose generous assistance the Nadia Gamal chapter could not have been written; Ibrahim "Bobby" Farrah, for his generosity and time sharing his great knowledge of Middle Eastern dance; Vivian "Yabby You" Jackson, for his time and insight; Joan Higgins, Patrick Lafayette, and Mikey Thompson, for sharing their insights about Augustus Pablo; David Nathan, Roger Steffens, and Peter Guralnick, for their encouragement and suggestions at crucial moments; Andrea Deagon and Neil "The Mad Professor" Fraser, for their reminiscences of Nadia Gamal and Augustus Pablo respectively; Peter Simon, Adrian Boot, David Corio, and Richard Horsey, for their generosity in making their photographs available; Simone, for allowing me to share her mother, Nina Simone's, poetry with the readers of this book; Greg Espy, for his help in connecting with Simone; Tom Jenkins of Enterplanetary Koncepts, for his gracious help with Sun Ra materials; Rikki Stein and Francis Kertekian, for their help with Fela lyrics; Mark Fried of Spirit Music, for graciously authorizing use of Bob Marley lyrics; Daniel Peters of Hal Leonard; the late, great Timothy White, for his inspirational example and conversations with me about writing; Sandy Fleishman and Martha McAteer, for their great proofreading work; Shamira, for her inspirational dancing; and all the great musical artists who have shared their creations with the world!

Invocation

We were perhaps forty miles north of Kabul, Afghanistan—myself, my friend John, and two Swedes—laboring up a rutted track over a rocky hillside in our battered little Citroën 2CV. As we pulled into a motley village of baked-mud dwellings, most of the population of the village—young and old, male and female, human and animal—surged toward us. At that time (1972), few foreigners visited that modest settlement perched half a mile off the main road running from Kabul to the Hindu Kush. As we lurched to a stop we were immediately surrounded; people gawked at the four of us and our strange-looking bundles inside the car. One item immediately captured their attention: the acoustic guitar, wedged behind the passenger seat and clearly visible through the side window. People pointed at the guitar and grinned. As I opened the door and emerged, I pulled the guitar out. It had lost a couple of strings since I had bought it in a Tehran bazaar, but I knew I could still get some music out of it. I began picking out some notes, imitating the scale of music I had heard in Afghanistan. Broad, astonished smiles of recognition broke out on people's faces and they began clapping in time to the rhythm of my playing. One boy about twelve years old began to dance, moving his head from side to side in a characteristically sinuous dance move which I had seen many times in Hindi films. Our welcome in the village was assured.

Music has opened countless doors for me in my wanderings around the world. It is easy to take music for granted, to forget what a powerful thing it can be. Music has a way of ineffably penetrating our hearts and minds and souls. Perhaps, then, it should not be surprising that the most recent theory concocted to explain the universe is string theory, which posits that the smallest, irreducible element at the core of any piece of matter is a single, vibrating "string." In other words, according to this theory, music is the essence of the universe: the cosmos is one massive symphony of vibrations and waves pulsating at myriad frequencies, tempos, and rhythms—an idea at least as old as the "music of the spheres." We are made of music! Some researchers say that an affinity for music is hard-wired into the brain, just as a capacity for language seems to be. The capacity of humans to relate to music may be simply an innate means for people to comprehend and connect with the cosmos at the most profound level. Nina Simone took this idea one step further; for her, as she once expressed in an interview, music is God.

Some music is regarded as transforming. You often hear someone say that hearing the music of a certain artist was a life-changing experience, as in "hearing the music of Bob Marley changed my life." What does such a statement mean exactly? The implication is that the music in question delivered more than a gorgeous melody, a memorable lyric, or irresistible rhythm—though those things can be transporting enough in themselves. Something about the music changed the listener's perception of the world. Maybe it unlocked emotions that had been unexpressed. Perhaps it portrayed a unique world of beauty that was new to the listener. Possibly it enabled the listener to transcend the limitations of his or her own psyche and connect with spiritual currents or a larger human essence.

This book is about life-changing musical artists— artists who intended their art to bring their audience to a heightened state, to act as a bridge to a higher consciousness. Often these artists have taken on a larger-than-life persona. Their impact can be seen in many ways. More than a million people—some say five million!—attended the funeral of Egyptian singer Om Khaltoum, whose weekly radio broadcasts were heard throughout much of the Arab world. Likewise an estimated one million people turned out for the funeral of Afrobeat icon Fela Anikulapo-Kuti. The day after the assassination of Dr. Martin Luther King Jr., a concert by James Brown was widely credited with preventing a riot in Boston. The premiere of Igor Stravinsky's *The Rite of Spring* provoked riots. John Lennon's ironic comment that the Beatles were more popular than Jesus may have been true. The music of Bob Marley and Peter Tosh helped inspire revolutions in southern Africa. Such artists made music at the highest level and in the process changed people's lives.

The artists in this book are "great spirits," the kind you cannot forget after even one encounter. All of them changed the world in ways great or small. Some are celebrated worldwide; others are known only to a relatively small group of devotees. In each case, I remember the first electrifying moment I encountered their musical art. Inevitably, I was propelled on a journey, a pilgrimage you might say, that led me to the creator of the music. It can be a complicated moment when you come face to face with someone who has touched your heart, fired your spirit, or enlarged your mind. At that point you must reconcile the person behind the art; you may understand the price paid by those who see things others do not see, give voice to things others cannot express, or give their hearts too completely to a fickle world. In every instance, I found the person behind the music to be as remarkable as the music they made.

So here are portraits of some "great spirits" I have personally encountered in one way or another. Artists such as Bob Marley and the Neville Brothers I came to know in a journalistic capacity, though I have known many in their extended families and networks. Others, such as Fela Anikulapo-Kuti, Augustus Pablo, and Yabby You, I came to know on a personal level, both as a fan and in a business context. In the case of Nina Simone, my personal encounter came when I arranged for her to do a performance in a Philadelphia club. With Nadia Gamal, my encounter consisted of witnessing her sole performance in the United States. Sun Ra, on the other hand, was my neighbor for twelve years.

In these portraits, my goal is not to provide a comprehensive overview of the artist's life or art. The life stories of some of these artists—Bob Marley, Fela, Sun Ra, and Nina Simone—have been told elsewhere. My hope is that through these portraits you will encounter these artists as I did and come to see what made them life-changing. My intention, especially with the better-known artists, is to give a personalized view, perhaps illuminating some aspect of personality or artistry that has been overlooked. If, after reading one of these portraits, you are inspired to listen to the artists' music—whether for the first time or anew—then I will have accomplished my prime goal.

No doubt some will find my inclusion of Nadia Gamal, a dancer, to be quixotic. But a great dancer is a musical artist whose instrument happens to be his or her body. Nadia Gamal truly was a "great spirit," as well as a musical artist of the highest order, one who inspired awe in those who encountered her. Yet she is hardly known outside of the Middle East and Middle Eastern dance circles, an injustice I felt needed to be corrected.

We live in a time when music surrounds us, emanating from radios, televisions, computers, iPods, CD players, restaurants, shops, and nightclubs. A great percentage of this music is mundane and random in its significance, even numbing to a degree—the musical equivalent of junk food. The proportion of music that truly affects people on some important level is probably smaller than ever before. Much wonderful music is still being made but it is harder to hear amidst the tidal wave of dross, what the great jazz singer Betty Carter dubbed "sheet rock music" because it is slapped together mechanically like drywall on a house. It is worth noting that all of the artists included here have either passed away or are of advanced age. This may reflect my personal vintage or it may indicate, as some suggest, that fewer musical giants have emerged during the past twenty-five years. Do the likes of Bono, Tupac Shakur, Lucky Dube, Youssou N'Dour, or Wynton Marsalis, to cite a random list of artists who have had worldwide impact since 1980, compare favorably to the "great spirits" in this book? Or, moving forward, what about the likes of Erykah Badu, Luciano, Angelique Kidjo, or Shakira? I leave the question open. In the meantime, I hope these portraits are a reminder of what music can be at its highest level. The artists I portray created musical art that truly mattered, that changed lives and, in some cases, made history. I celebrate them for that and hope you will be inspired to do the same. As Nadia Gamal often said: "always, remember the music!"

Great Spirits

Nina Simone, photo © David Corio, www.davidcorio.com

Nina Simone

The High Priestess of Soul

Montreux, Switzerland, 1976: On a darkened stage the shadowy figures of musicians waited; there was an anticipatory hush from the audience.

"Ladies and gentlemen," a voice intoned, "the High Priestess of Soul, Miss Nina Simone."

There was a swell of applause but no discernible movement on stage. The lights remained dim. At last, Nina Simone strode out, threading her way through the musicians and instruments until she reached the front of the stage. She was wearing a simple black evening dress, no earrings, her hair short and "natural," unwrapped. She dipped into a low bow that she held for a thirty-second eternity, rising with a severe, set expression as she critically surveyed the audience. Her expression was that of a grade-school teacher who has been away and has received bad reports about her students. She waited until there was complete silence. As always, Nina Simone was sussing out the audience, making up her mind whether those in attendance were worthy of her performance. She had been known to walk out if she found the audience below her standards of attentiveness or respect.

Without speaking, she abruptly turned and sat herself in front of the grand piano. Suddenly she spoke, frowning slightly.

"Do you hear all those other noises?"

Evidently the microphones were picking up some random sounds. It was a delicate moment. After all, what could be more annoying to an artist than persistent buzzing sounds when the person was trying to perform? A fit of temper seemed likely, even expected, at that point.

"Oh, it's better . . ." she said. She tested her microphone. "Hello?"

"Hello?" someone from the audience echoed. This moment of irrepressible humanity blindsided her, punctured her mask, tickled her. She let her head fall forward, tilting it slightly to the side, and chuckled.

"I haven't seen you since a very long time, since 1968, because I said I wasn't going to do any more jazz festivals. And that's still true!"

With that, she began to play, starting with delicate fugue-like fili-grees on the piano, a baroque version of "Little Girl Blue," one of her first recordings. She sang softly and tenderly, turning a poignant, sen-timental ballad into a haunting experience. At the end she played off the song's lyric "you're not on your own" by interpolating the repeated phrase "umoja! umoja!" the Swahili word for unity, and finished with an orchestral flourish of fanfares that built to a climax.

As rapturous applause washed over her, she abruptly stood up by the piano, like a concert pianist.

Resuming her seat at the piano, she said, "You didn't forget me, did you?"

There was a pause and she turned toward the audience with a mock threatening look: "I didn't *expect* you to!"[1]

Philadelphia 1979: In a small nightclub I waited for Nina Simone. I was not the only one. A club full of people was waiting for her. They were restless, but I was consumed with anxiety. After all, I was the one responsible for all those people packing Stars nightclub to see her. I was the one who had said she would show up. And now it seemed very foolish of me to have confidently stated that a legendarily mercurial artist whom I had never met and had only spoken to a few times by telephone would indeed come to that spot to perform on that night in Philadelphia. What had I been thinking? You could say a glimpse of a certain kind of beauty led me there.

Nina Simone was not conventionally beautiful. Some propose that overtly African features and a dark complexion automatically and unjustly put her in an "unpretty" category, given the Eurocen-tric standards of the United States, the country of her birth. My own experience living and traveling in Africa suggests that she would not necessarily be considered a great beauty there either. Yet her face was fascinating, irresistible . . . beautiful. Her beauty was not placid; it was dynamic, the roiling of a great spirit, an awesome beauty that was the result of some combination of her physical features and the animation of her spirit. Nina Simone was the most beautiful "unpretty" woman I have ever seen.

I was captivated by her beauty the moment I saw her face in the mid-sixties, staring at me from numerous LPs in the record racks of a local record retailer. Thanks to an early hit and major label recording contracts, her many albums were very much in the public eye. She gazed out from the album jackets, rarely smiling, her posture and features suggesting great melancholy and yet great strength. Her slightly puffy cheeks camouflaged regal cheekbones. Dark eyebrows arched over fierce, dark eyes, then plunged down to the bridge of her nose, giving her face a constant hint of a scowl. Voluptuous lips met in dismissive, downward intersection with her face. It was a radical contrast to the showbiz smiles and overtly sexy poses of most pop and jazz chanteuses of that time. Her appearance often suggested a lonely woman looking out her window at a cold, rainy day; sometimes it suggested something else—but always it was portentous. Who was she? She had the look of somebody important.

That look and mood were present from her first album. In that album's cover photograph, Nina is sitting on a park bench along a river lined by autumnal woods. Her head is tilted disconsolately down, propped up by her right arm. Her pose suggests that she had just been evicted from her apartment or perhaps just lost the love of her life. The title of the album was *Little Girl Blue*. The sub title read "Jazz as Played in an Exclusive Side Street Club," an enticing bit of marketing for the would-be hipster, the Playboy "man about town," for whom jazz at the time was an accouterment of sophistication. The date on the album was 1958.

Little Girl Blue opens with a version of Duke Ellington's "Mood Indigo." The sound is that of a standard jazz trio—bass, drums, and piano—and the groove has a buoyant swing. But as Nina begins to sing the mood is immediately and decisively altered by the sound of her voice, a smoky, bittersweet contralto with a built-in blue note and quavering vibrato. She often hits the notes sideways, with an exotic tonality, something that flowed in and around the demarcations of the Western scale. The sound of her voice is like her face—dark, brooding, and strong. A couple of tracks later, a loping, descending bass line and an emphatic, preemptory piano chord from Nina, set the stage for a sassy, exuberant "My Baby Just Cares for Me." A few tracks further on, Nina sings the opening arpeggio of the song that would assure her an audience forty years after its release: "I Loves You Porgy" from the Gershwin opera *Porgy and Bess*. She was hardly the first to do the song—indeed she had learned it from a Billie Holiday recording—but anyone who sang it after her had to reckon with her interpretation. She inhabits the song, makes it more than one woman's plaintive lament, makes it an anthem for human powerlessness. In its original context in the opera, the song conveys a woman's despair that the man she loves is unable to protect her from a stronger man who wants her. But, given the history of African Americans, it resonates on a larger level, recalling the powerlessness and humiliation suffered by black men and women, first under slavery and later under the segregated, subjugated reality that lasted until the triumphs of the civil rights movement, triumphs that were yet to come when Nina recorded the tune. In that reality, a man was often unable to protect his woman. Nina conveys the anguish, longing, and frantic despair of the situation so persuasively that she touches her listeners on the most elemental human level. It was a massive hit. Over the years, her audiences would greet the opening notes of "I Loves You Porgy" with such joyous affirmation that I had to wonder if the song's celebrity had overshadowed its meaning. For me, applause is the last thing the song invites. Tears maybe, somber silence perhaps. Most of all it invites a prayer that the vast cruelty of human beings could be vanquished. Perhaps for some in Nina's audiences it was easier to celebrate the song than to give themselves over to its pain. Or maybe there is a kind of relief in their applause, a sense that the pain and sadness it conveys is of the past.

If "I Loves You Porgy" had been the only highlight of *Little Girl Blue*, it still would have been an auspicious debut. The album is essentially a set list of songs she had been playing as a fledgling nightclub performer, although the nightclub she had started out playing in was far from exclusive. But there are a myriad of special moments on the album. Nina's piano playing, for instance, often interpolates a classical motif in the midst of a jazzy groove. The lyrical range of the songs, and Nina's ability to turn even a love song into a larger statement about the human condition, constantly reach for something deeper. And always there was that smoky, earthy, bittersweet voice. Nonetheless the album, and the kinds of venues she was playing pigeonholed her as a jazz singer, the first of many misappropriations of Nina's talent by the record business and the media.

Her first major television appearance, on the *Ed Sullivan Show*, was notable for the authenticity and uniqueness of her performance. Seated at the piano, she superficially looked the part of jazz chanteuse—her hair permed and cut short, her eyes set off by mascara, and wearing an elegant patterned brocade evening gown fitted out with spaghetti straps and sashes draped from each side down her back. She first played a very classically oriented version of "Love Me or Leave Me" and then delivered an unusual version of "I Loves You Porgy" that sounded nothing like the recorded version. In the middle of the song she stopped playing for a moment and sang a cappella: "Someday, someday . . . I know he's coming for me; it's going to be like dying." She then played an instrumental piano interlude filled with arpeggios and rumbling rolls. At the end, she stood up, smiled, and bowed her head slightly.

Nina was a prolific recording artist, so even in the early sixties there were quite a few Nina Simone albums in the racks. The range of her material started out wide and soon was pushing the boundaries of what could be considered popular music. Though she did not record many of her own compositions, some of her songs were as much a snapshot of their time as any of Bob Dylan's songs. "Mississippi Goddam," for instance was a cry of pain, a howl of rage. She lashed out the title phrase like a whip cracking. Written in 1963, in the wake of the murders of Medgar Evers in Mississippi and of four young black girls in an Alabama church bombing, it gathered up a boiling-over frustration in the hearts of African Americans—"We ain't gonna take no more!"—that two years later erupted in "Burn, baby, burn" with the Watts riots. It is hard to think of any song in the realm of popular music up to that time that was such a direct, naked eruption of anger. It was ultimately the most honest and righteous response to inhuman acts of pure evil.

And then there was her song "Four Women." Where "Mississippi Goddam" was a straightforward rant, "Four Women" was a conjuring of spirits—the spirits of African American women across four centuries of suffering. Each verse was the story of a woman, an archetype defined first and foremost by her complexion and hair texture. Speaking openly of these truths was a revolutionary act. Nina laid out in direct fashion the ways in which each woman's identity and life had been determined for them by society on the basis of their complexion, hair quality, sex, and race. Each vignette is haunted by the specter of rape. She presents them in turn—the mulatto "Siffonia," whose appearance is an emblem of the rape that created her; the dark, strong "Aunt Sarah," who, uncomplaining, carries the burdens and abuse of many upon her back; the alluring "Sweet Thing," who uses sex as her passport to get by; and the angry, defiant "Peaches," who lashes out like a wounded lioness. It is perhaps unsurprising that Nina Simone became the first popular African American entertainer to wear her hair "natural." This simple act was considered daring and controversial in the sixties, indicative of the truth of the issues she raised in "Four Women."

On her *High Priestess Of Soul*, the front cover illustration depicts a woman in profile—it apparently is intended to be Nina—wearing an Egyptian headdress in the manner of Egyptian royalty. By the time she had recorded this album, nearly a decade after her debut, her musical palette encompassed jazz, classical, gospel, blues, folk music from many cultures, rock 'n' roll, French *chanson*, Brecht-Weill, popular song, and more. She composed contemporary spirituals such as "Take Me to the Water" and hypnotic African-inflected chants such as "I'm Gonna Leave You." She delivers a jazzy romp with "The Work Song" and even does a version of rock 'n' roller Chuck Berry's "Brown-Eyed Handsome Man," making it an explicit anthem to swaggering cool black manhood. In every piece she molded the song in the crucible of her fiery spirit, infusing each one with the most elemental emotions. By the time of *High Priestess Of Soul*, Nina had become an icon, one of a handful of musical artists at the swirling vortex of social and political forces who encapsulated the zeitgeist of the times and transmuted it into truth-telling and inspiration.

Philadelphia, 1968: It was a long, hot summer in 1968. Martin Luther King Jr. was assassinated in April and riots had exploded in cities across the nation. The apostle of nonviolence had been shot down in cold blood. In that instant, Dr. King's big dream and millions of individual dreams were extinguished. In June Bobby Kennedy was assassinated. During the Democratic convention in Chicago, mass protests were met with what was later described as a police riot; Americans watched on television as police chased, beat, and gassed protesters. The nation teetered on a precipice. Nina Simone was playing a concert in Philadelphia, part of a summer concert series sponsored by Schmidt's beer. For the admission price of one dollar, you could see a triple bill featuring a top local act and two headline artists. On the night Nina appeared, the stadium was packed with a mostly black crowd for an impressive triple bill of the Delfonics, Nina Simone, and Ray Charles. There was a huge video screen at the back of the stage projecting close-up shots of the performers.

"You know Dr. Martin Luther King was killed of course . . ." Nina intoned. "This is in his memory."

She began to play the song that her bass player had written the very day he had heard the news of Dr. King's murder, just in time for Nina and the band to perform it three days later at a Westbury, New York concert: "Why? (The King of Love is Dead)."

She began singing in a deceptively languorous, whispery way:

What's going to happen now . . . in all of our cities?
My people are rising; they're living in lies . . .
Even if they have to die . . . at that moment they know what life is
If you have to die, it's all right.
'Cause you know what life is
You know what freedom is for one moment of your life
Folks, you'd better stop and think
Everybody knows we're on the brink
What will happen now that that the King of Love is dead?[2]

On the big screen, the closeup of her face was hypnotic. She was reaching deep within herself, and a burning aura emanated from her, somehow reminiscent of the glowing end of a cigarette at the moment when a breath is drawn, the ashes fall away, and the glowing fire intensifies.

Then she began to sing more deliberately, coming down harder on each syllable, gathering momentum as the bass drum began to beat a slow march.

But he had seen the mountaintop

And he knew he could not stop
Always living with the threat of death ahead
Hate was not his way
He was not a viii . . . o . . . lent man
Tell me folks if you can
Why he was shot down the other day![3]

She whispered "mountaintop," as though it were a secret vision. She squeezed out the word "violent," stretching it as her tone turned raw and raspy, encapsulating the intensity and destructiveness of the word's meaning. When she sang the word "shot" it rang out sharp and hard like a gunshot. You felt the violence of that gunshot, the shocking, contemptible violence of an unprovoked blow smashing a wholly benign human being.

And then her grief turned to rage, a rage that had been building since that moment when she was eleven years old and had been hit full force by the consciousness of racism that had enveloped her since birth. That rage had reached a peak in 1963 when a period of optimism engendered by President Kennedy's announcement of a civil rights initiative had been shattered by cataclysmic events: the murder of NAACP field secretary Medgar Evers in Mississippi and the Birmingham church bombing that had left four little girls dead. And now, in the wake of Dr. King's death, there was no limit to her rage.

"I've never been a pacifist," she had said on more than one occasion. "I had it in mind to go out and kill someone. I tried to make a zip gun. My husband told me, 'Nina, you don't know anything about killing. The only thing you got is music.'"[4]

So Nina made her artistic mission a dedication to fighting her people's battles with music as her weapon. In New York, she had met many key thinkers of the Movement: James Baldwin, Leroi Jones (later known as Amiri Baraka), Stokely Carmichael, and most crucially, Lorraine Hansberry, whose *Raisin in the Sun* had been the first Broadway hit by an African American playwright. She threw herself totally into her mission. Some concert promoters were put off by her "militancy" and some of her audiences became uneasy during her shows. She was not simply delivering entertainment, if indeed she had ever been; now, she was singing uncomfortable truths.

Nothing embodies her transformation more than "Mississippi Goddam," one of the strangest, angriest, most ironically bitter songs ever created. Her 1964 concert recording of the tune begins with her announcement: "The name of this tune is Mississippi God-*damn*! And I mean every word of it!" The audience laughs nervously. The musical backing she and the band play is a jaunty, bouncy, music-hall kind of setting that belies the caustic, often horrific, lyrics:

Hound dogs on my trail
Schoolchildren sitting in jail
Black cats cross my path
I think every day's gonna be my last[5]

At one point she intones over the vamp, "This is a show tune . . . but the show hasn't been written for it yet." In truth, the song's title says it all; the rest is mere explication, brilliant though it may be. Despite all the hand-wringing over the Jim Crow South by those with a conscience, no one on the national stage up until then had dared to be so emotionally honest about the reality of the situation. The only authentic response to the events in Mississippi in 1963 was a curse—one that Nina Simone had the courage to utter loudly and repeatedly. Copies of the recording, broken in half, were returned by Southern record distributors.[6]

As a result of this song and others, Nina was a frequent performer at civil rights rallies, marches, and similar events in both the South and the North.

"Her music was more than powerful," civil rights activist Stanley Wise recalled in *The Legend*, a documentary about Nina's life, "and it was more than just music. It was a philosophy and a belief that despite all of these problems we will get through this. And not only will we get through this, we will survive and triumph."[7]

Nina herself remembers such appearances as peak experiences in her life. "It was dangerous," she recalled. "We encountered many people who were after our hides. I was excited by it, though, because I felt more alive then than I do now because I was needed, could sing something to help my people, and that became the mainstay of my life, the most important thing."[8]

It was a source of great pride to Nina that her recordings were considered prized possessions by those on the front lines of the civil rights struggle. Yet she was acutely aware that she could be killed at any time for being black, female, and outspoken. But there was no hesitation in her; she threw herself wholeheartedly into the cause.

Durham, N.C., 1971: At Duke University in 1971, Nina performed a concert sponsored by the Black Students Association. In the three years since Dr. King's assassination, an undeclared war had been waged by the United States government against political activists of all types. Demonstrators had been shot at Kent State University and South Carolina State University; what was later described as a police riot at the Democratic convention in Chicago had resulted in numerous injuries to demonstrators as well as bystanders; Black Panther Party officer Fred Hampton had been murdered in cold blood in Chicago. And these events were merely the tip of the iceberg, as similar but less publicized events were occurring frequently across the nation; these provided the atmosphere of danger and incipient violence that was the backdrop for Nina's Durham concert.

Though open to the public, the concert was intended to be a communion between the black students and Nina—a state-of-the-black-nation séance led by Nina. She prowled the stage in front of the black audience members seated in rows arranged in front of her. A scattering of white folk sat up in the bleachers on either side; it was oddly reminiscent of the old rock 'n' roll shows in the segregated South where the white portion of the audience was seated either upstairs or down on the floor, and the black portion of the audience was in the opposite area. Dressed in a colorful African-print maxi-dress and head wrap, she preached to the multitude of young black folk in front of her as Afro-Caribbean percussion maintained an oscillating pulse behind her. Her tone was that of a teacher remonstrating with wayward pupils.

Her message was simple: "Don't turn the other cheek! Get a gun! Be ready to use the guns to shoot the white people before they shoot you!" As she chanted her prescriptions in a low, insistent, hypnotic voice, she began to dance. Her movements were African, her body bent toward the earth, her head turned slightly to one side as if listening for a vibration, her hips undulating gently, and her arms waving gracefully in the air. At that point in her life she had only been to Africa once, briefly, but she had met Nigerian drummer Olatunji in Harlem and witnessed his percussion-and-dance troupe. Her tremendous ability to assimilate the emotional and spiritual essence from anything she encountered enabled her to internalize elements of African dance. So, although her dance was not any specific African dance, it conveyed an African essence. She drew her audience into her dance, into her vision, into her truth, and people began to shout and clap; even the white members of her audience, from their perches in the peanut gallery, were moved to applaud her call to arms against people like themselves. Such was the power of Nina Simone in performance.

Tryon, North Carolina, 1930s: In order to understand Nina Simone, you have to travel back in time, to a specific time and place—to her birthplace in Tryon in the thirties. In this somewhat remote North Carolina mountain town, with its oddly cosmopolitan element devolving from its popularity as a vacation spot, the future Nina Simone was born Eunice Waymon in 1933. The twin vises of segregation and the Depression circumscribed her formative years. Yet her entrepreneurial ex-musician father and preacher mother each set an example of achievement in the face of these limitations.

Nina began to play the organ virtually from the time she could walk. According to her mother she was spontaneously playing hymns by age three, a miraculous manifestation that her mother regarded as a gift from God. Soon Nina was accompanying her mother to various churches, playing the piano at services. The supercharged atmosphere of the Holiness churches, especially, had a profound effect on Nina; church music was the vehicle to transform people, to enable them to reach exalted states through mesmerizing rhythms, soaring melodies and intense devotional spirit. Church was the cauldron and first pillar of her musical development. The transformational nature of her live performances years later was rooted in the collective ecstasy of church worship. As Nina grew older, she was also shaped by the more earthly appeal of the blues that she heard randomly around her.

Young Eunice was such a prodigy that her mother's white employer, for whom she worked as a domestic, offered to pay for classical piano lessons for her. As it happened, an accomplished piano teacher, an English woman married to a Russian painter named Massinovitch, resided in Tryon, and at age seven Eunice began formal piano studies. She was immediately captivated by the splendid logic and formal beauty of Bach. The discipline of classical training and the elegance of classical forms became the second great pillar of her psyche. Her mother wanted her to become the nation's first black female concert pianist, as did her white patron. Confirming her devotion to this path was the close relationship young Eunice formed with her piano teacher, whom young Eunice called Miss Mazzy. The teacher's genuine affection for and interest in the child gave Eunice emotional support and affirmation that was often missing from her mother who, since her ordination as a minister, was often away from home. The long hours of practice forged a close bond between Eunice and the woman she called her "white mother."[9]

Soon the town was talking about "the little colored girl" who could play classical piano, referring to her as "Mrs. Massinovitch's little colored girl."[10] To help her continue her studies, members of the community established the Eunice Waymon Fund. Though there was a patronizing element in their attitude toward her, it was nonetheless a unique initiative that afforded Eunice a highly unusual opportunity.

However, the specter of racism was never far away. When she was eleven, Eunice was about to commence a recital for her benefactors when she saw that her parents had been removed from their front-row seats to make room for some white patrons. Her parents had then been seated in the rear of the auditorium. Eunice stood up and stated to the assembled audience that she would not play unless her family was seated up front. They duly were seated in the front row. The incident crystallized for her the racism that was all around her but that she had accepted as normal. As she has stated in her autobiography, she never saw the world the same way after that incident.[11] It was telling that even as an eleven-year-old she had the courage to confront the issue in what had to be a highly charged situation. This experience of racism and her deep-rooted anger when confronted by it became a third pillar of her formative experience.

Aside from her innate musical talents, Eunice was an excellent student. She wrote poetry that was precocious to say the least, as evidenced by a poem that she wrote at age twelve that was later reproduced on her album *Here Comes the Sun*:

All music is what awakens within us
When we are reminded by the instruments
It is not the violins or the clarinets
It is not the beating of the drums
Nor the score of the baritone singing
His sweet romanza; nor that of the men's chorus
Nor that of the women's chorus
It is nearer and farther than they.[12]

The Eunice Waymon Fund paid for her to attend a private Methodist-run secondary school for African American girls, located fifty miles away in Asheville, so that she could prepare to apply to a conservatory of music. There, she was a straight-A student and valedictorian, an achievement all the more notable considering that she was devoting five or more hours a day to piano practice throughout her secondary school years.

At age fourteen, Eunice—who was beginning to "feel like a freak," as she noted in her biography,[13] because she was the only one of her circle of girlfriends who did not have a boyfriend—met the love of her life, Edney Whiteside, a boy her age of mixed African American and Cherokee blood. It was mutual love at first sight, but when she was away at school the relationship was difficult to maintain. Nonetheless, it continued, with both of their families anticipating that they would marry. When they both turned seventeen and Eunice graduated, she was offered a scholarship to the Julliard School of Music. Edney made it clear that if she left for New York, he would marry someone else. It was a wrenching choice, but, for Eunice, the collective weight of her mother's dreams, Miss Mazzy's plans, the expectations of the community, and her own investment of ten years working toward that goal were too much for her to resist. She went to New York and Edney ended up marrying her best friend. It was a loss that permanently marked her. As one who loved fiercely and deeply, the pain of love lost and the need for love became a fourth crucial element of her character. Indeed loneliness became a recurring theme in her life.

Many years later, when she and Edney were both in their sixties, they were reunited for a visit during the making of *The Legend*. It was the first time they had seen each other in decades. The camera captures them as they sit in the back of a car, being taken on a drive. They sit close, holding hands. Edney, an amiable-looking, fine-featured light-skinned African American man with glasses, sits with his arm around Nina, a benevolent smile on his face. Nina looks distraught and torn. She moves her mouth as if to speak but hesitated. She sings along a bit to a melancholy ballad playing on the car's sound system; it is one of her songs.

"That's my music, too," she murmurs absentmindedly. Suddenly her face collapses and tears stream from her eyes. She dabs at them with a white handkerchief. Edney steals a glance at her and then looks out the window.

"I don't know what life is supposed to be anymore," Nina says, staring mournfully straight ahead. "When you don't have anybody at home, it doesn't mean much."

"Well . . . ," Edney begins, searching for some word of comfort. "You've got your daughter."

He has taken Nina's hand in both of his hands.

"I don't see her often," Nina objects. "She's singing now, she's got a career . . . I saw her yesterday. I have a grandchild I've never seen . . . seven years old! I have sacrificed my whole life to do songs for this race of mine!"

"Well," Edney says, "that's what you wanted. . . ."

"It *isn't* what I wanted," Nina interjects, turning to look directly at him.

"And you were successful . . ." Edney continues, trying to comfort her or perhaps ward off some uncomfortable truth.

"It was what Miss Mazzy wanted for me, she and Mama," Nina says. "They made up their minds what I was supposed to do!"

Edney turns away to look out the window, as though unable to cope with her unspoken accusation.

"You wanted me to stay here. . . ." Nina says.

"Well, I didn't exactly want you to stay *here*," Edney says, patting her hand and grasping it more tightly. He smiles helplessly at her. "It is what I said yesterday . . . things just . . . (he shrugs) . . . stray apart."

He caresses her hand.

"But we're still alive!" Nina exclaims, her voice rising.

"Yeah," he said, nodding, his eyes closing momentarily.

"We're not dead yet!" Nina says, looking at him intently.

"No," he murmurs. "But we have different lives now."[14]

Another pivotal experience in Nina's life was her rejection by the Curtis Institute in Philadelphia. Such a rejection would be deeply disappointing to anybody who had spent the better part of their life dedicating themselves to the goal of being a concert pianist. But in Nina's case, it was shattering because in addition to the normal disappointment there was the feeling that she had let down the community that had sponsored her years of lessons as well as her mother who had dreamed that she would become the first black female concert pianist.

"It was as if all the promises made to me by God, my family, and my community had been broken and I had been lied to all my life," she wrote in *I Put a Spell on You*.[15]

Then came the suggestion that the rejection may not have occurred simply because she "wasn't good enough" but because she was black. Her brother Carol, who was living in Philadelphia at the time, heard from various people that while the Curtis Institute was open to having a black student, it did not want to establish the precedent with a "poor, unknown black girl."[16] Wracked by uncertainty, Nina came to believe this. In the *Legend* documentary, Vladimir Sokhaloff, a member of the Curtis faculty with whom Nina studied, stated definitively that racism did not play a role in the decision.[17]

"It had nothing to do with her color or background," he says. "She wasn't accepted because there were others that were better. She had talent . . . oh, not genius, but she had great talent. And I accepted her (as a private student) on the basis of her talent and the understanding that I would prepare her for an audition at Curtis. It was during the early period that she demonstrated her ability to play jazz. I remember distinctly telling her: 'Why don't you pursue this?' And she said, 'Oh no, my first love is classical music and I want to be a pianist.'"

As Nina noted in her autobiography, the terrible thing about such discrimination is that you really do not know for sure to what extent racism is the problem or one's abilities are the problem.[18] Sokhaloff himself might not have been sensitive to the subtleties of racial discrimination operating at the Curtis Institute. His suggestion that Nina pursue jazz may have been sincere or may have been a reflection of a subtle racial attitude of his own. In any case, her rejection from Curtis solidified her feelings about racism.

Atlantic City, 1954: At The Midtown Bar and Grill, a dive a couple blocks off the boardwalk, Nina Simone was born. Knowing that her mother would disapprove of her performing in a nightclub but needing the money, Eunice came up with the performing name of "Nina Simone"—Nina, a name she had been called by a Hispanic boyfriend, and Simone, the first name of actress Simone Signoret. Nina walked into the Midtown as though about to make her professional performance debut at Carnegie Hall, dressed in a long chiffon gown, hair styled, and impeccably made up. She gave a seven-hour concert for an audience of barflies, improvising a mix of popular song, classical music, gospel, and jazz. Between sets she sat at the bar, drinking milk. The owner liked her playing just fine but told her if she wanted to keep the gig she would have to sing. Since she needed the money, the next night she threw impromptu vocals into the mix. It is safe to say that her performances were totally unlike anything being presented in any other nightclub. In *I Put a Spell on You*, she says she played one song for three hours, constantly improvising and embellishing.[19] She began to develop a reputation that spread by word of mouth, and the clientele of the Midtown morphed from barflies to music fans. Soon, offers to perform in Philadelphia and New York nightclubs came in. Yet Nina had never intended to become a nightclub performer and did not consider herself a singer. The money she earned helped her continue pursuing her dream of becoming a concert pianist.

That dream was realized with her breakthrough concert at New York City's Town Hall in 1959. She was thrilled to be playing in a venue that had none of the distractions of a nightclub, a place where the audience had come for one reason only—to hear her perform. She wore a long white gown, with a drape over one shoulder and white satin shoes. Accompanied only by drummer Tootie Heath and bassist Jimmy Bond, Nina delivered a tour-de-force performance of a diverse set of impeccably selected material transformed by her into something highly personal. She began the concert with a haunting version of the folk song "Black Is the Color of My True Love's Hair," starting with an impressionistic classical motif, then singing almost a cappella with very deliberate, almost meditative phrasing, until the song built to a climax.

She then kicked into a swinging jazz number, "Exactly Like You," very much in the vein of "My Baby Just Cares for Me." Her highly moving version of "The Other Woman" demonstrated Nina's uncanny ability to bring to the fore songs that had been overlooked gems. At the same time, she showed at the Town Hall concert that she was equally likely to take the most familiar material, such as "Summertime," "Fine and Mellow," or the melodramatic film theme "Wild Is the Wind,", and create an original experience. It is notable that at her New York concert debut, out of fewer than twelve selections on the program, she chose to perform two original instrumentals, the blues "Under the Lowest" and an Afro-Cuban number, "Return Home," which she introduced by remarking slyly: "We're all out in the jungle right now . . . and we're going to see what happens when we're out there."[20]

Four years later she performed at Carnegie Hall and was deeply gratified that both her parents and Miss Mazzy were in the audience. It was the closest she had come to achieving what they had envisioned for her. Though Miss Mazzy and her father both expressed their pride in her, her mother said nothing. She was evidently still not willing to endorse her daughter's secular career.

With Nina Simone the question always arises: What sort of artist is she? Although she utilized elements of classical and baroque music, she clearly was not a classical artist, though she sometimes referred to her music as "black classical music." She drew on too many different musical strands and combined them far too spontaneously to be categorized as a classical artist. In the beginning of her career she was marketed as a jazz artist, the most convenient way to pigeonhole a black female singer/pianist who wore gowns and played in nightclubs, often accompanied by a small combo. She emerged at a time when jazz was an accouterment of sophisticates or would-be sophisticates who might have an abstract painting on their wall and Miles Davis on their turntable. (Indeed, many jazz albums of the era had abstract paintings on their covers.) Nina herself explicitly rejected the "jazz artist" label, considering it to be a stereotypical identification of a black artist. While it is true that she or her musicians sometimes took improvised solos, jazz is ultimately a spontaneous exploration of the various musical possibilities of a given composition, and that was not the essence of her artistry. Rather she explored the emotional and spiritual possibilities of a composition or, more to the point, she used a piece of music as a vehicle to achieve heightened emotional or spiritual states.

When asked to identify herself artistically, Nina often declared: "I'm a folk artist." It is an apt description. She drew on all the music she heard, including much traditional material. This led to an astonishingly broad repertoire. Her earliest musical experiences involved gospel music, blues, and rhythm 'n' blues, which she heard and absorbed as part of her daily life. So it was completely natural for her to play a song such as "Wade in the Water" or sing a blues. But she also played traditional songs such as "Cotton-Eyed Joe" and "Black Is the Color of My True Love's Hair." Her version of "House of the Rising Sun" predated those of Bob Dylan and the Animals. It is obvious that her sojourn on the Greenwich Village scene in the early sixties, keyed by her frequent performances at the Village Gate, put her in touch with the many cutting-edge personages from the jazz scene and the progressive black thinkers. But the Village was also the epicenter of the new folk movement, with everyone from Bob Dylan to the Clancy Brothers performing regularly in Village clubs, so she was exposed to a diverse folk repertoire as well as to emerging singer-songwriters. She also drew on popular song—both standards and hits of the rock era such as the Bee Gees' 'I Can't See Nobody," the Beatles' "Here Comes the Sun," Bob Dylan's "Just Like a Woman," and even seemingly slight pop confections such as "Everyone's Gone to the Moon." As early as 1961 she was playing African material such as "Zumbi," Israeli folk songs, and songs drawn from French artists such as Jacques Brel. She had an extraordinary ability to take a song from any source and shape it into a unique, personal, and usually deeply moving expression. As such, she was probably the foremost interpreter of song of her time. Every performance she gave was unique, and many were radically different—in song selection, dynamics, and mood—from any other performance she had given.

She also composed, not in great quantity but often quite meaningfully. "Young, Gifted, and Black," co-written by Nina with Lorraine Hansberry, became an anthem for African American empowerment. "Four Women," "Mississippi Goddam," and "Backlash Blues," with lyrics by her friend, poet Langston Hughes, were all powerful statements about racism. "Nobody's Fault but Mine" and the sexy "I Want a Little Sugar in My Bowl" touch on love, sex, and romance in a way that harks back to classic blues and jazz styles so effectively that some assume they were simply standards that she was covering. "Come Ye" is an African-inflected, chantlike spiritual composition. Out of the hundreds of songs she recorded, just over thirty are original compositions; yet the quality quotient is high, begging the question as to why she did not write more.

The essence of Nina Simone as a performer goes beyond an explanation of repertoire or style. She titled her autobiography *I Put a Spell on You* for a very specific reason. The song, a powerful, more serious version of Screaming Jay Hawkins's original, is an exact description of her performance strategy—which was to cast a spell on her audience and transport them to another reality. This goes a long way in explaining why her relationship with her audience was so important to her. It was not simply diva-ish behavior. In order to do what she intended to do, she needed the audience members' attention and she needed to be in tune with them. Part of her preparation for concert performances involved going to the venue earlier in the day, to size up the room, sense the atmosphere, and evaluate the ways the layout of the venue would affect the audience. What she perceived determined which songs she chose to perform later, choices she rarely made until she went onstage or just before. As a person with extraordinary sensitivity, she felt even small fluctuations in the people around her. Thus audience members who might be restive or unresponsive affected her strongly and interfered with the mood she was trying to create. At Montreux, as she began playing a song, an audience member apparently stood up, possibly to go to the restroom. She immediately stopped playing and snapped, "Hey you . . . sit down!" There was a nervous titter in the audience, which was perhaps hoping she was joking. Evidently the guilty party, no doubt frozen in shock, had not sat down. "Sit down!" Nina commanded again. She would not resume until the person had taken a seat. Other times she might say to the audience, "Don't push me, don't push me, we'll get there," if she felt its expectations too keenly. On other occasions she complimented the crowd, saying, for instance, "You're such a nice, mellow audience, I can really appreciate it."

"I had a technique and I used it," she explained in *I Put a Spell on You*. "To cast a spell over the audience I would start with a song to create a certain mood which I carried into the next song and then on through into the third, until I created a certain climax of feeling and by then they would be hypnotized. It was always an uncanny moment. It was as if there was a bigger power source somewhere that we all plugged into and the bigger the audience the easier it was—as if each person supplied a certain amount of the power.

"These moments are very difficult for a performer to explain. It's like being transported in church; something descends upon you and you are gone, taken away by a spirit that is outside of you."[21]

It is telling that Nina compared the heightened effect of her concerts to transcendent moments of church worship. She herself often attained a trancelike state when she performed. Thus it was particularly apt that she became known as the High Priestess of Soul. This appellation may have originated with the release of her *High Priestess of Soul* album in 1967, shortly after Aretha Franklin's breakthrough as "The Queen of Soul." The record company may have thought of it as a way to position her in the music market. But it was very appropriate as a description of what she did. Though she was not a soul music artist per se, her musical performances tapped the souls of her audience and, like a priestess leading worshippers, she drew them into a heightened state.

Philadelphia 1979: At Stars nightclub, the audience was becoming irritable. It was a small club, holding perhaps 300 people, and was packed to capacity for a rare appearance by Nina Simone. The problem was that it was near to the time that she was scheduled to go on and she had not even arrived yet. There had been an opening act—a comic—but he had decided to do a set laced with racial humor for a racially mixed crowd that was not in the mood to hear it. People began heckling the comic. Instead of using the hecklers' comments as grist for his mill, the comic snapped an epithet and walked off. So, at that point there was no opening act and, as yet, no Nina. People began stomping their feet and clapping a demand for what they had paid for. During this period of her life, Nina's concerts had become more unpredictable. Often she kept her audience waiting for an hour or more. Other times she would walk offstage after three numbers, sometimes returning to play in response to the fervent, somewhat desperate applause that was driven by the thought—what if she doesn't come back? It had become almost a cat-and-mouse game between her and the audience.

Knowing all this, I nevertheless had arranged for her to be booked into Stars. I had been talking to a radio colleague, a gospel radio host who also worked for a local concert promoter; he had happened to mention that Nina was in somewhat difficult straits, out of money and no longer with her husband and manager, Andy Stroud. It is a double blow to be simultaneously without the linchpin of both one's domestic life and one's professional life; complicating the matter was a huge debt to the IRS, due to poor handling of her taxes. She and Andy had split up in 1972, but she soon found the task of managing herself overwhelming, which contributed to some of the problems attendant to her concerts. When Andy offered to resume management of her affairs in the late seventies, she had accepted, noting later that "he was a bad husband but a good manager."[22] But that arrangement had not lasted long and so once again she was without manager, husband, or money and was living in a small apartment in Philadelphia. As evidence of her desperation, she had asked my colleague, whom she had just met, if he would be her manager. He was stunned. As he told me later, "I nearly dropped on the floor! I was not a promoter and certainly had no experience being a manager!" He concluded by telling me that Nina was thinking of playing a show at Dino's Lounge, a small club in West Philadelphia, in order to raise some badly needed cash. I was amazed to hear this. While Dino's Lounge was a decent enough place and had historically booked some prominent jazz artists, by 1979 it was only intermittently presenting live music and was functioning just a step or two above a neighborhood bar. It did not seem right that Nina Simone, accustomed to playing major concert halls, would have to play a rare Philadelphia show there. I knew the booker for Stars, a relatively new club that had emerged as a prime showcase venue and had a much better media profile. I asked my acquaintance if he thought Nina would like to play there. He thought she would and gave me her number.

I called the number and Nina picked up, her familiar contralto forming a very tentative "Hello?" I explained why I was calling, and naturally she sounded very hesitant, not knowing who I was. But when I mentioned that the club would guarantee $3,000 for one show, a sizable sum at the time for a small club, she quickly said she would play it. At that point, all signs of tentativeness disappeared and she began listing her requirements: a certain type of piano bench, a limousine to transport her, flowers in the dressing room, a bottle of champagne, and so on. I had heard that she believed it was necessary to act like a star in order to ensure decent treatment, so her demands did not really surprise me. The nightclub's booker promised to accommodate her every wish. Foolishly, I assumed everything would be fine.

At Stars, the crowd was making mutinous noises. Many in the audience were well aware of Nina's idiosyncrasies, and no doubt there was a real fear that she would not show. From the start it had seemed almost too good to be true that she would make a rare Philadelphia appearance at such a small club. Another thirty minutes passed before word came that Nina's limousine had arrived. Moments later, Nina herself, in a splendiferous white gown, swept into the club, and headed directly for the stage. Amazingly, the crowd greeted her with a standing ovation, which brought a smile to her face. She sat down at the piano, adjusted the microphone, and a hush descended on the crowd in anticipation. Nina turned her head to the audience and asked, "Do you love me?" It was a question she often asked her audiences at one point or another, but here it seemed particularly unnecessary considering the rapturous welcome she had just received despite having kept everyone waiting and not having played even one note. Could it really be that she was so needy of emotional affirmation? Or was this just part of her game with the audience? In any case, the crowd erupted into applause again and someone shouted out "We love you, Nina!" and she beamed again. Then she launched into the opening chords of "I Loves You Porgy." Bathed in love, with her audience close around her in the small club, she gave an intimate, personal performance, just herself and the piano.

Between songs, she talked about her African identity but also about her love of Switzerland. She spoke with a bizarre accent that seemed half French, half African, or perhaps that of an African living in France. It was an interesting juxtaposition—her deep identification with Africa as her spiritual home and her deep-rooted love of the European classical tradition and countries such as Switzerland, France, and Holland that had accepted and celebrated her. They were her refuge as she became estranged from the United States due to her bitterness at American racism. Part of her had become European and another part of her African. Ultimately her performance at Stars was wonderfully relaxed and personal. She played a good long set. The audience demanded three encores, which she accommodated.

After the show I went backstage. Nina was surrounded by admirers in the cramped backstage area. I approached, intending to introduce myself. As I came into her field of vision, she looked at me with a penetrating look, as though she knew who I was. She smiled. Nina's smile was a wondrous thing, the sudden radiance of the sun breaking through storm clouds.

"Well, you see, it turned out all right, didn't it?" she said. But before I could say anything, another fan caught her attention. Her relationship with her fans was very important to her. Even after an intense performance that left her drenched in sweat, she would spend an hour greeting well-wishers backstage.

There were sides of Nina the public rarely saw. Often, what people saw and heard was her imperiousness, her seriousness, her anger, her eruptions. Interviewers often were confronted by a reserved or cold or very formal Nina—until, that is, she saw that you understood some things about her and were serious yourself. Then she would open up.

Paris, France, 1990: Nina is backstage in the midst of a sound check at a concert venue.

"I guess I am a little capricious," she says to the interviewer, during the making the documentary film of her life. In the film her comment is juxtaposed with a recording of her reading the riot act to the concert promoter: "You better bring all those *contracts!*" she is heard shouting, "or I'm going to *kill* your fucking concert! I know you're rich, you son of a bitch!"[23]

Later, Nina, standing on the street next to a lamppost, smoking a cigarette, is asked if she is angry. At first she denies it.

"No, I don't think I'm angry." Then she catches herself. "I am very emotional . . . if I don't like something I say something immediately, so people would say I have a hot temper."[24]

There were many dimensions to her anger. For one thing, she often had good reason to be angry. First, there was the racism of the country she was born in, which was destructive to her people and had been a direct threat to her personally. Anger at U.S. racism led her to live abroad for much of her life after 1972. There was also her husband, who in a drunken rage had beaten her on the night of their engagement. Although he did not repeat that physical abuse, she found their relationship abusive in other ways. He habitually wrote on a blackboard in their kitchen such statements as: "Nina will be a rich black bitch by 1965."[25] Though he was devoted to her in his role as manager and endured some abusive behavior from her in turn, she felt he pushed her to the point of exhaustion in pursuit of the goals he set for her. She also felt the abuses suffered by so many artists—seeing bootlegs of her recordings for sale in Europe, watching other artists have hits with her own compositions, and, of course, not seeing much in the way of royalties from her record companies.

But Nina could also erupt in anger at seemingly minor irritations, and, being a highly sensitive, all-or-nothing personality, she could see red over a small irritation or offense. An unlucky fan who approached her at the wrong moment could be on the receiving end of hostility. For instance, Art D'Lugoff, owner of the Village Gate, recounts in *The Legend* an incident when an unsuspecting female fan approached Nina at his club and asked her to autograph an album, only to have her snap "Is that all you want?"[26] At one point she alienated both David Nathan and his sister Sylvia, who over a couple of decades had formed a close relationship with her and had worked devotedly to promote her in England through the fan club they had established there. In their book, *Nina Simone: Break Down and Let It All Hang Out*, Sylvia describes an episode when Nina telephoned her at 4:00 a.m. to demand that Sylvia round up some fans and bring them over. "Where are my fans?" she had raged in a manner suggestive of Gloria Swanson in *Sunset Boulevard*.[27] For someone who professed not to enjoy the showbiz aspect of performing, Nina placed a surprising emphasis on having her fans show up to see her outside of the performance venue. When Sylvia objected to the request, given the hour, Nina blasted her with withering anger.

And, most significantly, she did not speak to her father during the last several years of his life because she had overheard him telling her brother things that she knew were not true. She was shattered by hearing her father, whom she loved more than any man in the world and whom she had never known to lie, say something untruthful about an important issue. The only way she could deal with her hurt and feelings of betrayal was to not speak to him. She did not attend his funeral.

Another dimension to Nina's anger was the undeniable fact that on occasion she indulged in self-oriented, diva-like behavior. Most telling, though, is the one component of the "angry" Nina Simone that was not publicly known, namely that she suffered from a chemical imbalance that in the absence of medication could result in severe depression and outbursts of rage.[28]

Often her seemingly hostile or severe attitude was a defensive action, the first line of defense for an essentially shy, emotionally vulnerable person who, based on both her experiences and her own insecurities, found it difficult to trust others. Those whom she did trust got to see the person behind the formidable public mask.

Tryon, North Carolina, 1989: Nina had not been in her hometown for twenty years. She had stayed away from the United States because it was the locus of too much pain. As she arrived in her old neighborhood, people she had not seen in years came out to greet her. She hugged one after another, saying: "Goodness gracious, so good to see you!" She walked up to the house she had lived in as a child and said, "It brings back so many memories . . . I don't know how I'm going to stand it. I feel like killing myself."[29]

Then she visited her father's grave, staring down at the simple marker embedded in the earth. "It was my father who had a sense of humor," she mused, "It was my father who I could lean on all the time." Tears began streaming down her face. Though he had died years before, the devastation she felt from his death was still with her. Perhaps she was allowing herself to truly confront it for the first time. "He meant more to me than any man in the world," she said, sobbing like a child. "I wish he was here right now!"[30]

Later she visited her mother who, at ninety years of age, was still vibrant. With her daughter, Lisa, by her side, Nina banged out gospel songs on the piano as she, her mother, and her daughter sang together. Her joy in the simple pleasures of family was evident. She smiled and her smile swept away the melancholy that seemed so to often cloud her public face. At that point, the down-to-earth, wickedly funny, even sensual Nina Simone, the one who took pleasure in bantering with friends or family and just having a good old Southern time, was revealed.

"I wasn't able to raise Lisa well," she later said regretfully. The reunion had brought home to her what she had sacrificed. "I think I can make up for it."

"I made a world for myself, just like Jimmy Baldwin said," she reflected in *I Put a Spell on You*, "and the best thing of all is that I'm still happy to live in it after all these years. Right now I'm as happy as I could be without a husband to love . . . looking back over a life which . . . I have no regrets about. Plenty of mistakes, some bad days and, most resonant of all, years of joy, hard but joyous, fighting for the rights of my brothers and sisters everywhere; America, Africa, all over the world, years where pleasure and pain were mixed together. I knew then, and still do, that the happiness I felt, and still feel, as we moved forward together was of a kind that very few people ever experience."[31] This statement seems a little too pat, perhaps a little forced, a nice tidy ending to her autobiography. But those who love and admire her hope it is true.

Paris, France, 1990: Nina sat at a grand piano on a large, tiled veranda, bounded by the huge marble columns of an imposing manse. She was resplendent in an orange-and-yellow African *boubou* and head wrap. Arranged around her was a chamber ensemble—six string players and a harpist, all in formal attire. Seated on chairs on the stone patio in front of her was a small gathering of guests, also in formal attire. She played the "Fantasy Overture" from Tchaikovsky's *Romeo and Juliet*, accompanied faultlessly by the chamber orchestra, performing as the concert pianist she had always wanted to be. She was claiming the European classical tradition she had embraced from an early age, but she was doing so on her own terms, clad in African garments, an emblem of her true spiritual identity. The scene was a felicitous unification of two streams of her identity.

Nina Simone, as a person and as an artist, was able to draw on the deepest wells of human experience and transport her listeners to higher realms. As such, she was a psychic alchemist who, instead of transmuting lead into gold, transformed her listeners' psyches. For those who were open to her art, she was capable of anything.

"Who am I?" Nina asked. "I am the reincarnation of an Egyptian queen!"[32]

She has also said that, for her, music is God. "I know what God is," she told an interviewer in 1985. "I do not believe in any particular denomination. I know that ritual is necessary and whatever people need, they should do it. I do need the solitude, the quiet and I often do meditation. I'll go to any church but I will not get to the point where it dominates my thinking. Music is my God. The structure, the cleanliness, the tone, the nuances, the implications, the silences, the dynamics . . . the *pianissimo*, the *fortissimo*, all having to do with sound and music. It is as close to God as I know."[33]

Sun Ra, photo © David Corio, www.davidcorio.com

Sun Ra

Composer from Saturn

On a hot, humid day in the summer of 1979, the scruffy block of Morton Street in the Germantown section of Philadelphia was uncharacteristically empty. The relentless heat had driven everyone, even the children and dogs, indoors. Silent stone row homes lined one side of the block; a tangle of trees, shrubs and weeds dominated the other side. One house in particular, #5626, drew the eye, though at first glance its appearance was identical to the others. Unlike the others, though, its big casement windows seemed opaque. It was hard to tell what was covering them but whatever it was, it did not resemble curtains or blinds. Also, if you looked closely enough, you could see some whimsical swirls of pink paint on the door trim. The house seemed to emanate a brooding, portentous atmosphere. It was easy to get the impression that there was something unusual about it.

Appearances can be deceiving, and perceptions are easily influenced by what we know or what we think we know. I had known about the occupants of 5626 for nearly a decade, yet only recently had I learned that their residence was in such close proximity to my own. It was surprising to find them in such a prosaic setting. You see, Sun Ra, who lived there with a number of his followers, claimed to be from outer space. He was a musician who had gained notoriety as one of the world's most unique and prolific jazz artists, albeit one whose music was strange, oddly compelling to some yet very disturbing to others. People who heard his music were either repelled by its discomfiting harmonics or entranced by its uniquely subversive character. Some embraced it as a revelation.

The musical impact of Sun Ra was only part of the story. Sun Ra intended his music to be a bridge to an alternate reality; and he and his musicians talked, dressed, and behaved in a way that set themselves apart from most people. That made his presence especially incongruous on that scuffling, run-down block of a poor neighborhood in a city that has often seemed more a conglomeration of numerous small villages than a single cosmopolitan city. His presence there was a mystery, one of many mysterious aspects of Sun Ra, not the least of which was his seemingly dead-serious assertion that he had not been born on Planet Earth. His mission was nothing less than the salvation of humanity.

Sun Ra had not been at home that day. Perhaps it was the day that he stood in the Egyptian Room of the Philadelphia Museum of Art a few miles southwest of Morton Street. Standing amongst Egyptian statuary, most notably a bronze sphinx, he made a declaration to the cameras of filmmaker Robert Mugge. Gazing dreamily upward, his head tilted back slightly, a half-suppressed, knowing smile playing at the corners of his mouth, he recited one of his poems:

They say history repeats itself
But history is his story
You haven't heard my story
My story is different than his story
My story is a mystery
My story is not a part of history
Because history repeats itself
Nature never repeats itself
Every sunset is different
Why should I have to repeat myself?
Those of this reality have lost their way
Now they have to listen to what myth has to say[1]

Though the museum was only a few miles from Morton Street, it was another world. Most of the residents of Morton Street had never been there. Yet Sun Ra was as comfortable there as he was on Morton Street. His neighbors were only somewhat aware of his accomplishments. Though most knew that he and his band members traveled to Europe, they generally did not know the extent of his worldwide following. To many of them, Sun Ra and his musicians were a novelty, people who often wore futuristic or African-style clothes, and talked about space and played strange music. Other than that, Sun Ra and his group were friendly. They hung out on the block and chatted with their neighbors. They were truly part of the neighborhood.

When strangers—music journalists or documentarians or other musicians—would come in search of Sun Ra, the neighborhood youth would answer questions about him with neighborly pride. After all, they knew that Sun Ra must certainly be someone important if outsiders were coming all the way to Morton Street to see him. Not much happened there that was of any interest to the outside world—the important world of television and politicians and businessmen down in Center City, which, though only a few miles away, might as well have been on another planet as far as they were concerned. Sun Ra and his people were undeniably strange, but they had chosen to come to this neighborhood, whose residents were black and poor, so folks figured they might as well claim him.

And of all the neighborhoods of notoriously provincial Philadelphia, Germantown probably was the best choice for what turned out to be Sun Ra's last stand. It is a polyglot mix of working poor, doctors, artists, social activists, construction workers, clerks, students, musicians, welfare recipients, and the insane (for some reason Germantown has more than its share of mental health facilities and residential group homes). The Quakers were a strong presence, and both George Washington and Walt Whitman had sojourned there. So a man from the planet Saturn was just one more colorful personage in the endless diversity of Germantown, like the gray-beard with a beret and burning black eyes who stood out on Lincoln Drive brandishing a placard urging immediate nuclear disarmament, or the "peanut man," a peanut vendor who wore peanut shells as earrings, or Rufus Harley, who played jazz on bagpipes, not to mention the mentally ill regulars panhandling on Chelten Avenue. There were a fair number of jazz musicians in Germantown: legendary drummer Philly Joe Jones, trail-blazing female guitarist Monette Sudler, avant-garde drummer Sunny "Big Chief" Murray, and noted free-jazz saxophonist Byard Lancaster, who played every day on the streets of Center City, not so much for the tips he received but as a mission to take jazz directly to "the people."

Yet Sun Ra stood apart, and in the Philadelphia jazz community opinions about him were more negative than positive. Quite a few looked askance at his "man from space" persona; folks did not know how to take it. The fact that his band members wore costumes that seemed a combination of *Star Trek* and ancient Egypt suggested some kind of charade. Quite a few musicians on the scene figured that Sun Ra was running some kind of cult or perhaps a scam. When he had moved to Philadelphia from New York in the late sixties, some of his musicians came with him to live in the communal house on Morton Street. Others would come when summoned from far-flung locales, as though he had cast a spell on them. How else to explain a musician like saxophonist John Gilmore, who had been playing nearly exclusively with Sun Ra since the early fifties even though he had the skills and reputation to play better-paying gigs with such well-known artists as Earl Hines and Art Blakey? In fact, several of Sun Ra's group—Gilmore, Marshall Allen, and Pat Patrick—had been with him since the fifties and it was not because they were making much money. On the contrary, playing with Sun Ra meant endless unpaid rehearsals, a strict, almost monklike lifestyle and inconsistent performing opportunities—in short a scuffling, poorly remunerated existence.

Then there was Sun Ra's music. Like Ornette Coleman, Thelonius Monk, and even Stravinsky, Sun Ra had been derided as a charlatan. Many considered his music profoundly unmusical and without substance. Quite a few musicians found Sun Ra's music impossible to play because of the difficult and unusual harmonic intervals he used, as well as his habit of writing parts beyond the normal range of the instrument the part was written for. Very few jazz venues in America would consider booking him. Yet those who "got it" found Sun Ra's music to be profound, commensurate with some of the greatest jazz ever created, and on a par with the great composers of "serious music." Those who embraced Sun Ra and his music claimed that their lives had been changed.

John Gilmore, tall, lean, sharp-featured and smooth-skinned even in middle age, looks somewhat bemused as he matter-of-factly describes his conversion to Sun Ra's music to Robert Mugge, in Mugge's documentary film *Sun Ra: A Joyful Noise.* He smiles when Mugge asks him what led "one of the most respected saxophonists in the country" to commit so much of his musical life to Sun Ra. Gilmore's smile turns mischievous, and his eyes twinkle, as though he knows his answer will baffle or outrage his questioner.

"Well," Gilmore begins, drawing a deep breath, "he was the first one to introduce me to the higher forms of music, you know . . . past what say Bird and Monk and the fellows were doing. I didn't think anyone was ahead of them . . . until I met Sun Ra!"

He chuckles as he says this, the laugh of one who has gained secret knowledge. He shakes his head in wonder and smiles broadly. But then his expression turns serious and his gaze sharpens as if seeing the past unfold again.

"I played with him on and off for about six months. I had just come out of the army playing solo clarinet so reading was no problem. Any music that he showed me I could read it pretty well . . . but I really didn't understand it! I couldn't hear it for about six months. Then one night (and now his grin returns) . . . I *heard* it!" (and he chuckles again giddily).

"This number 'Saturn,' I'd been playing it for six months, every time we worked. But then I really *heard* the intervals one night . . . and I said 'my gosh, this man is more stretched out than Monk!' (He shakes his head wonderingly from side to side.) It's unbelievable that anyone could write any meaner intervals than Monk or Mingus, you know? But he does! His intervals, his knowledge of intervals and harmony are very highly advanced. So when I saw that, I said, 'well, I think I'll make this the stop!'"

And he smiles the blissful smile of a believer.[2]

Gilmore's discourse sounds very much like that of a convert, one who has had a mystical epiphany or found a guru. It is the sort of talk that adds fuel to the argument of those who say Sun Ra was a cult leader. The fact that several musicians, including Gilmore, lived communally in the Morton Street house only reinforced this line of thinking. So did the fact that Sun Ra forbade any of his musicians the use of drugs or alcohol. Involvement with women was strongly discouraged. Sun Ra wanted anyone who played under his direction to have the same single-minded focus on music that he had. All else was a distraction, according to Sun Ra. He was known to ostracize or otherwise punish band members who strayed from the strict guidelines he had laid down.

Sun Ra espoused his philosophical and spiritual outlook to anyone who happened to come in contact with him. Band members often spoke of Sun Ra's knowledge and wisdom. Some attributed quasi-supernatural powers to him. Many expressed that he gave them an understanding of life and the cosmos that they had never had before. Marshall Allen, a conservatory-trained multi-instrumentalist whose father owned the Morton Street house, had also been with Sun Ra since the mid-fifties. Like Gilmore, Marshall absorbed Sun Ra's cosmology and made it the mundane reality of his life.

"He used all the musicians in Chicago," Allen recalled in the UK television documentary *Brother from Another Planet*. "Everyone respected Sun Ra because he had something different and they could see it and hear it but they couldn't do it. He was writing all these rhythms against rhythms and odd melodies and stuff like that. Now I go to play in his band, and I could play my horn, I'd been studying music, but he's telling me about history . . . telling me about space!

"You watched [him] and you were kept busy. You were kept so busy you would just cry . . . 'cause you were in the Ra jail with Sun Ra! And he was a busy man. Didn't even sleep; he cat-napped. And when he woke up he'd start out on the same note he'd finished on. At Slug's, Sun Ra had fifteen, sixteen people there playing from 9:00 p.m. until 4:00 a.m. without stopping.

"He made the music according to the musicians. Everything you do that's right, it's wrong! That's not what he wanted. It's not that you're wrong but it's not what he wanted. So I began to play what you call (he chuckles) . . . anything! The sound . . . mixing the sound!"[3]

I had discovered that Sun Ra was a neighbor quite by accident, shortly after I had moved to Germantown two years earlier. Someone had told me that he was listed in the Philadelphia phone book as "Ra, Sun" and that if you called the number, whoever picked up the phone would answer with the salutation "Space!" in spectral tones. So, one day, just for the hell of it, I looked up his listing in the phone book and, sure enough, he was there. The address was right around the corner, which was intriguing but also oddly disquieting.

One thing about Sun Ra's spaceman persona: it was great for press and for media attention in general. Some people considered it simply a publicity gimmick, a showbiz routine, which was anathema to jazzmen who came up in the fifties and sixties. Even Dizzy Gillespie had been criticized for his crowd-pleasing stage antics. Gimmick or not, Ra's space conceit had all the ingredients for a great story, one that most journalists could not resist: a jazzman whose band wears far-out costumes, plays "revolutionary" music, and claims to be from outer space. As a result, Sun Ra has been one of the few jazz artists to receive substantial media attention outside of the narrow world of jazz journalism. It was easy to write an entertaining story about Sun Ra without spending too much time on his music. Only a few who wrote about Sun Ra truly understood his music or had listened to it in depth, but even cursory listeners sensed something momentous in it. In any case, the outer space conceit engendered coverage in outlets that were not even music-oriented. The pageantry of his performances (which often featured a light show and costumes), along with the freewheeling ebb and flow of his music, had high entertainment value, especially for people who did not normally listen to jazz. It enabled Sun Ra to obtain bookings at rock festivals, for instance. For audiences who were also encountering the atonality, drones, feedback, distortion, and electronics presented in the music of Frank Zappa's Mothers of Invention, Jimi Hendrix, Pink Floyd, the Soft Machine, and Parliament-Funkadelic, Sun Ra was accessible, perhaps more readily so to them than to jazz fans. The many articles about him were like seeds scattered far and wide, planting opportunities for inquiring minds to discover him, a crucial dynamic since, during much of his artistic life, he had limited opportunities to perform publicly.

It was in one such article around 1970, in *Down Beat* or perhaps *Rolling Stone*, that I first encountered Sun Ra. His name alone demanded attention. Who or what was Sun Ra? Some people might remember that Ra was the name of the Egyptian sun god, which would seem to make his name oddly redundant. In the article Sun Ra was quoted as saying with apparent seriousness that he was not from Earth and in fact had been born in the region of Saturn. He stated that his "arrival zone" was Birmingham, Alabama. He had led a large musical ensemble, which he had called the Arkestra, since the early fifties, one of a small number of large-group jazz ensembles to survive the decline of the big-band era. Sun Ra's compositions, as played by the Arkestra, were some of the most unusual music ever heard in the jazz world—or any world, for that matter. The article heralded Sun Ra's music as a unique, wide-ranging achievement that brought together elements of free jazz, Ellingtonian compositional prowess, orchestrated big-band tonalities, electronic keyboards, African percussion, and bizarre pageantry involving outer space themes. It was like nothing else on the planet.

Anyone remotely interested in new forms of music, on reading such an article, would feel a compulsion to hear Sun Ra's music. At that time, if you lived within striking distance of New York City, the place to find esoteric music was Sam Goody's flagship store at 49th Street, a stone's throw from Radio City Music Hall. It was there that I found one of the few available albums by Sun Ra. Though by that time he had recorded and released dozens of albums, most were available only on his own Saturn label and were stocked in very few stores, because Sun Ra had no distributor and they had been manufactured in very small numbers (often as small as one hundred copies). There were three Sun Ra LPs in Sam Goody's bins: *The Sound Of Joy*, *The Heliocentric Worlds Of Sun Ra Vol. 1*, and *The Heliocentric Worlds Of Sun Ra Vol. 2*. Of the three, *The Heliocentric Worlds Of Sun Ra Vol. 2* immediately attracted me. It had been issued by ESP-Disk, a strange record label known for releasing some of the most esoteric, uncompromising free jazz, as well as recordings by such underground fringe folk and rock artists as The Fugs, The Godz, Pearls Before Swine, and unconventional vocalist Patti Waters, whose singing, the label's promotional literature promised, would "shatter the unwary." ESP-Disk's name reflected its dedication to the propagation of Esperanto, an artificial language intended to serve as an international lingua franca to facilitate world peace. In short, it made a lot of sense that ESP-Disk would issue works by Sun Ra.

Heliocentric Worlds' cover was dominated by an ancient diagram of the solar system. A two-inch-wide strip at the bottom featured portraits of scientific and mathematical visionaries whose thinking had led to the discovery of the solar system: Leonardo DaVinci, Galileo, Copernicus, Tycho Brahe, and Pythagoras. In the middle of them was a photo of Sun Ra, eyes closed, head tilted slightly heavenward as if in meditation, his head covered by a turban-like headdress with a sun-shaped jewel affixed in the center of his forehead, where the so-called "third eye" has been presumed to be. The other men pictured were major historical figures. Who, then, was Sun Ra? It was a fascinating and slightly humorous conceit. On the one hand, adopting such a name was a spiritual assertion bordering on audacious. On the other hand, he appeared to be comparing himself to some of the greatest scientific visionaries of all time. And yet Sun Ra was a musician—though some might recall the affinity of mathematics and music. On the back cover, a headline proclaimed, "you never heard such sounds in your life!" A photograph captured Sun Ra in shades, holding a metal sun-sculpture in his hands. A short poem by him also graced the back cover, reading in part:

There is a land
Whose being is almost unimaginable to the
Human mind.
On a clear day,
We stand there and look farther than the
Ordinary eye can see.
Far above the roof of the world,
We can encompass vistas of the worlds.[4]

It was not a typical album jacket, not for jazz or any other music. To any moderately curious person, it was irresistible.

There are only three pieces on *The Heliocentric Worlds Of Sun Ra Vol. 2*, two of them very long. The album opens with "The Sun Myth," which begins with an improvised bowed bass solo, not at all typical of what you hear on most jazz recordings. There follows a percussion interlude using tuned bongos as well as trap drums, and then a soaring, screeching saxophone enters in conversation with the bass and percussion. The music is, like much so-called "free jazz," chaotic on the surface, with no obvious melodies. At times it is a cacophony. But at other times it evokes an odd and compelling beauty, as something magnificent forms out of the chaos, like the worlds that formed out of the primordial cosmos. It is not easily digested or enjoyed but it is unlike any other music. Even if you do not fully grasp it, bits of it will tug at you long after the music ends.

Hearing *The Heliocentric Worlds Of Sun Ra* was like a door opening, beckoning to a new reality. Finding other Sun Ra recordings was no easy task. Living in Philadelphia was an advantage: because Sun Ra had come to trust Jerry Gordon, a Sun Ra fan who owned an independent record store in downtown Philadelphia called Third Street Jazz, the limited pressings of various Saturn releases were intermittently available there. Sun Ra or members of the Arkestra created the cover art by hand.

At its most basic, a cover design might simply be the album title scrawled in quasi-psychedelic ink letters. A more elaborate design might feature an illustration, done in magic marker or crayon overlaid with a dappled, transparent urethane. *Cosmic Tones for Mental Therapy* featured abstract swirls of blue with a vaguely Van Gogh feel; the form of a person seems to appear in the midst of the swirls. *We Travel the Spaceways* has an illustration in blue, red, and black of a piano keyboard breaking apart and keys ricocheting into space interspersed with elongated musical notes and small unicellular entities with single eyes, all against a backdrop of oceanic swells. *Jazz in Silhouette* has a black cover dominated by a portrait of Sun Ra's head bathed in a reddish glow, a knit hood cascading down either side of his head and strings of cowrie shells hanging over his face in the manner of certain West African kings. In any case, aside from Third Street Jazz and a few other trusted outlets in the United States and abroad, the Saturn albums were most likely to be found for sale at performances by the Arkestra. But there was no rhyme or reason to the Saturn releases. Music recorded in 1958 might be issued in 1970, dates noted might be wrong—some say a result of Sun Ra's penchant for obfuscation. The titles listed on the LP jackets were sometimes wrong. Whenever the small pressing of a particular title sold out, it became unobtainable, to the dismay of the handful of stores who had sold out and wanted to sell more. This do-it-yourself (DIY) approach to issuing recordings may be the earliest example by a notable artist of the DIY phenomenon—pre-dating the trend by punk rockers and rappers in the eighties and nineties.

Fortuitously, through a licensing deal in 1973, Sun Ra's music began to be issued with major-label distribution via Impulse Records. In addition, a new recording, the soundtrack to a low-budget independent film *Space Is the Place,* was issued by major-label-distributed Blue

Thumb Records. Suddenly more than a dozen old and new Sun Ra recordings were readily available.

The immediately striking thing about this multitude of releases was the vast range of Sun Ra's music, which stood in stark contrast to the formulated structure of the overwhelming majority of jazz recordings. The music varied wildly from album to album, even track to track. Dissonant bebop, blues, free-flowing sonic explorations, funky percussion-driven grooves, tone poems, swing romps, quasi–chamber music, solo piano musings, and much more made up his universe of expression. In addition to the conventional arsenal of a big band— saxophones, brass, trap drums, acoustic piano, electric guitar, string bass—Sun Ra utilized bass clarinet, oboe, flute, bassoon, African percussion, and a host of exotic instruments from around the world. There was also electric piano—Sun Ra was one of the first musicians to incorporate electric piano into his music—electric bass, organ, and synthesizers (he obtained one of the earliest Moog synthesizers). And then there was clavinet, clavioline, euphonium, tympani, gong, and adapted instruments whose names he altered: space dimension mellophone, cosmic side drums, Egyptian solar bells, space lute, and more. One track might feature twenty or more instruments while another track might use only a handful.

The multitude of Sun Ra albums bore track titles reflecting either cosmological themes or ancient mythology: "Atlantis," "Space Is the Place," "Outer Planes of There," "Ankh," "Planet Earth," "Tiny Pyramids," Lights of a Satellite," "Spiral Galaxy," "Ancient Ethiopia," "Sunology," and the like. Almost every title referenced space, ancient Egypt, or some philosophical concept. What did it all mean? Was it a gimmick? Was it serious philosophy? Or was Sun Ra simply delusional? It is often difficult to categorize a given Sun Ra recording as "good" or "bad" by any conventional musical aesthetic. The music creates its own reality and is often not amenable to conventional critical standards. In fact, at strategic points in the music Sun Ra deliberately included elements that disrupted accepted standards of melody, harmony, or rhythm. He did this to jar the listener—and the musicians!— out of normal patterns of listening and perceiving. He wanted to take the listener someplace else, and that was difficult to do as long as his listener held on to conventional earthly aesthetics. One either enters the music's cosmos or stands outside, uncomprehending.

This is most easily seen in his solo piano recordings, such as the 1979 recording *Solo Piano, Vol. 1.* His performance of the traditional song "Sometimes I Feel Like a Motherless Child" begins with an ostinato in the bass register, a device that often appears in Sun Ra's own compositions. He then begins to hit chords with dissonant intervals, often in hauntingly beautiful clusters. The dissonant intervals undermine the conventional ideas of melody and harmony that dominate Western music. The ostinato dissolves before long into something else, as though maintaining it is unbearably predictable. Often Sun Ra, in his piano playing, seems to rush a phrase, giving a herky-jerky, push-pull feel to the music. At other times his playing is more lyrical, but never for long. Like many great improvising musicians, it is difficult to tell whether certain notes are deliberately played or are simply the result of a mistake. The notes may be wrong according to conventional thinking but somehow sound right in context. He uses the full range of the piano, hitting chords in the extreme lower register, which most pianists usually reserve for single notes because the fullness of bass notes becomes very dense when combined in a chord. He also hits chiming clusters of notes in the extreme upper register, where the piano can take on a shrill or bell-like tone. This approach renders Jerome Kern's popular standard "Yesterdays" virtually unrecognizable but often gorgeous.

Few take Sun Ra's claim of extraterrestrial origin seriously. Still, there is often something in the music that is hard to explain by earthly rules of logic, physics, or perception.

An entertaining exposition of Sun Ra's view of himself can be found in *Space Is the Place*, a low-budget feature film shot in 1972 that combines elements of *Star Trek*, low-budget science-fiction films of the fifties, and early-seventies "blaxploitation" films. Sun Ra not only stars in the film, playing himself, but had a major role in the creation of the script. The film opens on a distant planet where conditions are more advanced than those on Earth. Sun Ra decides to bring the benighted black population of earth to this higher realm. He sets out in a yellow oblong spaceship with huge eyelike orbs at either end; the spaceship is powered by energy generated from music played by Sun Ra and the

Arkestra. They land on earth, in the Oakland, California, ghetto—coincidentally the spawning ground of the Black Panther Party—and set out to awaken and rescue black folk from the corrupt, oppressive reality that is manipulated by an evil "overseer." At one point, playing piano in a decadent nightclub, Sun Ra creates music that causes glasses to shatter, winds to blow, and smoke to appear as the nightclub is ultimately blown apart.

Sun Ra rarely answered questions with a straight answer, and he deliberately obscured the early parts of his life. This only made those who encountered him more interested in unraveling his biography. His sojourn on earth did indeed begin in Birmingham, Alabama. His birth date is most often reported as 1914, but it has also been given as 1910 and 1912, a result of his obfuscation. Virtually all accounts agree that his given name was Herman Blount. From an early age he was fascinated by and drawn to music, teaching himself to play piano. A dreamy, introverted boy, he soaked up knowledge of all types by reading voraciously. His reading touched on subjects that were to become lifelong obsessions: Egyptology, black history, religion (particularly the Bible and the writings of various Spiritualists), and cosmology.

The Birmingham of his youth was one of the most cosmopolitan Southern cities, though also a city where the racist Jim Crow laws were rigidly and brutally enforced. Nonetheless young Herman was able to sneak off to watch the many touring big bands that played clubs in town. He absorbed the music of church choirs, the swing records that his brother bought, the society orchestras and party bands, stage shows that his mother took him to see, and the street musicians they passed on the way. He taught himself to read music. Soon he was playing in the high school band that had long been directed by John Whatley, an extraordinary music teacher whose students went on to play with Duke Ellington, Fletcher Henderson, and other notables. His first professional experience came with Whatley's touring band, which traveled as far as Chicago, where he was designated leader of the band. He adopted the nickname his bandmates called him by—Sonny. This was the first step toward his Sun Ra identity.[5]

In 1947 he left Birmingham for Chicago, cutting all ties with the city, his family, and his life there. He did not return for nearly half a century, when he was near death. Chicago, with its wide-open nightlife, was a cauldron of black culture. There he encountered Fletcher Henderson, one of his heroes, and soon was playing in his band. Though not as popular as Ellington, Basie, Goodman, or other swing-era bandleaders, Henderson was an important figure, as many of the top bands used his arrangements. Around this time Herman legally changed his name to Le Son'r Ra and launched his own ensemble, finding musicians who could—or, more importantly, would—play the challenging music he was creating.

Describing Sun Ra's music as *challenging* is like describing the moon as *circular*. It was not merely the difficulty of the music that made it challenging; the whole process of playing under Sun Ra's direction was demanding, often deliberately disorienting. Musicians were admonished to "play what you don't know." Rehearsals typically lasted for several hours, if not longer, and were often instructional and compositional sessions directed by Sun Ra and interspersed with his long philosophical monologues. To play with Sun Ra, a musician had to learn to think—and, ideally, to live—in a different way. Music was a means to an end, a bridge to a different, higher reality; for that task he needed musicians who would devote themselves completely to his music. If the music sounded strange it was because its purpose was different than that of other music. Nonetheless, saxophonists Marshall Allen, Pat Patrick, and John Gilmore joined Sun Ra during this period and stayed with him for the better part of the next forty years. Other notable musicians who played with Sun Ra were bassist Ronnie Boykins, saxophonist Pharaoh Sanders, trombonist Julian Priester, and drummer Clifford Jarvis.

When the possibilities of Chicago had been exhausted, Sun Ra migrated with several of his musicians to New York in 1961, summoning others to join him, and they came like hypnotized subjects responding to the conjurer. New York offered an even broader spectrum to draw upon. In 1966 the band established a Monday night residency at an East Village dive called Slug's. In a typical Sun Ra gambit, he had taken the worst night of the week because he knew musicians were usually off on that night and there would not be many other musical performances going on.[6] The Arkestra's music expanded like a supernova, the pieces getting longer, the Arkestra growing larger, and the last bit of conventional limits stripped away. On recordings such as *The Magic*

City, *The Heliocentric Worlds of Sun Ra*, *Nothing Is*, and *Outer Planes of There*, the band began to attain Sun Ra's ideal of pure expression.

By 1968 New York had become untenable to Sun Ra and the Arkestra: the landlord was raising the rent and the neighbors were intolerant of the band's incessant rehearsing. Marshall Allen's father owned the house on Morton Street in Philadelphia that became the Arkestra's final refuge. They continued playing Monday nights at Slug's, taking the train to New York in full regalia. No doubt early-morning commuters were startled to find a group of black spacemen as fellow travelers as Arkestra members returned the next morning from their performances, which often ended a couple of hours before dawn.[7]

Knowing that the person responsible for such mysterious and fascinating paradoxes was a neighbor, I felt a special urgency to learn the truth about him. He was not someone who existed only in the grooves of his recordings or onstage. Sun Ra and members of the Arkestra were part of the workaday world of the neighborhood. I often passed Marshall Allen on the street walking up to a store on Germantown Avenue. He was a short, wiry light-skinned man with a scraggly hipster's goatee and a bushy reddish-brown Afro contained by a multicolored cap. He moved through the neighborhood with an easygoing amiability, a bebopper's dip and sway in his walk. On occasion I encountered Sun Ra himself with a small entourage in the hardware store a few blocks down the Avenue. Sun Ra often wore an immense silver tunic or smock made of material that looked like a medieval knight's chain mail, his helmetlike headdress made of the same material. Sun Ra's outfits were not just stage attire. His facial expression was as set as that of a priest presiding over a religious ritual. But he was buying hardware supplies. There was something profoundly incongruous about such a personage engaged in such a mundane activity. One might wonder why he could not simply materialize the supplies in some way. But even a space traveler needs to make certain repairs, and where else could he get materials on Planet Earth? They would complete their purchase and leave without fanfare.

It was not unusual to glimpse Sun Ra in a local diner, partaking of a meal alone. Though reportedly a vegetarian in his younger days, his culinary tastes ran to basic, "down-home" cooking. After the meal, you might see him outside leaning up against a telephone pole, reading a comic book. But if you stole a glance at the comic book, you saw strange, unrecognizable images that seemed not of this earth.

Danny Davis, one of the band members, ran a little grocery store, the Pharaoh's Den, on a run-down block of Chew Avenue, just a few blocks from the Morton Street house. Amidst the snacks and groceries were hand-carved percussion instruments and philosophical pamphlets. Neighborhood kids coming in for candy and chips got a dose of cosmic philosophy at no extra charge.

On more than one occasion, Sun Ra brought the entire Arkestra to play at the Red Carpet Lounge, a narrow little bar located on Chelten Avenue around the corner from Morton Street. Despite its humble setting and size, the Red Carpet was a place where name jazz musicians regularly played in the sixties and seventies. In 1979 it still occasionally presented the likes of Groove Holmes, Houston Person, Etta Jones, and others. But those were small groups; the twenty-odd members of the Arkestra could not fit onto the small stage and so they ranged along the wall opposite the bar, effectively demolishing the barrier between audience and performer. In Europe, the Arkestra played major concert halls; at home, they were not above playing a corner bar. So Sun Ra and his cohort were part of the community, even as they stood apart from it in many ways. Like everything else about Sun Ra, it made sense and nonsense at the same time.

Sometimes I walked down Morton Street at night and stopped to gaze at the Arkestra's lair. In the dark, it emanated an even more suggestive, brooding atmosphere. No light escaped through the windows; I later learned that the windows were covered completely by foil. Probably it was just my imagination, but I sensed something alien within. If it was after 10:00 p.m., I would likely hear the pulsing sounds of music from within. When the band was in town they would rehearse every night until the early hours of the morning. The music swelled and crashed and surged. It was nothing like the party music that streamed out of the other houses. Cries and squawks of ancient beings coalesced into unnerving crescendos. I wondered how the neighbors dealt with it.

The music inside that house exerted a strong pull. It was tempting to walk up to the door and knock, to catch a glimpse of the Arkestra in action. However it just did not seem right—or advisable—to intrude.

Still, walking away from that music was no easy task. It was like walking out of the ocean with the receding waves sucking your feet backwards. A strong forced emanated from that house.

Around that time, Sun Ra's Arkestra began performing more frequently in Philadelphia. The name exhibited Sun Ra's penchant for puns and double meanings, as it played on the words *orchestra* and *ark* to reflect Sun Ra's vision of music as the salvation of mankind, like Noah's ark. The exact name he used frequently changed: the Solar Myth Arkestra, the Solar Arkestra, the Myth Science Arkestra, the Intergalactic Research Arkestra, the Power of Astro-Infinity Arkestra, and so on, in dozens of permutations. These variations were not arbitrary. Each one related to a specific musical mode or direction. Whatever the name, it always suggested that the ensemble was concerned with more than just music. And that was true; they were on a mission, nothing less than the spiritual salvation of humanity, and they were very, very serious about it.

One night he and the Arkestra were performing on South Street at the appropriately mythologically monikered club Grendel's Lair, a modest-sized club that booked all kinds of music, both local and nationally known artists. Gazing at the array of instruments crowding the stage, the audience's anticipation grew. What would they play? With Sun Ra anything was possible. Suddenly, without an announcement, Marshall Allen walked out dressed in a multicolored space tunic and peaked headdress, blowing a flute. He played solo for several minutes, the flute implying a pastoral mood even as he ranged into unusual scales. And then he walked slowly off, still playing. A tall, lean man walked out and began playing the huge, hand-carved African-style drum standing on one side of the stage. It looked like an elongated conga drum, and had been fashioned from a tree that was struck by lightning across the street from the Morton Street house. Sun Ra had decreed that a drum should be made of it. Some say he had predicted that the tree would be struck by lightning. The drummer established a pulse and oscillated between various cross-rhythms; it was nothing like what most drummers played when they took a solo. As he played, other members of the Arkestra, all in space tunics and caps, began drifting in, picking up their instruments.

Suddenly they kicked into a big-band romp, a swing piece in the classic mode of Fletcher Henderson, possibly "One O'Clock Jump" or another swing standard. As that song drew to end, the Arkestra launched a cacophony, the horns squalling and shrieking, the drummers furiously pounding and the bassist running his hands frantically up and down the neck of his big string bass. From the left, Sun Ra entered, majestically making his way to the various electronic keyboards arranged in a semicircle stage right. He moved with the deliberate inevitability of an ocean liner docking; he was a big man, six feet tall with a sizable, vaguely potato-shaped physique rendered shapeless by his garb. A glittering, gold togalike garment was draped over a sparkling, black, sequined tunic trimmed with gold fringe. He wore reddish-gold pantaloons and a gold skullcap. Suddenly I recognized the cacophony. It was exactly like the fanfare musicians played for the arrival of a king or emir of West Africa; I had witnessed a dozen *algeita* (reed horn) players and percussionists doing exactly the same thing in Kano, Nigeria, as the Emir of Kano's procession drew near. I realized that it was not meaningless noise but a robust hosanna, intended to salute a great personage and possibly to invoke the spirits of the ancestors.

Sun Ra moved impassively to a synthesizer, which was tilted slightly forward so that the audience could see his hands move over the keyboard. As he touched the keyboard, the rest of the musicians abruptly stopped playing. Sun Ra began coaxing a series of unearthly sounds from the synth—whooshes of white noise, jagged roars, and oscillating whines—as his hands moved, nimbly twisting knobs and pushing buttons with purposeful, precise movements which suggested that every sound was precisely calibrated even if it superficially seemed random. If anything could be said to be space music, this was it. He was playing pure sound without reference to melody or rhythm. At a climactic point he ran his fingers all over the keyboards, orchestrating a rapid-fire series of burbling bleeps. Suddenly he whirled around, and without missing a beat, continued his assault on the keyboard with his hands behind his back, hitting the notes without seeing them. The patterns did not sound arbitrary. It was reminiscent of the showmanship of old-time blues guitarists playing the guitar behind their back. He whirled around so that he was again facing the keyboard, and jabbed at it nonstop; at one point he spun around completely, his face deadpan as he executed what seemed like a cheap parlor trick, as if sending up the portentous aspect of the Arkestra's presentation thus far. It was a very funny moment and could lead one to suspect that it was simply a put-on. Many people fail to realize that Sun Ra, serious and "cosmic" though he may have been, did have a dry sense of humor and was not unaware of the impact of his presentation. Then again, he was serious about humor, which to him was a natural response to what he considered the almost unbearably stupid and negative character of much of earthly existence

After a while, June Tyson walked regally out. It was generally be-lieved that Sun Ra did not like women, or at least did not like hav-ing them around. Some say he considered them a distraction; others attributed his attitude to latent homosexuality, although it would be more accurate to say that Sun Ra was asexual than homosexual. A ma-jor exception to his animus was June, a tall, slender woman with a serene mien, whose face was reminiscent of a Yoruba priestess. She often stated to interviewers, who wondered how she felt as virtually the only female member of the Arkestra, that when she performed with Sun Ra she was not a woman but an angel.[8] She was referring to Sun Ra's concept of angels as beings of a higher order than humans. For over thirty years she provided haunting contralto vocal expression of Sun Ra's cosmos, demonstrating a complete ability and willingness to sing Sun Ra's abstract cosmic poetry with seriousness and devotion. On tour she was his frequent companion as he moved about whatever city they were in. She would walk with him, clad in the costume of an Egyptian mythological animal, or move closely with him onstage in space costume, like a female familiar, a channel for the spiritual energy he was tapping into.

June sang in her clear, resonant voice cryptic words carried by one of Sun Ra's prettiest melodies: "Astro-black . . . mythology . . . astro-timeless . . . immortality . . . astro-thought . . . in mystic sound . . . . astro-black . . . of outer space. Astro-natural . . . dark is dark . . . be-yond the stars . . . out to endless endlessness . . . astro-black . . . cosmo earth . . . the universe . . . is in my voice . . . the universe . . . speaks through this sound."[9]

And so it went. The Arkestra oscillated from space to the earth, from atonality to haunting melody, from free jazz cacophony to in-terludes reminiscent of chamber music, from big-band swing to Afro-funk grooves. Some two hours later, the performance climaxed as two female dancers appeared in back of the audience, striking abstract, quasi-African dance postures and singing "we are members of the angel race, coming to you from outer space," as the band vamped. The band joined in on the chant and members of the group began following the dancers around the room, singing all the while, It was like a gospel choir's exit, conga line, and showbiz finale all at once. One could argue that it was oddly similar to the floor show at Club De Lisa where Sun Ra had played when he first came to Chicago in his thirties. The entire Arkestra snaked through the crowd and out the door leading upstairs singing and playing tambourines and shakers all the while; Sun Ra himself had simply disappeared.

Like everything about Sun Ra, the Arkestra's performance was a strange mix of improvisation, orchestration, spirituality, solemn ritual, apparent nonsense, humor, showbiz spectacle, and astonishing musicianship. It was a totally unique experience that was more than the sum of its parts and seemed to have a profound effect on a fair percentage of those listening. Sun Ra and the Arkestra was a mass of contradictions coexisting within one entity. Just when you thought you had begun to fully grasp what Sun Ra was all about, you would hear of some new incident or aspect of his being and your conception would be challenged.

It was not hard to meet Sun Ra. *Philadelphia* magazine commissioned me to do a piece on the jazz scene in Philadelphia. Although many in the jazz community would disagree, it seemed vital to include Sun Ra. Even though he stood apart from the various musical cliques in Philadelphia, his presence in the city could not be ignored. A phone call to the Morton Street house was answered by one of the musicians. He said it might be possible to arrange an interview with Sun Ra and asked me to call back. On calling back the next day, I was informed that Sun Ra was willing to grant me an interview and a mutually satisfactory time was arranged.

A few days later I left my house and walked down the block toward Sun Ra's house. I was not the first to make the trek and far from the last: in ensuing years pilgrimages to 5626 Morton Street became common as the legend of Sun Ra spread. I rang the bell of the Morton

Street house. All was silent within. After a while, I heard footsteps approaching the door and a slight, middle-aged man opened the door, his face a mask of silent inquiry. I introduced myself and he ushered me into the dim interior, past the stairs to a parlor off to the left and motioned me to a seat. The room was packed with musical instruments, amplifiers, lights, and an astonishing collection of art covering the walls. Ancient murals nestled among modern abstract paintings of infinite keyboards stretching into space. Small Egyptian and West African statuettes perched on the mantle and elsewhere. Every surface was covered with books, sheet music, and small objects of one sort or another. This, then, was the Arkestra's rehearsal room, the cauldron of sound and rhythm and nightly incantation.

After a few minutes waiting in the stillness, I heard slow, heavy footsteps coming down the stairs; I turned in time to glimpse Sun Ra descending the last few steps majestically, attired in a silver robe and tiger-stripe cap. He came into the room and settled in the chair behind the electric piano, which was painted in oranges and reds. An old black rotary-dial telephone was perched on top of it.

"This is my office," Sun Ra declared gravely.

It was hard to know how to begin. An interview with Sun Ra is not an interview in the normal sense. You merely come within range of thoughts he is already broadcasting. At any given moment he could and would discourse endlessly in philosophical terms about anything—music, history, religion, his approach to daily life. His response to a question might or might not directly answer the question. But no matter what the topic might be, the trend of his discourse always tapped into the same themes—the illusory nature of life on Planet Earth, Sun Ra's otherworldly perspective, humanity's misguided and mistaken existence, the role of music in bridging the gap between illusory reality and higher, substantial reality, the special history of the black man, and so on. Asking a question of Sun Ra might lead him to direct some of his monologue to the question, at least as a departure point. When you left his presence, he continued the broadcast silently, until someone else came within range to receive it. He gave the impression of thinking or meditating continually.

On one occasion an interviewer for *Down Beat* asked him a question about the idea of music as a universal language. Sun Ra instantly responded with a couple of thousand words of abstract discourse, of which this paragraph is only a sample:

> As far as intergalactic music is concerned in its relationship with jazz, it is related just like I have been to the world and just like some other black people have been, a part of and yet not a part of. I have to face the fact that some people are materialists and there is such a thing as a spiritual man. At that point, there is an expansion and diversion of the word "brother" . . . different orders are in being. There is an infinity between the every thing of everything, so I am still talking about music and jazz, and I still say that jazz did serve as a bridge, like everything else does, to somewhere or nowhere at all or some no place unknown like intergalactic; but from the point of view that I did not cross the bridge of jazz to go to intergalactic, I crossed the bridge of jazz to come from where intergalactic music is, or perhaps I should say is a fundamental phase of being.[10]

He could emit this sort of monologue endlessly and effortlessly, all delivered in a soft, evenly modulated drone; it was the voice of a hypnotist. Often he appeared to be talking double-talk but at other times it all seemed to cohere into something big and visionary. His facility with words and abstraction came from a lifetime of voracious reading. Since his youth he had been drawn to the writings of mystics, spiritualists, philosophers, and historians, most especially from hybrid spiritual/philosophical thought spawned by theosophy, esoteric Christianity, alchemy, Gurdjieff, so called "New Thought" spiritualists, and much more, all mixed in with his investigations into Egyptology and other currents in the ancient world.

I imagined the scene of one of the endless rehearsals that took place in the room, filling in dialogue recounted by various Arkestra members. Sun Ra would sit behind the same electric piano he was sitting behind at that moment. Band members would be ranged before him helter-skelter in the cramped space, sitting on chairs, boxes, or any available surface, if indeed they could find a place to sit. If it was summer, the air would be hot and close; there was no air-conditioning. Sun Ra would play a line on the piano and point at one of the musicians, a saxophonist perhaps, who would attempt to replicate the line.

"No, you're playing it wrong!" Sun Ra would say, as trumpeter Michael Ray remembered in *Brother from Another Planet*. He would point to an apple perched on a crate. "An apple has a vibration. It's red, it's round, red is a shocker. So it's a very energetic thing. Play with your pinky up." He'd play the line again on the piano and again the musician would mimic what he played.[11]

"No, it's wrong! Omigod, you're just human! You know, I have a hard time with human frailties!"

He might digress on a philosophical tangent, talking about the special responsibilities of musicians perhaps or lecturing on the extraordinary life-sustaining properties of a certain variety of beans. Then he would return to the painstaking process of leading his musicians to play some new music. It was always new, often composed on the spot.

In order to ground the conversation as much as possible, I asked him how he happened to come to Philadelphia, not noted (when he arrived in the late sixties) as a particularly vibrant or progressive place. As usual, he had several different answers to the question, all of them probably true in one way or another.

"Marshall's father had a house here, so we came to visit. I saw the trees," he said, without levity, "and the roses. I like trees, so I moved here.

"The revolution in music will be here. The Philadelphia Orchestra is the best in the world, so why shouldn't the avant-garde be previewed here?"

Yet on other occasions he has said that he came to Philadelphia because it was the "worst place on earth . . . the headquarters of the devil."[12] This is typical Sun Ra reverse logic. To him, if you are dedicating yourself to saving the human race, it makes sense to start at the most negative place on the planet.

No doubt the availability of Marshall's father's house as a base for the Arkestra was a huge factor, based on simple economic need. Keeping a big band going twenty years after most big bands disappeared in the face of the high costs of maintaining a large aggregation (and when there was no longer any big band live circuit) was no small feat.

He continued on the Philadelphia theme. "Philadelphia doesn't know what I'm doing. Some people play for money, for ego, but not me. I improvise and create classically. I play rhythms that have nothing to do with this planet. I've given up everything to do this."

When he uttered that last sentence, for the first time I discerned hints of emotion, a subtle look of hurt in his eyes. Truly, he had given up everything to create and play original music, true to his vision and without compromise. In spite of the undeniable power of his music and the international acclaim he had received, he nonetheless found himself in a decaying row home located in a shabby neighborhood in a city where people had no idea what he was doing. Survival was a daily challenge.

"Playing is like being a preacher," he said. "You got to put in discipline. There is no freedom without discipline. We play here until four in the morning every night; we don't know what time it is."

This was a recurring Sun Ra theme. Even the most chaotic passages of his music were part of a designated structure, a precise composition. Sometimes even the solos were written out. For this reason descriptions of certain of his works as free jazz are not really accurate.

It is doubtful if any group of musicians anywhere rehearsed as relentlessly as the Arkestra. Even on days when they had concerts, they would rehearse. Often they would play ten or fifteen hours a day. The work ethic of Sun Ra himself was stupendous. When he was not rehearsing the band, he was composing (there is a vast treasure trove of hundreds of his composition manuscripts, including many works never recorded or performed) or writing arrangements. Michael Ray has said that stacks of music manuscripts were often kept in crates in the rehearsal room and that once when he opened the refrigerator he saw music sheets in there as well.[13] When not composing, rehearsing, or performing he was talking about music or philosophy and, of course, the cosmological extensions of music-making, which were infinite. He also wrote poetry (a collection of his poems has been published) and created illustrations for the Arkestra's LPs. He oversaw the logistics of the band, which were not inconsiderable, as well as the needs of its members. It seemed that he hardly slept; it has been reported that he suffered from insomnia and slept in brief catch-as-catch-can stretches.

But it is not really accurate to call the band's all-night sessions rehearsals. They were more often collective composing sessions. Often the Arkestra might work on tunes for several hours during the day and then at a performance the same evening play none of the material they had rehearsed. From Sun Ra's point of view, it was all about simply playing music, something he felt a real musician should be doing virtually every waking moment.

"There are lots of musicians in Philadelphia now," he continues. "But we need a club where there is something for jazz every night."

After an hour of conversation, mostly Sun Ra talking and me listening, he mentioned that he had another appointment. But he wanted me to send him the article when it came out.

Walking out of the house into the bright sunshine, I blinked, as much from encountering again mundane earthly reality as the brightness. Having looked Sun Ra in the eye at last and heard his cosmological talk from his own mouth, I had to answer the question everyone one asked: was Sun Ra for real? Or, more urgently, was he crazy?

Let's face it, when someone looks gazes unblinkingly at you and declares that he was not born on this planet but that he was from a region near Saturn, there are three likely possibilities: he could be putting you on; he could be delusional; he could be telling the truth.

As quoted in John Szwed's *Space Is the Place*, Sun Ra's sister Mary sets the record straight pretty directly: "he's not from no Mars . . . he was born at my mother's aunt's house over there by the train station . . . I know, 'cause I got on my knees and peeped through the keyhole."[14]

So, literally, physically, Sun Ra, named Herman Blount and called "Sonny" early on, was not from Saturn. He was an earthling. But Sun Ra did not live a literal life. He was quite direct and specific about his intentions. One of his common homilies, which he often dropped into conversations, were two lines from the poem he recited for Mugge at the Art Museum.

"Those of this reality have lost their way," he would intone. "Now they must listen to what myth has to say."[15]

He was not concerned about literal truths of the material world he found himself in. Confronted with a dysfunctional, oppressive reality, Sun Ra looked for an alternative. His approach was to create a myth, a narrative that portrayed another reality. Of course, mythology has been used in many cultures to explain or illuminate things beyond man's experience. The Greek myths described a world of supernatural beings—gods and goddesses who existed by a different set of rules from humans. Sun Ra was born a black male in the segregated South, a sensitive, creative artist in a society dominated by ego, power struggles, and greed. His response was to create a narrative, a myth that would liberate him and all humanity from the oppressive reality into which he had been born. For that reason, one of the many names he used for the Arkestra was the Myth-Science Arkestra. "Ark" recalls Noah's ark, which was the salvation of humanity; Sun Ra's "ark" used myth to save humanity.

But Sun Ra also has recounted a very specific experience which was the catalyst for his space mythology and his assertion that he was "not from this planet." He related to Francis Davis, during an interview at the Morton Street house in the early nineties, an anecdote he has told many times.[16] In *Brother from Another Planet*, Yahaya Abdul Majid, a musician who played with the Arkestra, mentioned that Sun Ra had been ridiculed by other musicians when he was younger because they found his diary and read his account of the incident in question. Yahaya Majid referred to it as a "trans-molecular" experience;[17] to most people it sounds like a classic "abducted by spacemen" tale. According to Sun Ra, beings from beyond Earth came to him and identified him as someone with special potential. So they transported him to another planet, which he identified as the planet Saturn, and showed him many things there. According to Ra, he was given knowledge that no one on earth had and was told that when he returned to earth he had the ability to change the destiny of humanity by imparting the special knowledge he had gained. Sun Ra describes this event utterly matter-of-factly. His assertion that he was "from Saturn" most likely is simply a straightforward statement that the person he became was from the planet where he was transformed. Or perhaps it was shorthand for the transformative experience he had. From this perspective, his original physical birth was irrelevant.

In an interview for the television program *New Visions* in 1989, Sun Ra laid out his point of view in what was, for him, an unusually straightforward way. His attire for that interview was uncharacteristically subdued as well. Sitting on a stool next to the host on a stark studio set, he wore a bulky gray woolen sweater over a tie-dye patterned shirt with a brown, woolen scarf wrapped turban-like on his head.

"A sense of humor is demanded in this age," he stated in his soft southern lilt, with a slightly effeminate, mincing cadence. "People have to see how ridiculous this situation is and when you see something ridiculous you're supposed to laugh. All they have to do is look in the mirror and have a good laugh. Because they've been put in a trick bag by someone. I'm supplying an exit out of problems. I give my music as a sound bridge to something more than psychic, more than spiritual. And they call that 'spirit sound.'"[18]

His face was turned slightly away from his interviewer, speaking like a child shyly reciting something, occasionally rolling his eyes over toward the host. Now and then he suppressed a smile—was it shyness, pride, or mischievousness? When he spoke only his lips moved; the rest of his face was immobile.

"But you were talking about outer space, right?" his interviewer prompted.

"That's right," Sun Ra answered, now turning his face toward his interviewer. "I was talking about space. A lot of musicians felt it was too far out for people but it's not, really. They had the wrong impression about people. They underestimated their intelligence. I realized that a lot of people got feelings. I reached toward their feelings, not toward their minds because their minds had been brainwashed. Why should I try to reach someone who had been brainwashed? But their spirit hadn't been brainwashed and it's pure. I know what they're supposed to be and potentially *will* be.

"I'm not really a man, you see. I'm an angel. If I was a man I couldn't do anything. Man always fails, you know. He doesn't have the right to do things. But angels are not the same as man. Angels can do lots of things. An angel is a little step above man."

This, then, is Sun Ra's myth: There are spiritual beings existing in a higher spiritual reality. The goal for humanity is to reach that higher reality. Music is a way to access it. It is important to bypass the conscious mind in order to accomplish this. Stated this way, there is nothing particularly unusual about Sun Ra's outlook. Similar viewpoints have been presented by countless philosophers and spiritual leaders. Sun Ra simply outfitted his mythmaking with space costumes, cosmological terminology, and destabilizing music that pointed to a different reality. Other spiritual leaders have used other trappings or devices to get people's attention.

Sun Ra's music is a potent means to an end. It is often deliberately jarring. It is intended to shake listeners out of their complacency. Sun Ra chose melodies, harmonies, and rhythms at odds with what most listeners were accustomed to hearing. They open a pathway to a new way of hearing, a new way of experiencing music. Some of the sound frequencies and harmonics he used seem disturbing. The first adjective that comes to mind is "unearthly." The vibrations created by his music penetrate to the marrow, sometimes seeming to have magical effect. And what is magic but the accessing of a different perspective or knowledge not generally known?

Sun Ra often said he was not a musician but a scientist, a "tone scientist." His music is composed to have a certain specific, significant effect on those who hear it.

"You've got these equations," he has said. "Music is based on equations. There are certain overtones, a certain number of notes, if you divide them wrong you'll be disharmonizing. Music is language. Music is saying things. I got a lot of tapes that I made. The other night I was listening to one of the tapes and it frightened me. What was being said in that song was something else . . . it took me outside the universe. It was my composition and it still frightened me!

"I was playing in Chicago one time and a medical student came up to me and said, 'You're playing nerve music. There's nerves all over a man's body.' So, we play 'nerve music' . . . I have to watch it![19]

"One time at Slug's, a man came up to me and said, 'Have you been to India?' 'No,' I said. 'You're playing forbidden temple music . . . no one's supposed to hear it!'

"Strange things happen to me all the time."

So Sun Ra simply organized his life along nonmaterial lines. Since he perforce had to function among the vast populace of Planet Earth, the majority of whom do not look beyond the material reality of their lives, he had to speak metaphorically, indeed live metaphorically. So when he said he was from Saturn or "somewhere else," he was metaphorically expressing that he was not functioning on a material plane. When speaking to the average person, it is easier to say you're from outer space.

And even though he saw humor in the clash of realities—and the general absurdity of human existence—he was deadly serious about his mission: creating music as a bridge to non-earthbound realities. In

Sun Ra's view, human existence is so self-defeating, so destructive, so wasteful of human potential, that it is imperative to be from "someplace else."

Still, certain elements in his music suggest he might not be from Earth—especially the intervals he created in his music. Intervals are the gaps between notes. When several notes are played together, the different intervals create the distinctive sound and harmony of a chord. Sun Ra orchestrated some of the most unusual intervals ever heard in music. I saw him play a solo piano piece once in which he hit some chords in the lower register that I had never heard before. They were strange and highly disturbing. The first word that came to mind was "unearthly." The vibration created by those chords penetrated to the marrow, giving a sense of some sort of magical effect.

The last time I saw Sun Ra was when Fela Anikulapo-Kuti, the Afrobeat king of Nigeria, came to perform in Philadelphia at the Trocadero Theatre. It was Fela's first U.S. tour after being jailed for eighteen months on trumped-up charges in Nigeria, where he had dared to openly criticize the government and had articulated a personal philosophy of Africanism. So his appearance in Philadelphia was more than just a show.

As a guest of Fela, I was watching the twenty-odd singers, dancers, and musicians of his band Egypt 80 from the side of the stage. A movement of bodies attracted my attention to my right and I was surprised to see Sun Ra, resplendent in leopard print cape and hat moving slowly with a few members of his entourage through the crowded narrow passage alongside the backstage. It was not his habit, at least in his later years, to come out to see other artists perform, so it seemed highly significant that he was there to see Fela. It made perfect sense, as there were many similarities between the two. Fela and Sun Ra drew from the same well. Ra, though claiming to be from outer space, identified with Egypt; Fela's Afrocentrism had roots that led to Egypt. The Yoruba, some believe, had migrated from Sudan and upper Egypt and, of course, Fela's band was called Egypt 80. Both created music that was unique and complex—Fela's compositions often took up to an hour to perform live and he, too, used singers, dancers, costumes, and pageantry as part of his presentation. Both maintained large, semicommunal organizations with far larger musical ensembles than most.

Fela and Sun Ra both articulated a philosophy and spirituality that each had created out of diverse threads of spiritual and cultural tradition. And the music of both men was meant to convey far more than entertainment. Both of them saw their ultimate arena of expression as spiritual. Sun Ra had traveled to Nigeria in 1977 to perform with the Arkestra at the Second World Black Arts Festival. Fela had boycotted the festival but invited many musicians to his own venue, the Shrine; Sun Ra and many of his musicians had encountered him there. Sun Ra's presence at Fela's concert was a statement by him that Fela was a kindred spirit. Perhaps they were communicating on some spiritual level.

Some years seeing Sun Ra at The Trocadero, I heard he was seriously ill and confined to the Germantown hospital. Electronic keyboards were brought to the hospital so that he could continue to compose.[20] On May 20, 1993, he passed away, not long after suffering a heart attack, at the age of seventy-nine. Of course, he would not say he died; he departed this earthly plane . . . passed on. I have only listened to a portion of the hundreds of recordings released by him; yet, in this portion I have heard things that challenged most concepts of what music could be and on occasion affected me deeply in ways I cannot articulate. Having witnessed Sun Ra at work and having met him face to face, I know that he presented directly to people things that seemed impossible, and dared them to deny their reality and power. Unless your senses and mind are hopelessly dulled, it is impossible to ignore Sun Ra or his music. If you listen to his music on its own terms, your view of music, and perhaps life itself, will very likely be permanently altered. Though he has been gone more than ten years now, I think of him often and smile. Sometimes when I have felt that life is untenable, I am reminded of the message of Sun Ra's life and work: there is another way, another "place," another reality, another spiritual realm to be found. Sonny Blount from Birmingham, Alabama, traveled unimaginably far from the unacceptable reality of his birth and, in so doing, showed new possibilities to us all.

Fela Anikulapo-Kuti, photo © David Corio, www.davidcorio.com

Fela Anikulapo-Kuti

The Afrobeat Rebel

Sometimes music is more than entertainment. Sometimes music is a weapon, a tool for the powerless to confront the powerful. Often a musician can transmit certain messages, certain rallying cries more effectively than a political activist using polemical means of communication. Music is a fluid, fundamental aspect of life that cannot be easily suppressed and that can communicate in subtle, even subliminal ways. One might as well try to stop a river from flowing as suppress music. Some musicians have, in certain times and places, become avatars of the collective spirit of a people, conveying their collective fear, rage, hope, and determination.

Such musicians, of course, incur the wrath of those in power. They proceed at their peril. Some have been censored, banned, jailed, or even killed. A select few choose to continue in the face of serious consequences. It is a special sort of person who is willing to die for his or her beliefs. That kind of stand takes a deliberate kind of bravery, quite different from the spontaneous, instinctive bravery some exhibit in the heat of battle. This kind of courage involves the conscious decision to stand in front of guns and play a forbidden song or sing provocative lyrics. I knew one such man who stared death in the face many times, who was beaten, bombed, burned, and jailed. And yet, repeatedly, he picked himself up and resumed his truth-telling through music. Perhaps he felt protected. His name literally meant, in the Yoruba language, "he who carries death in a pouch" or, more figuratively, "he who cannot be killed."

I first encountered his voice. The sound of that voice conveyed an absolutist mindset and boundless energy. It was the voice of a man without doubts. Its emphatic, resonant cadences conveyed certainty, yet its rising inflections gave it a caustic, sarcastic edge that was leavened by lighter tones of impish humor. It was a voice equally suited to mocking authority, puncturing pomposity, or reveling in human folly. Hearing that disembodied voice once was enough to make the unique strength of his spirit instantly comprehensible. Nothing about Fela was a surprise after that.

I was sitting on a spacious, immaculate patio surrounded by the graceful, curving stone-and-glass walls of the Magwan Waterworks Café, an upscale watering hole in Kano, Nigeria, when I first heard Fela's voice. At that time—1974—Kano was a fairly large city on the edge of the Sahel in northern Nigeria. It boasted only a couple of Western-style nightspots, which were little oases of sophistication and comfort in a scuffling, improvised new city negotiating twentieth-century technology on the flanks of the ancient, walled old city, where life had not changed much during the previous hundred years. A few feet away from where I sat beggars squatted in the dust; a few blocks away, women carried buckets of cistern water on their heads. A few miles away, nomads in long cloaks and pointed, almost oriental hats herded their cattle, and black-turbaned desert men in their blue robes led lines of camels at the beginning of a caravan route that, in ancient times, had stretched to China. But on the restaurant patio elegantly dressed men and women—European, African, Asian, and Arab—sipped cool drinks brought by deferential waiters in starched, white jackets. Tiny speakers suspended from light poles piped in music—popular African sounds and fashionable American soul and disco—at a discreet volume, as a convivial soundtrack for the fortunate few.

Then a musical selection abruptly changed the mood. It featured a sort of driving African boogie bass line and drums overlaid by a chiming, jazzy electric piano. A stentorian voice aggressively chanted pidgin English over the groove. The unmistakably male voice was heavy, with an edge, and no vibrato. Unlike the elastic lilt of so much African popular music, with its smoothly pulsating rhythms and liltingly lyrical vocalizing, this singer's phrasing conveyed defiance, assertiveness, even sarcasm. I could not quite catch the words other than a single phrase repeated frequently: "Open . . . open and close." I had no idea what those words meant, but the singer's phrasing of them seemed conspiratorial, as if the speaker and listener were in on a joke, a dirty secret. Whoever the singer was, he seemed to speak his mind without the slightest restraint. "The hell with *you*," the voice seemed to say. "This is what *I'm* about!" It was the voice of a rebel, a trash-all-limits rock 'n' roll spirit. I had not heard anything like it in African music before that moment. West African cultures tend to be oriented toward social harmony, at least in their surface conventions. Such a voice was at odds with the complacency of the elite and made it difficult for them—or anyone—to ignore the dirty realities surrounding their little comfort zone.

Who was it?

"Oh, that's Fela!" Isaac, one of my Nigerian friends said, chuckling with relish and shaking his head in bemusement. Others at the table broke into hearty laughter. Evidently, Fela was somewhat notorious but loved for doing things other dared not do. Indeed, Fela's name had been on everyone's lips during the few months I had been in Nigeria. His throbbing Afrobeat sound blared out from shops into the streets. Newspaper headlines trumpeted the news of his latest arrest, usually for hemp (marijuana) possession, and the reported beating of members of his extended communal organization. Some of his recordings had been banned by the dictatorship. Rumors of the making of his first film, *The Black President,* abounded. The daily newspapers ran Fela's ads for his performances, including juicy quotes from Fela, "the Chief Priest," that often lambasted the authorities. Magazines carried photos of Fela, standing in the yard of his communal compound in Lagos, clad only in briefs, saxophone in hand; exclusive shots of bare-breasted young girls lounging idly around his house titillated the public. The word on the street among young Nigerians was that if you showed up at Fela's compound with no place to go and nothing to eat, you would be given a place to stay and food, in exchange for doing work for his organization. At times more than a hundred people lived there. It was the sort of thing that would have created an innocuous stir in Western countries; in Nigeria it was a major scandal. Nonetheless, his was a voice for the dispossessed. Teenagers idolized him and university students championed him. Many of the elite despised him, but he had plenty of admirers among that group as well; they were not isolated from the common man's lot, since even the affluent had many less privileged relatives in their extended families. The man in the street shook his head delightedly.

"That Fela!" they laughed.

In the United States a musical artist who becomes a rebel may pay a price, but that price is not necessarily very heavy; just as often it is a ticket to fame and fortune. It is very different for a rebel in a country in which a military dictatorship controls the government and traditional cultures still envelope a large portion of the population. Those who have never lived under a military dictatorship may find it difficult to imagine the many ways that life is circumscribed. Superficially, everyday life under a dictator may not seem so bad unless the ruler is a hyper-dictator along the lines of Joseph Stalin, Saddam Hussein, or Kim Jong Il. People may seem to go about their business easily enough. But a magazine on the newsstand might have had certain pages ripped out by the authorities, or the magazine's editors could be jailed; a policeman may oversee rush hour traffic with liberal use of a whip; the guard at the post office may brandish an automatic weapon. And if a citizen for any reason incurs the displeasure of a government official, his or her life could be complicated in ways ranging from annoying to lethal. Troublemakers often disappear. At such times the realization hits home that there is no recourse. Those in charge do not need to justify their actions.

Life under a dictatorship is most notable for what is not said or done—protests that are not made, objections that are unspoken, initiatives that are avoided. People automatically avoid any action that might invite the attention of the authorities. Nigeria in the seventies was a representative example of this syndrome. When the popular head of state Murtala Muhammad was assassinated, rumors abounded that the CIA was behind it. Gerald Ford, president of the United States at that time, proclaimed that he thought it perfectly reasonable that ordinary Americans—journalists, teachers, aid workers—should act as CIA agents. In Nigeria, this statement reinforced existing suspicions. Some Americans in Nigeria were rounded up for questioning. Anyone could be picked up and tossed into jail indefinitely. Some Nigerian dissidents had been in jail for years without charges ever being brought. Public executions were not infrequent.

As a man living under a military dictatorship, Fela's focus was not just winning the right to express himself in an outrageous manner or to live an alternative lifestyle. He spoke for the dispossessed. He wrote and sang about those who did not frequent the Magwan Water Works—those beggars in the street, those women carrying buckets long distances because their households lacked running water, those young people who could not afford to finish school and were desperately seeking some way to a decent life. On their behalf Fela threw down the gauntlet to the elite powers. He took his protest a step further than others did; he named names. In most traditional African societies, social critics use indirect means such as satire or parable to criticize the powerful. Their audiences get the point but without it being expressed overtly. This acculturated politesse, encouraged by authoritarian governments, still held sway in much of urban African society in the seventies. Fela did things differently. He baldly stated that those in power were corrupt liars, thieves, and hypocrites. It was the first of many ironies I was to discover about Fela—that a man so outspoken about the need for African authenticity and tradition would be so untraditional in his behavior. His courage was impressive because the price paid by a cultural or political rebel in Nigeria at that time could be beatings, prison, even death.

It was Fela's mix of controversial lyrics and powerful music that captivated people. During the mid-seventies, he seemed to be releasing a new album every three months, although most only had two songs on them, each running twelve to twenty minutes, often filling an entire side of vinyl. The covers of Fela's albums were often garish, anarchic illustrations. *Gentleman*, for instance, depicted a giant ape wearing a Western business suit. The lyrics of the title track satirized Africans who adopted European ways that did not make sense in the African environment, such as wearing a suit in tropical heat, or eating only a small portion of food out of politeness even when they were hungry. *Algabon Close*, which referred to the location of the central police headquarters in Lagos, featured an illustration of Fela breaking out of shackles and capsizing a patrol boat, with the crumbling police station and Fela's graffiti-emblazoned home base, Kalakuta Republic, in the background. Not every album cover featured an illustration. One sported a photograph of a bevy of topless, young women standing behind a barbed-wire barrier with Fela standing bare-chested among them. All concerned have raised, clenched, fists and shit-eating grins—a new kind of Black Power salute. The name of the album? *Expensive Shit*. The title referred to one of Fela's arrests for marijuana possession. Evidently, the authorities, convinced that Fela had swallowed the evidence, monitored his bowel movements in jail and probed his excrement for said evidence. This led Fela (as usual making a joke and a point at the same time) to conclude that his shit was very valuable indeed.

The music was stupendous. Fela called it Afrobeat, and it was one of those rare events: something entirely new. The essence of Afrobeat was a deep, heavy, pulsing, polyrhythmic groove created by electric bass, multiple percussion—trap drums, congas, *sekere* (a beaded gourd), sticks—electric guitars, and keyboards. The rhythm was an original amalgam of James Brown funk and West African rhythms: traditional Yoruba beats, primarily, but also highlife, itself a mixture of African and West Indian rhythms. Over the groove, a full horn section of saxophones and trumpets blared choruses that stated melodic themes and answered the vocals in the traditional African call-and-response pattern. Soloists, including Fela on tenor and alto saxophones as well as electric piano or organ, would take turns playing rambling, declamatory jazz solos, rhythm-based excursions verging at points on free improvisation. The overall effect of the Afrobeat groove was a massive, oceanic rhythmic pulse. At some point Fela would begin to declaim or sing, as the mood struck him, delivering sing-song lines in pidgin English or Yoruba, as a chorus of six or more female singers answered him with charged refrains. On record, the average song lasted ten or twenty minutes. In live performance, one song might end up going on for an hour.

Funk, African rhythms, jazz, and political lyrics; that was the unique Afrobeat mix invented by Fela. It was so completely an expression of his persona that no other artist could really bring it off. Others—Sunny Ade, Sonny Okosun, the Lijadu Sisters—incorporated Afrobeat elements into their music but the results were generally pale imitations of Fela. Unlike blues, jazz, highlife, juju, funk, or any number of other styles of music, Afrobeat was invented, defined, popularized, and successfully practiced by one man: Fela.

Fela orchestrated the new Afrobeat sound, but it is hard to imagine without the contribution of trap drummer Tony Allen. Fela met Allen in 1964 and recruited him to be the drummer in Koola Lobitos, a group he founded with the express intention of reinventing highlife by injecting it with jazz and, later, funk elements. Fela approached Allen because he had seen Allen's unique ability to maintain the power of African rhythms even as he embellished them with jazz drumming techniques. Even more important, considering the importance of multiple percussion parts in West African music, Allen played his Western drum set in a way that worked organically with the African percussion. His style was an uncanny combination of power and subtlety; he never overplayed, leaving lots of space in the rhythm for the kinds of dramatic accents and statements that make the African use of rhythm so sophisticated and compelling. It is an open question whether Fela's creation of Afrobeat would have come to fruition without the abilities of one of the world's great drummers.

Fela renamed his band Afrika 70, espousing the unity of the seventy then existing African nations. Fela's ascendance coincided with Nigeria's emergence from the disastrous effects of the Biafran civil war as well as the nationalization of the country's oil industry, which injected vast amounts of money into the national economy and gave Nigeria political clout internationally. In 1974, Fela and Afrika 70 hit a peak of popularity just as Nigeria hit a peak of optimism about its ability to be a leader among Third World nations, to be the dominant power in Africa, and to bring unprecedented affluence its people. But it already was becoming clear that the masses in Nigeria were not benefiting from the oil boom in any meaningful way. In his music, Fela directly raised the question of who was benefiting from the oil wealth and then answered his own question by indicting the Nigerian elite as corrupt, greedy, and incompetent abusers of the people. "Go Slow," for instance, used the infamous Lagos traffic jams as a metaphor for a country whose modern infrastructure did not work because of governmental incompetence and neglect. "Algabon Close" described the abusive activities of the police against "undesirables" and ordinary citizens alike. "Jeun K'oku (Eat and Die)" criticized the rich elite with its portrait of gluttonous greed, consuming everything within reach. Fela became a major thorn in the side of the Nigerian government and its private-sector accomplices. That is when the arrests and random attacks on began.

From accounts in the daily newspapers, the *New Nigerian* and the *Daily News*, the authorities seemed to act against Fela or his followers on a nearly weekly basis. Fela or members of his organization were constantly being arrested and jailed, often for petty offenses; usually the charges were dismissed. Fela and the authorities played a cat-and-mouse game. Every time Fela and his entourage set out to play a show outside of town, the Lagos police arrested the singer, most often on charges of possession of hemp (at least that charge had some basis in reality!). Soon he would be freed, largely through the efforts of his mother, the formidable Funmilayo Ransome-Kuti.

Born in the western Nigeria town of Oshogbo, Fela came from a prominent Yoruba family. His father, the Rev. Oludofun Ransome-Kuti, was a well-known minister and educator. Rev. Ransome-Kuti was a straight-laced, take-no-nonsense Nigerian man who had been schooled by missionaries and who became one of the few Nigerians allowed by colonial authorities to flourish in those pre-Independence days. His mother, on the other hand, was an anti-colonial activist who once led all the market women of a certain town in a strike when a local chief refused to rescind a tax imposed by colonial authorities. Since the market women were at the hub of the town's daily commerce, the chief had to back down. Fela's mother was a rebel, a champion of women's rights, and an intimate of the pan-African crusader Dr. Kwame Nkrumah, the first president of independent Ghana. Although she was just as strict and demanding as Fela's father during her son's formative years, he was clearly her favorite child, and when he was arrested she would use her connections to get him released. The arrests often triggered protests and demonstrations, mostly by students, which only intensified the government's desire to suppress Fela and to jail or expel the protesters.

Fela had not always been a rebel. Those who knew him in his student days describe him as somewhat diffident, even shy around the ladies.[1] He had always been stubborn, though, with an acute sense of injustice. He told me in later years that between his father and mother—both of whom subscribed to old-fashioned notions of parenting—he had received no fewer than three thousand blows between the ages of seven and seventeen. Then he was packed off to London to study music, which he defiantly insisted on pursuing instead of a more respectable career. In London he hung out in the jazz clubs and experienced camaraderie with musicians from all parts of the African diaspora—Africa, the Caribbean, and the Americas. He also met and married a British-Nigerian woman named Remi.

When he returned to Nigeria, after some desultory work at the Nigerian Broadcasting Corporation (he was fired due to a combination of lateness and intransigence) he formed Koola Lobitos in an effort to forge a progressive blend of jazz and highlife. But Koola Lobitos was not especially popular. At this point in his career, Fela was simply a moderately talented, struggling musician whose relatively affluent background gave him the opportunity to pursue his musical dreams.

A trip to the United States in 1969 changed all that. America blew Fela's mind. A financial angel had arranged for him to travel to the States with Koola Lobitos to play a series of shows arranged by some stateside Nigerians. Koola Lobitos had been struggling in Lagos, so the trip must have seemed like a heaven-sent opportunity. Unfortunately, the tour fell apart and the band ended up stranded in Los Angeles hustling gigs anywhere it could. Fela was overwhelmed by the impact of America's marvels, which is surprising considering he had spent so much time in London.

"Africa is nothing," he recalled thinking when I interviewed him many years later. The United States' riches and technological wizardry, its superhighways, spectacular buildings, and intoxicating cultural explosion of the go-go sixties was daunting. Fela felt uncharacteristically humble and small. But then he met a woman, one of a series of women who had crucial impact on him. Sandra Isidore was a political activist heavily involved with radical organizations such as the Black Panthers. She gave him a book to read: *The Autobiography of Malcolm X*.

"I hadn't read a book in years," Fela later told me. But he devoured the *Autobiography*. Its description of the self-actualization of an oppressed person, combined with Sandra Isidore's perspective of pan-Africanism, struck a deep chord in Fela. It was an antidote to the feelings of powerlessness he had been experiencing as an African in America. Almost immediately, a vision coalesced in his mind, a vision of African empowerment rooted in African identity and culture. This vision found its natural expression in his music, through the creation of Afrobeat. After finishing the *Autobiography,* Fela sat down at the piano and composed a song—which he later described as his first African composition. It was based on a chantlike melody and drew on African vocal styles and a rhythmic concept influenced by seminal African drummers such as Guy Warren, whom Fela had known in London, and Ambrose Campbell. It also incorporated the traditional rhythms he had heard all his life.

When Fela returned to Lagos in 1970, he and the band, now renamed Nigeria 70 but soon to be called Afrika 70, hit like a rocket ship from the future. Fela, fired by a revolutionary vision of Africa—which, ironically, he had found in America—shed all notions of propriety and convention; he had absorbed the ethos and ambience of America's counterculture—hippies, communes, the Black Panthers, protesters, and the like. He and Afrika 70 quickly became a sensation, especially among Nigerian youth. This was the unfettered Fela I had been hearing and would eventually come to know.

However, in 1976, although I had been in Nigeria for two years, I still had not been to Lagos, except for an overnight stay on my arrival in Nigeria. I had not seen Fela in the flesh. Because the police were making it difficult for Fela to travel, a pilgrimage to the Shrine, the venue where Fela performed, was the way to make it happen. A chance meeting with a Nigerian pop group called Bongos and the Groovies made it happen. I had gone with Nigerian friends to see the group perform at the Central Hotel in Kano. Apparently the band's keyboard player had suddenly deserted and when they learned I was a keyboard player, I was immediately invited to sit in. My efforts proved satisfactory and I was asked to join the group on a regular basis and on its upcoming nationwide tour. Bongos and the Groovies played a wide range of material: American funk and R&B; highlife; Congolese styles, known collectively as "Congo"; reggae; and Afrobeat. Playing with this band gave me an opportunity to experience Afrobeat from the inside. Chris, the bass player, usually led the Afrobeat tunes, laying down a hypnotic bass figure. I filled in a two-chord *ostinato* on electric piano as Ajiboye, the guitarist, picked out funky little riffs, and Mike, the drummer, kept a pulse going on the high hat and snare. This added up to a powerful, oscillating current that the musicians rode like surfers sliding up and down giant ocean swells. It was as entrancing to perform as it was to hear. When our tour hit Lagos, Joe, Bongos' conga player, offered to take me to see Fela at the Shrine.

It was about 11:00 p.m. on a still steamy Lagos night when Joe and I pulled up in front of the club in my Volkswagen Beetle. The Shrine was located in a scruffy neighborhood on the edge of the vast slum of Mushin, a part of Lagos where thousands of men and women ended up when they came to the city from the country to seek their fortune. An open sewage ditch, a common sight in most Nigerian cities, ran between the Shrine and the street. Groups of young men hung about outside the entrance, a couple of vendors were selling *suya*, a barbe-cued, spiced meat on a stick. The Shrine was actually located in the courtyard of the Empire Hotel; in Nigeria, it is common for open-air nightclubs to be attached to hotels. As Joe and I walked up to a dimly lit doorway, the pulsing throb of bass and percussion vibrated the walls. A surly gatekeeper patted us down for weapons; after passing muster we paid the few Naira—the equivalent of fifty cents—admis-sion, walked down a semi-dark hallway, and turned the corner into the club.

The scene before us formed an indelible tableau; it seemed more a communal rite than a show. The courtyard, open except for a portion around the perimeter covered by a corrugated iron roof, was dimly lit by the lurid glow from red light bulbs. A haze of hemp smoke hung over the heads of a jam-packed crowd of hundreds. Around the pe-rimeter hung paintings of the flags of all seventy African nations. On raised platforms, young women in skimpy, fringed two-piece outfits wriggled their hips in time to the Afrobeat pulse, like African go-go dancers. Many in the crowd echoed the dancers with a less flamboyant hip-shake. The heaving sea of humanity was tuned into one frequen-cy—Fela—who arguably was at the absolute pinnacle of his power and influence.

Onstage, the band, more than twenty strong, generated a boiling cauldron of sound. A trap drummer, three or four hand drummers playing traditional African drums reminiscent of conga drums, and a bassist created the foundation pulse as two percussionists, one playing sticks and the other playing *sekere,* advanced and retreated on either side of the stage. Three electric guitarists played funk riffs, one playing chords and two others picking out staccato single-note lines that amplified the groove. A half dozen horn players, saxophonists, and trumpet players blew choruses. Eight female vocalists, resplendent in lime-green African-print maxi-dresses and elaborate, brightly colored head wraps, jiggled in place behind the microphone, their hips replicating the beat. In the center of it all was Fela, shirtless, his left arm and shoulder swathed in a white bandage, the result of an altercation with the police. He had a slight, wiry build, a small head with cross-cropped hair, and striking if not overly handsome features. Fela's tight, white pants were embroidered with swirling talismanic designs in turquoise and gold thread. He was blowing an alto saxophone, playing hard with his legs apart, his eyes bulging slightly and his chest heaving. His playing was ragged and jazzy, sometimes with an atonal squawk, sometimes sounding like a harangue, other times mocking and humorous. After several minutes he stopped playing and held his instrument to the side. A young boy who had been sitting by the side of the stage ran to him with a tenor saxophone, and took away the alto; years later, I realized that this small boy had been Fela's son, Femi. Fela embarked on yet another raging solo on the tenor saxophone, lasting several minutes. This time, when he stopped blowing, the young boy ran to him and took the saxophone but did not bring another. Fela whirled around and jumped behind the electric piano, jabbing at it, sometimes mis-hitting a note, intentionally or not, to create a dissonant interval as he played a percussive, pentatonic solo.

When he was finished with the piano, Fela strode out to center stage, a large spliff in one hand. He began pacing like a panther getting ready to stalk its prey, pausing only to take prodigious draws on the spliff. He began talking about the police, recounting the story of their attack, and denouncing their brutality. Then, he began to sing over the groove in pidgin English (singing in pidgin was a political statement because pidgin was the lingua franca of the multi-ethnic urban masses; singing in Yoruba would have reinforced ethnic divisions that had torn the country apart only a few years earlier):

When trouble sleep, yanga [a provoker] go wake am
Wetin [what] him de find? Palaver [trouble] him go get

My friend just come from prison
Him de look for work
Waka waka [walk all over] day and night
Police man stop am [him] for road
Him say "Mr. I charge you for wandering"
Wetin he de find?
Palaver him de find?[2]

Then one of the saxophonists started to play a solo, and Fela jumped back behind the electric piano, to comp behind the solo. And on and on. Many songs lasted an hour. The band played for many hours without a break. Afrika 70 usually played until daybreak. It was called the Shrine for a reason: Frequently, the night's proceedings would begin with a libation poured to the ancestors and a Yoruba priest said a prayer. The night's proceedings were designed to gather spiritual energy.

As Fela chanted and sang his satirical lyrics in pidgin or Yoruba, his chorus singers answered him. As Fela sang, his lips formed a petulant pout and his jaw thrust out defiantly. Now and then, he laughed lustily and bantered with the audience. His every gesture proclaimed a defiance and an assertion of self that were rare in African music. His manner was that of a rock 'n' roll rebel except that his music was funk, jazz, and African beats. He was charismatic and riveting, a natural star. No wonder he was a hero to African teenagers and university students.

As it turned out, I had seen Fela just in time, at his creative and charismatic peak. Storm clouds were gathering as the Nigerian government became more repressive. The government was heralding a showcase event—FESTAC, the 2nd World Black Arts Festival—which was to gather artists of African descent from all over the world for a spectacular cavalcade of performances on the scale of the Olympics. The event, which was to present musicians, singers, dancers, and other kinds of artists, was also intended to assert Nigeria's leadership of the pan-African world. It was a massive undertaking, financed by Nigeria's petrodollars at a time when many Nigerians lacked basic amenities. The country watched in early 1977 as hundreds of governmental entourages and thousands of artists descended on Lagos for many weeks of performances, pageantry, and conferences. It was in many ways a fascinating undertaking but also fantastically expensive, so some Nigerians questioned the government's priorities. People wondered where all the money went, and Fela was one of those raising his voice.

Originally Fela had been invited to be on the festival's steering committee, but he soon resigned. His weekly ads in the newspapers proclaimed: "I cannot be a part of anything that is not first quality."

Years later he expressed his feelings in detail.

"FESTAC!" he sneered. "One big hustle. A rip-off! They tried getting me in it. They started out being nice to me and that sort of thing. So I presented a nine-point program to make the festival meaningful. The first point of my program called for the participation of the people. Then, I denounced the way in which the cultures of Nigeria were being treated trivially. But Maj. Gen. Haruna rejected those proposals. Then I resigned."[3]

So Fela did not participate in the official FESTAC, but he held a kind of counter-FESTAC at the Shrine. Artists from Europe, the United States, and the Caribbean (among them members of James Brown's band and Sun Ra's ensemble) came to the Shrine because they wanted to see Fela. It was highly embarrassing to the Nigerian authorities.

"All the big musicians and artists FESTAC brought in wanted to see me, man," Fela noted with satisfaction. "For one whole month, every night, Shrine was packed by blacks from all over the world. And since they wanted to know what was happening in Nigeria, I told them!"

Shortly after FESTAC ended and the spotlight of world attention disappeared, the government made its move. There had been rumors that Fela had political ambitions; he was involved with a youth-oriented political group, Young African Pioneers, as well as a group called Movement of the People (M.O.P.), and some believed that Kalakuta Republic, as he had dubbed his communal base of operations, was Fela's attempt to set up a sovereign state within Nigeria. He had also started work on a film, *The Black President*. One day a band of soldiers showed up at Kalakuta. They surrounded the property and demanded that one of Fela's "boys" be handed over because of an alleged altercation with the police. Fela refused. The soldiers cut the power to the compound and attacked, going on a rampage that resulted in scores of people injured, the house ransacked and burned to the ground. Fela's irreplaceable master tapes as well as his musical equipment were destroyed. Women were raped, some violated with broken bottles. Fela's mother was thrown out of a window and suffered a broken leg. Not long after the incident, she died. Fela was badly beaten.

Fela was devastated by the attack and his organization was shattered. I spoke with Sandra Isidore in Los Angeles a couple of years after the fact. She had spent time at Kalakuta only a year before. I asked her how Fela had dealt with this blow.

"The destruction of his home and the death of his mother had a very serious impact on his life," she said. "I didn't realize how serious until I went there. The destruction of Kalakuta had broken him to some degree. The government practically destroyed the man. They beat him to his knees, then they began beating his knees."

The outrage generated by the attack led to an official inquiry. It concluded that "an unknown soldier" had been responsible for the fire that had destroyed Kalakuta. Fela released a recording called "Unknown Soldier"; it was dedicated to his mother. He also led a procession carrying his mother's coffin to the home of the head of state, Gen. Olusegun Obasanjo; this act was memorialized on a new recording, *Coffin for Head of State*.

The attack was not the end of Fela. Friends, family and supporters came to the rescue. Someone donated land in Ikeja, on the outskirts of Lagos, to build another Shrine. The government allowed it to exist only because it was considered a shrine, not just a nightclub. In a grandiose gesture, Fela married twenty-six women of his organization all on the same day, in a traditional Yoruba ceremony. Henceforth, the women were known as Fela's Queens. The thoughts of Remi, his wife of more than a decade, were not made public. Fela later said that he married the women in recognition of their loyalty and suffering and to give them social respectability. But from that moment on, any Western media attention made prominent mention of Fela's twenty-seven wives, a titillating conflation of the West's harem fantasies.

Back in the United States, much had changed. The political activism and countercultural movements of the sixties were largely dormant. On the music scene, hedonistic disco, overblown rock, and self-referential singer-songwriters dominated. The harsh realities of Nigeria seemed far away, but Fela's music began to surface in the States. Mercury Records released *Zombie*, which had been banned in Nigeria by the military, and it was reviewed in *Rolling Stone*. I found a copy of Fela's new recording *Johnny Just Drop*—a devastating critique of the Nigeria bourgeoisie—in House of Oshogbo, a small Afrocentric craft shop in the heart of the north Philadelphia ghetto. Like a disciple spreading the prophet's word, I felt compelled to tell people about Fela and to play his music for them. One of my more quixotic efforts came when I persuaded the deejay at a bar on the edge of North Philly to play "Zombie." The spot was a rough-and-tumble neighborhood joint for a crowd of hard-drinking, mostly African American, regulars, who crouched over their drinks and kibbitzed with their neighbors. A go-go dancer named Smoke shook her rear end onstage to the latest disco and funk hits. According to some sociopolitical theorists, the white-dominated media prevented African Americans from embracing African culture. Would a lightning bolt from the motherland galvanize the denizens of a bar at 22nd and Erie in North Philly? The deejay liked "Zombie," but nobody else showed signs of interest.

"These people aren't going to be into that," the deejay said dismissively. "It's too progressive."

When I began presenting a world music show on a local radio station, I was able to more effectively showcase Fela's music. I faithfully played at least one Fela cut every show, and often got calls from listeners who wanted to know who he was. Across the country, similar shows on community or college radio stations also were playing Fela's music. He was the underground artist of choice for pan-African culturists. Along with Bob Marley, Fela became a beacon of substance in a politically vapid landscape.

By the early 1980s Fela had renamed his band Egypt 80, signaling a change in both consciousness and musical direction. His compositions were longer, the tempos slower, the melodies less buoyant. His music carried a more reflective spirit, tinged with melancholy, but the lyrics were as hard-hitting as ever. In "I.T.T. (International Thief Thief)", Fela named Chief Abiola, the head of the Nigerian branch of I.T.T. (International Telephone and Telegraph), as a thief. Arista Records unaccountably licensed and released Fela's *Black President* album, which contained "I.T.T.," in the States.

In 1984, the news came from Nigeria that Fela would tour North America. It seemed miraculous. Possibly, despite all his setbacks, Fela would triumph. Concert dates were announced and plans laid for Fela's fifty-strong entourage to fly to New York City. The buzz was fierce among African music fans, Afrocentric politicos, and others from the grass-roots underground: the Afrocentric messiah was coming!

On the eve of the tour, I received a phone call from a friend in New York who was involved with some of the tour arrangements. Fela's band had arrived, but he had not; Fela had been arrested by the authorities at the Lagos airport. I went to the Gramercy Hotel in New York where the band was staying. Emerging from the elevator on the floor that Fela's group was occupying, I encountered a scene reminiscent of a refugee camp. I found dispirited band members and various "Queens" hanging around their rooms or sitting morosely on the floor in the hallway, smoking hemp. Luggage and belongings were scattered around as clouds of hemp smoke drifted down the hallway. Fela's entourage hoped that the arrest had been a misunderstanding or that perhaps the authorities were just messing with Fela. Maybe someone had not paid a bribe.

The charges against Fela supposedly involved the illegal export of currency, a ridiculous charge. Fela had sent the band on ahead, saying he would catch another flight when the problem was sorted out. But the scenario was all too familiar, harking back to the early seventies when Fela and Afrika 70 would set out to tour and immediately be arrested as they headed out of town. The government did not want Fela on tour in the United States, speaking to the media with his usual lack of restraint and haranguing his audiences about injustices in Nigeria. The elite of Nigeria depended on oil revenues and the support of American oil corporations, as well as the U.S. government.

A couple of days went by and Fela had still not arrived. The scheduled New York show went forward with Fela's son, Femi—who had been playing with the band for a few years by that point—fronting Egypt 80. It was a depressing night; the performances were disorganized and the band uninspired.

Soon word came from Nigeria that Fela was to be tried for violations of currency laws. Despite a complete lack of evidence, Fela was convicted and sentenced to ten years in prison. The fix was in. Photos appeared in the press of Fela being led to jail, clenched fist raised, by three grim-faced soldiers. In the photos he grins ruefully as if recalling an old joke that had been played on him before. His grin looked a little forced and I felt that maybe this time there would be no happy ending. I wondered if he was thinking the same thing.

However, Nigeria's rulers had made a mistake. They were used to carrying out their travesties of justice with impunity, but they had underestimated Fela's worldwide following. An immediate outcry ensued. Stories ran in the international press, on radio, and on television. Benefit concerts were organized. Amnesty International got involved. I wrote a long article for *Spin* magazine recounting Fela's musical and cultural exploits as well as detailing his arrest and imprisonment.

Fela always felt protected. "Anikulapo means 'he who can't be killed,'" Fela once told me. "I don't fear death."

The spirits that protected Fela seemed to intervene once again. The judge who had sentenced Fela visited him in jail and apologized, saying that he had succumbed to pressure from the authorities to convict despite a lack of evidence. The press got wind of this, and the judge later wrote a letter urging that Fela's sentence be commuted. In 1986, Fela walked out of prison, a free man after having served only eighteen months of the ten-year sentence. I was the first journalist from abroad to interview him following his release.

I had been given the telephone number of Fela's brother Beko, a respected physician and activist. Beko worked for change from within the establishment—although that did not spare him from frequent arrests. As I dialed the number of Beko's home, I suddenly realized that this would be the first time I would actually speak with Fela. I struggled to make myself understood over a noisy connection. At last, Fela came on the line. I wondered how open he would be, talking to a stranger from America, considering his precarious situation.

"I'm glad to be speaking to you at last," I said.

"Yes, well, I'm happy to be speaking to you as a free man," Fela replied, his resonant voice triumphing over the static on the line.

"You've been in prison before," I noted. "How was this time different?"

"Oh, it was real prison, man. I'd never stayed more than thirty days for any kind of grievance before. This was eighteen months. Our prisons are very bad. When I was in Ikoyi Prison, people were dying every day. They were carrying bodies out of the prison every day. The hy-

giene is nil, no good food anywhere, medical care is nil. Prisoners have
to buy their own medicine."

"What sort of treatment did you have from the jailers?"

"Oh, most of them were friendly. Most, not all. They were ordinary
Africans. They suffer the same things we suffer. They just work for
their pay. They don't necessarily have to be hostile toward me because
they understand what I am doing. They really aren't against me."

"What did you do to keep your spirit alive and maintain yourself?"

Fela chuckled. "When I was going to prison, I said to myself, 'If
these people want me to suffer, then I must learn to suffer!' That was
my first thought. When I got to jail, man, I saw that it was very bor-
ing. To kill boredom, I had to either read books or play games. Then I
decided that these things only create an artificial interest. I decided to
not play games, *not* read books, and just try to let the time go and see
whether I could conquer boredom that way—try to think, if possible,
think only of the future, if possible, to think of the past, then remix it
toward the future. It was difficult at first, but things moved faster."

"Will you sue the government for imprisoning you for no reason?"

Fela laughed sardonically. "How can I sue a government in a court I
have already said is corrupt? I've sued them many times and they didn't
pay me anything. It's a waste of time. There isn't any court. We just
have people putting on wigs—that's all we got here!"

"Some people might say if you'd been a little more subtle, a little
more calculating, you would not have been so persecuted. Is there
sense in that?"

"Yes, there is sense, but there is also sense in just acting the way
you feel, without compromising, rather than acting on the concept of
being afraid of being punished for one thing or another. I'm not your
average politician. I believe in higher forces. I believe that suffering has
a purpose. I cannot suffer like this for no reason. I'm not working for
any selfish reason or ulterior motives. I'm working for the improve-
ment of my fellow man. So I have nothing to fear. I suffered a lot, but
I feel fine now. I'm happy for the suffering because I believe it's opened
the eyes of many people. I have accomplished so far two things: People
finally know the honesty of my struggle and the potentiality of my
leadership. People now want to hear what I'm saying. I will make a
very final statement—what I think the government should do, what I

think the country should do. I'm going to finish making those state-ments and then go back to work. I'm going to make my statement that I'm still going to run for president. The rest I can't tell you until I say it in the open. I don't want anyone to say I'm telephoning the CIA in secret." He laughed.

"Your manager said you don't believe in marriage anymore."

"I didn't say that. I said that I wasn't going to allow the marriage institution to tie me down anymore. I said I'm going to play down my marriage, make my environment more open because I want to have more women around me. Not only because I like women but also because of my business, many women want to come around me. The marriage I had several years ago has made many African women who want to participate in my art stay away. Those around me have used marriage to try to envelop my life—to make my environment inaccessible to other women. My wives created a jealous ring around me. Women couldn't speak to me. Women who weren't married to me were being harassed, which is not at all in the African concept of married life. You know, this is very colonial. The women are influ-enced by foreign lifestyles. So now I will do as I was doing before I was married. I have a new life now and I don't want anything to stop that freedom."

It all sounded like the old Fela. And the best news was that he was coming on tour to the States with Egypt 80. He suggested I meet him in Philadelphia, the first stop on the tour. Not long after, I found my-self in the middle of the Trocadero Theater, an old burlesque house that had been converted into a concert facility. The rows of seats had been removed, and so I stood in the empty space watching techni-cians and equipment people setting up a vast array of instruments and amplifiers onstage. Fela's road manager had gone backstage to let Fela know that I was there to see him. Something caused me to turn around and, suddenly, I saw Fela striding toward me, a broad grin on his face. He seemed smaller up close, slighter than I remembered. He was wearing a full-length, multicolored fur coat, which he habitually wore when touring colder climes. It was only November, so I could not help thinking that the fur coat was more than just protection against the cold. Perhaps it was Fela's way of saying that the West was spiritu-ally inhospitable so he had to gird himself against the chill of spiritual alienation.

As he approached, Fela threw his arms open wide and embraced me warmly. I was surprised by the warmth of his greeting. I had assumed he was only dimly aware of who I was. Perhaps he had heard about the articles I had written about his plight when he was in jail. Maybe he remembered our interview. Possibly the fact that he knew I had lived in Nigeria gave me credibility.

"How are you?" I asked. His youthful countenance seemed perceptibly less vibrant, as though something vital had been sapped from him. A quantum of life-spirit had been taken away. Could it simply be that he was nearly a decade older than when I had last seen him? He was, after all, only 48, his face still unlined. No, the change was not caused by age. I was seeing what Sandra Isidore had mentioned to me—the results of years of repeated physical, psychological, and spiritual blows over a period of years. The miracle lay in how much vitality Fela still possessed.

"Welcome to Philadelphia!" I said, drawing out my words slightly to underline the irony of the factors that had led to us meeting there, rather than, say, in Nigeria.

"I am *very* happy to be here!" he said, his grin widening. The unspoken remainder of that sentence was: "Rather than where I've been."

"We must talk," he said. "But after the show. I'm doing sound check now. Come backstage after the show."

The show that night—the first one of his long-delayed U.S. tour—was powerful. He commanded the stage full of musicians as authoritatively as ever, conducting them with emphatic jabs of his hands, orchestrating the successive layers of sound and rhythm. The newer Egypt 80 sound set a more languid, melancholy, ruminative mood. He had decided never to play anything he that had already recorded; he would only play newer, unrecorded compositions. Anyone yearning to hear "Zombie" or "Lady" or "Black Man's Cry" was to be disappointed. The absence of Tony Allen, who had left the band in 1978, loomed large. As bandleader and drummer, Tony had helped invent the Afrobeat pulse, and it was so much a product of his unique, subtly propulsive style that any other drummer produced only a lesser version of it.

Fela prefaced each song—and there were only three—with a long monologue. Unlike the old days, the band did not vamp behind him as he spoke his mind. Each time he held forth for fifteen minutes or more, talking about Africa, America, corruption, brutality, and thievery in order to provide a context for the upcoming piece of music. Each song's title was expressed as an acronym: "B.O.N.N.—Beast of No Nation"; "O.D.O.O.—Overtake Don Overtake Overtake"; "J.L.T.— Just Like That." At key moments in his perorations, Fela would pose a question or set up a statement whose punch line was the title of the song. He would cue the audience to deliver the punch line, which they did dutifully, setting up a call-and-response dynamic.

Any other audience would have lost patience after five minutes of lecturing, but these people were charged by pent-up anticipation. The mere fact that they were in the presence of the legendary Fela after years of waiting was enough. Even so, there was some restlessness when he launched into a third long monologue. In general, though, the wall-to-wall crowd at the Trocadero did not mind Fela's speechifying. Some fans had waited years to see him, having long ago been electrified by his recordings. Others, Nigerians mainly, saw him as a conquering hero helping them to reconnect with a lost part of themselves, the progressive, prosperous Nigeria so many had hoped for at independence nearly three decades earlier. Still others had come because they were drawn by the myth, the larger-than-life image of an authentic African rebel rocker. They had come if for no other reason than that they could tell people that they had been there. Among this group, any small gesture—the lighting of a spliff, the waggle of a hip, a sarcastic aside, a flatulent saxophone squawk—could ignite a small frenzy.

At one point in the show, as the band vamped, Fela stepped to the microphone with his a knowing grin and announced: "And now it's time for a little old-fashioned African butt-shaking!" With that his four female dancers wiggled onstage, wearing skimpy, shredded two-piece outfits and an abundance of jewelry, their faces daubed with chalk-white lines of spiritual powder that turned their faces into fantastic African masks, and thin strips of leather wound around their arms and legs. One by one they each took a solo, using their rear ends as instrument, to demonstrate that African butt-shaking was a higher order of expression than the American variety. But the way Fela had introduced the dancers seemed odd— as though he were the ringmaster at a circus. Was he cynically indulging in a showbiz device, knowing it was part of the spectacle that would keep journalists writing and people coming to his shows? Or, since female dancers had been an integral part of his performances since the early Afrika 70 days, was he mocking his own devotion to this earthy bit of entertainment amidst his high-minded crusading? Or was he making an ironic comment on the differences between Western and African attitudes toward this sort of thing? There was no way to tell.

At the end, as the band hit a final cacophonous fanfare, Fela raised his clenched fists, his own version of the Black Power salute (out of fashion by a decade in the United States) and turned, grinning, first left, then right, then toward the band, and finally toward the audience, his fists still raised. He was acknowledging spirits. The band members raised their fists as well—echoing Fela's eternal gesture of defiance and determination.

I had witnessed the final song from the side of the stage and was startled at one point by a wave of motion in the throng hanging out there. Moving toward me was the massive shape of Sun Ra, in full regalia, accompanied by several members of his entourage. Sun Ra, at that point in time, did not come out to see many musicians. Sun Ra's presence at The Trocadero was a benediction.

After the show, I made my way upstairs to the dressing rooms. The stairs and passageways were crammed with admirers, scenesters, band members, singers, dancers, and handlers. I pushed my way to the doorway of one dressing room and saw Fela sitting on a chair against one wall. A dreadlocked young African American man was seated next to him, talking earnestly. Fela was listening distractedly, like a village chief deigning to hear a supplicant. The room was filled with band members chilling out, laughing, conversing and chatting up the many admirers who were milling around, just happy to be part of the scene. I stood by the door and waited. Finally the young man received a Black Power handshake from Fela, got up, and moved toward the door. Fela looked up and saw me. He patted the now-empty chair meaningfully. This was his style at home or on the road: he would summon those who wanted to see him when he was ready to give them an audience.

I sat next to Fela. He was lighting a huge spliff.

"So, what did you think of the show?" he asked in his characteristic clipped tones.

"I think maybe people wanted to hear some of the old songs," I answered.

"Ah! I no longer play them. I will only play my new compositions now. I don't want to dwell in the past. I have so much new music. How was the sound?"

"It sounded fine out in the crowd."

He took a prodigious draw on the spliff.

"Well, I'm glad of that. I couldn't hear shit!"

"That last song you did as an encore reminded me of some of your old tunes," I ventured.

Fela smiled and nodded. "Yes, well, that's because it *is* an old tune. One I never recorded."

"You should record that one."

"You think so? Perhaps I will. In any event, Francis tells me that your company would like to release some of my recordings."

This was true. On behalf of Shanachie Entertainment, I had contacted Francis Kertekian, Fela's French manager, who had been licensing classic Fela recordings to European companies. We had entered into a preliminary agreement to release his newest album, *Beasts of No Nation*, in time for Fela's next U.S. tour.

"You must contact my lawyer in New York," Fela directed. "We are trying to clean up the mess with all these thief-thief companies who have been releasing my shit. Francis will give you the contact."

I agreed, but my mood was wary. It is dangerous to enter into business with one of your musical heroes. It is so much easier to admire and celebrate from afar. And, of course, Fela was more than a musical hero to me. Anyone who knew his history and personality knew that with Fela there would likely be twists and turns on the road. First of all, Fela was an artist, and artists operate on a different plane of reality from most people. Art and business make an uneasy mix in the best of circumstances. Second, Fela regarded record companies as thieves, and I was not looking forward to ending up in that category. Finally, Fela was a man of many often contradictory facets. He was a righteous crusader who nonetheless could be a rascal when he felt wronged. And despite his willingness to sacrifice himself for the good of others, he had a tremendous ego that bordered on megalomania at times.

Almost a year later, I was in Los Angeles on the way back from a bank where I had just picked up $10,000 in cash to take to Fela, who was in the midst of his second full U.S. tour. He was staying in a small suite of rooms in Santa Monica. Predictably, there had been a few complications with business arrangements for releasing his music in America. With the start of the new tour approaching, Francis Kertekian still had not returned the contract nor had he sent the master tapes and negatives necessary to manufacture the album. My phone calls and faxes went unanswered. Meanwhile, I had called Fela's New York lawyer, an African American woman named Yolanda Owens who was the latest in a long line of people devoted to helping Fela succeed in the international arena. Francis Kertekian was one of those people, as was Fela's London-based manager, Rikki Stein. Owens said that, according to Fela, Francis did not have the right to license *Beasts of No Nation*. That seemed doubtful to me, but Francis was dealing with the situation in a typically French way—by acting as if it did not exist. Nonetheless, the tour was approaching, and promoters and media were clamoring for the new album. It was crucial to time the release for the sake of both ticket and album sales. When Francis finally came to New York, he said that I should deal directly with Fela on the licensing of the album and back catalogue. I could tell from the way Francis spoke that he felt did have the rights to license the album but that he had decided to let Fela have his way. Francis held on to his position as long as he could—hence his lack of communication with me—but in the end he felt obligated to accommodate Fela and absorb the loss.

I arrived at Fela's hotel with cash and contract in a small fabric overnight bag; Fela had demanded that his advance payment be in cash. The door was answered by a very beautiful African American woman who looked to be in her thirties. She turned out to be Yolanda Owens. Fela, wearing only the embroidered pants he in which he performed, was in an ebullient mood. The three of us sat down to talk business. Yolanda had already gone through the contract, which provided for the release of *Beasts of No Nation*, the right to release a number of Fela's older titles, and an option for an unnamed future album. It was a beautiful California day, with sunlight streaming into the room through the sliding doors that led to a balcony. At one point, Fela got up, spliff in hand, and walked toward the balcony. When he stepped forward through the open sliding door, however, he did not notice that the screen was still closed and he collided with it. It popped off its tracks, and he grabbed it as he stumbled. Instead of expressing annoyance, Fela turned toward us and gave a grin that was both sheepish and amused. It was as though he felt that his inadvertent attempt to walk through a screen door was just a reflection of the human condition. Fela was not afraid to laugh at himself.

The meeting went smoothly enough. We talked of the upcoming tour and the release of the album. Before long, Yolanda had some business to attend to. Fela walked her to the door and gave her a far-from-platonic kiss on the lips to send her on her way. I wondered how many people kiss their lawyers. But it was true to form; Fela loved women.

A couple of years later, Fela was back in New York to play a concert at the Apollo Theater. I got a call from Yolanda, who said that Fela would like to record an album while he was in New York, and she asked me to make the arrangements. This was not necessarily simple. Not many studios could accommodate, let alone know how to properly record, an ensemble of over twenty musicians. Nonetheless, I arranged a session at Sound On Sound studio, a state-of-the-art facility in the theater district. Fela and his musicians arrived around 11:00 p.m., taking over the studio like an occupying army. Fela directed everything. The plan was to record "U.S.—Underground System," a song that asserted that Fela had embarked on an astral flight during which he had seen that George Bush and Nigerian dictator Babangida were both manifestations of the same spirit entity. He also said he would record "Pansa Pansa," the older number I had suggested in Philadelphia that he record. The rehearsal of the tunes was laborious as Fela taught each musician his part and orchestrated the arrangements. Nonetheless, by dawn the tracks were finished.

A few months later I was surprised to see *Underground System,* the recording my company had paid for, released in England by another company. I called Yolanda Owens, who was as surprised as I was. After checking with Fela, she said he had changed his mind about my company releasing the album and we could just apply the recording costs to his royalties. I was not completely shocked by this news. I felt a sense of wry confirmation. But if anyone had earned an indulgent response, it was Fela. It was pointless to fight about it. At that moment I felt a certain kinship with Francis Kertekian. Fela's record sales were not especially high in any case, so it was preferable just to write off the loss.

A short time later, Rikki Stein sent me a message saying Motown wanted to sign Fela and the rights to his entire catalogue for a reputed $1 million. Someone at Motown had been seduced by Fela's aura and great media profile. They felt they would be signing a Third World superstar, which Fela in many ways was—though not if measured by record sales. At the last moment Fela nixed the deal. His spiritual advisor, a Ghanian mystic known as Professor Hindu, reportedly had advised him not to sign the contract. This was the same Professor Hindu who had stirred controversy in Europe by conducting spectacles wherein he would allegedly resurrect individuals buried alive onstage at Fela's shows. Some considered him a charlatan, but Fela took him seriously. Fela's finances were not in great shape, so it was indicative of his regard for Professor Hindu and the value Fela placed on spiritual considerations that he passed up such a big payday as well as the prospect of a major-label promotional push.

Years went by, and the news from Nigeria was not good. A new regime there, headed by the dictator Sani Abacha, racheted up the oppression, and the suffering of ordinary Nigerians increased. A political activist, Ken Saro-Wiwa, was executed amid an international outcry. The country had fallen under a black cloud of oppression. Fela still played at the Shrine but it was rumored that his health was failing. One rumor even suggested that he had AIDS.

Then in June of 1997 I got a phone call from a friend.

"Did you hear? Fela died!"

My first thought was that it could not be true. He was Fela "he who carried death in a pouch" Anikulapo-Kuti. Surely Fela would never submit to death! But, in the end, he had not been killed. Fela had wasted away on a mattress, spread on the floor as was his custom, until his spirit left his body. The unconfirmed rumor was that he had died of complications from AIDS, which would not have been surprising given his freewheeling sexual lifestyle and disdain for precautions. When I heard about his last days, I felt that his spirit must have left his body days, weeks, or even months before his life ended. He had been preparing to join the spirits of his ancestors in the higher realm he had been accessing ever since the government had nearly killed him in the attack on Kalakuta, more than twenty years earlier. He would never have been content to merely exist, imprisoned on Earth in a weakened state. So his spirit had moved on. According to Rikki Stein, who was in Nigeria at the time, one million people turned out for Fela's funeral in Lagos.[4]

Not long after Fela's death, his managers finally concluded that million-dollar deal for his catalogue with Universal Records. The money would benefit his estate. Fela had no use for it and, truth be told, he never really had much desire for money. It was just a transitory tool for him. As a result of the major-label deal, albums from the entire breadth of Fela's recording career began to be released; many of them had never previously been issued outside of Nigeria. The media in America and Europe brought Fela to the fore as never before. His son Femi—who played a faster, more concise form of Afrobeat—began to tour extensively and, because he was not so rigid in his prescriptions for Afrobeat, there was a possibility that he would become more popular than his father. More recently, Fela's younger son, Seun, has been performing with Egypt 80, often performing his father's tunes and generally staying closer to Fela's style of Afrobeat. A few years after Fela's death, Afrobeat bands began sprouting up in Nigeria, Europe, and the United States. While he was alive, Fela's larger-than-life persona seemed to have left no room for other Afrobeat practitioners. Now that his physical presence is gone, others have had the space to create within the idiom he had invented. Even hip-hop artists and dance music producers have appropriated elements of Afrobeat. I wonder what Fela would have thought of that. Probably, he would have been annoyed if the music did not meet his standards. He would find their efforts wanting. In the end, no one was big enough or brave enough to stand as Fela had stood.

Bob Marley, photo © UrbanImage.tv/Adrian Boot

Bob Marley

The Reggae Shaman

"Let's take a shortcut through the ghetto," Rita Marley remarked matter-of-factly.

It was 1989 and I was riding with Rita Marley, the putative Queen of Reggae, through the streets of Kingston, Jamaica. Rita, clad in a long African-print dress and elaborate red, green, and gold head-tie, was at the wheel of her Mercedes. We pulled away in the late evening gloom from the Tuff Gong studio complex on Marcus Garvey Crescent, located on a barren industrial edge of the city. The area she was proposing to cut through was Trench Town, one of the poorest, roughest urban landscapes on the planet. It was a warren of narrow dirt alleys, where rickety hovels were bounded by makeshift fences that had been cobbled together from random sheets of tin, crushed cans, and wire. Here and there cinderblock housing compounds and stucco storefronts anchored the sprawl. It was a place where outsiders seldom ventured unless they had a compelling need. I had no such need, but then I was not the one driving.

We had just finished listening to some mixes of Rita's new album, her first in several years. I had come down to Kingston to see how things were going with the new project; a lot was riding on it. Rita had been one of the first reggae artists signed to Shanachie Records in 1981, just months after her husband Bob Marley's death from cancer at the age of thirty-six. Ironically, Rita had then just recorded a whimsical, infectious ode to herb-smoking entitled "One Draw" and the single had been blowing up in Jamaica. The shock of Bob's death had hardly been absorbed by millions around the world. The release of the "One Draw" single and subsequent album had created an international sensation, with Rita being hailed as the "Queen of Reggae" in the press.

But Rita's follow-up had not done as well and soon thereafter she had been sucked into a maelstrom of events that effectively put her recording career on hold.

In Kingston, people talk about "the pressure." They speak of it as a tangible thing, a heavy, malevolent presence hanging in the humid air. The pressure they refer to is the pressure of hunger, the daily struggle to survive amid the desperate rabble, and the incipient violence that could erupt at any moment. If you had money, someone else wanted it. If you had no food, you had to find some way to get it, enough at least to get through the next day, the next week. If you had enemies or were simply in the wrong place at the wrong time, the police or a gang of thugs might cut you down. People were killed simply for walking in the wrong neighborhood; graffiti spray-painted on walls marked different neighborhoods as PNP (People's National Party) or JLP (Jamaican Labour Party) territory. These demarcated turfs were controlled by rival political parties that maintained gangs as enforcers. This daily pressure was a fact of life for most people who lived in Kingston. Kingston may be only one of many desperately poor cities on the planet but, at times, it seems to have its own special atmosphere of lingering dread. Sometimes it seems as though the doomed spirits of brutalized slaves, bloodthirsty pirates, and feral prostitutes of centuries past hover about, seeking revenge.

When Bob died, Rita Marley was at the center of a vortex. As Bob's widow, she suddenly was in charge of his studio and his label as well as the estate, which included the rights to royalties from his vast record sales and songwriting. Millions of dollars were up for grabs. Bob had supported hundreds of people. These people now looked to Rita Marley for sustenance. She had banned the idlers and hangers-on from Tuff Gong, the multitudes that Bob had tolerated for years. They were not pleased. The knives were out for her.

As teenagers, Bob and Rita had lived in Trench Town amongst "the sufferers." Indeed, they themselves were sufferers, poor youth with big ambitions. When Bob sang of "hungry belly," he was singing from personal experience, as only a Kingston youth with a growling, empty belly could do. Even after his international stardom, Trench Town was very much with Bob and Rita, always reaching to pull them back, like a receding tide sucking at their feet. So Rita could navigate those streets in a way that no outsider ever could. Some people would have never returned to Trench Town after they had escaped to a better life. Rita was not one of those people.

She nosed the Mercedes off the paved road and onto a dirt track that ran through what looked like small hills. As we passed through them, I could see that actually the hills were huge trash heaps. I realized that we were probably in the notorious area known as the Dungle, where people lived amid the mounds of garbage. Rita knew this area like the back of her hand and navigated it expertly even in the dark. Suddenly we emerged out of the rough onto a paved street. Rita kicked the Mercedes up a notch and we sped down the street, which was nearly deserted at that hour. A solitary man, dressed in rags, eyed us with the hard, suspicious stare of the ghetto dweller. A few minutes later we were turning off Halfway Tree Road toward New Kingston, which might as well have been another world. The pressure eased off, became less palpable, although it still floated in the shadows.

Bob Marley sang about Trench Town, made hit songs about suffering, and became a global figure of messianic proportions. It is doubtful that any other artist in history has made such popular music out of such an uncompromising picture of poor people's lives. When he sang "No Woman, No Cry," the lyrics painted a picture of a couple sitting together in a "government yard in Trench Town." "No Woman, No Cry" is a love song but it is also a song about emotional sustenance in harsh circumstances. When he wrote "Dem Belly Full (But We Hungry)," he described an intolerable gap between the affluent and the desperately poor—that breaking point at which raw need becomes the engine of revolution. How strange it is that he rocked so many concertgoers with that song! He took his stories of life in Trench Town around the world. More than anyone else, Bob Marley made reggae— a music that was created and developed in just a few districts within and nearby the city of Kingston—a global phenomenon.

Just as many people can remember exactly where they were when they heard that John F. Kennedy or the Rev. Martin Luther King Jr. had been shot, countless thousands can tell you where they were when they first heard Bob Marley, when they first heard reggae. In 1972, Paul Simon's "Mother and Child Reunion" hit the charts. I was immediately mesmerized by its utterly original, stuttering rhythm. The drummer was dropping cymbal crashes and high-hat fills in unexpected places, while the bassist played short bursts of notes that meshed with the drums to create a strangely hypnotic, off-center pulse. I could have listened to that circular yet asymmetrical groove for hours without ever getting bored; it was like a musical Mobius strip. The music offered an alternate, non-linear mode of perception. Paul Simon had recorded it in Jamaica with Jamaican musicians; it was reggae.

Shortly after hearing "Mother and Child Reunion," I was in a record store where I spotted an LP designed to look like a giant square cigarette lighter. A brass eyelet on the left side held the two horizontal halves of the cover together, the top of the lighter and the lighter itself. You could pull the top half of the cover up and back to reveal a cardboard flame jutting up inside, in front of the record encased in its paper sleeve. The album was titled *Catch a Fire* and it was by a group called the Wailers. Word among aficionados was that the Wailers were the best reggae group in Jamaica. Turning the LP over, I gazed at the picture of the five Wailers in the photo on the back. Five lean and hard-looking young black men stared at the camera; they had the aura of a gritty funk group such as the Meters or War or Kool and the Gang but there was something different about them.

The LP was a promo copy, on sale for $1.97, which made it an inexpensive gamble. The first track opened with an ominous burbling, rumbling rhythm created by clavinet, bass, guitar, and drums. It was a hellacious groove with an edgy, aggressive vibration that hit harder and deeper than the reggae by Jimmy Cliff or Desmond Dekker or Toots and the Maytals. The track's title said it all: "Concrete Jungle." A reedy, urgent tenor voice delivered lyrics that described a grim reality:

No sun will shine in my day today
And the yellow moon won't come out to play
I said darkness has covered my light
And it's changed my day into night
Where is the love to be found?
Won't someone tell me?
Must be somewhere for me
Instead of concrete jungle
Where the living is harder[1]

This was not entertainment. It was gripping, the sound of raw human spirit grappling with anti-human forces. The singer was Bob Marley.

Within a year I was in Nigeria and there I encountered Bob Marley's music on a deeper level. Reggae was popular in West Africa, its popularity a kind of African diaspora in reverse. Browsing through a selection of LPs imported from Britain (a happy result of postcolonial trade patterns), my fingers stopped at an album. A burnt-sienna border framed a large illustrated portrait of Bob Marley, his hair fringing out in an imperfect, wild Afro, a precursor stage to dreadlocks. The album was credited to Bob Marley and the Wailers. Flipping over the LP jacket, I saw song titles I had never heard of before: "Trench Town Rock," "Lively Up Yourself," "African Herbsman," "Duppy Conqueror." Clearly these were earlier recordings than what was to be found on the major-label albums. I bought the record, walked through the dusty streets to my hotel, and put the LP on the cheap, battery-operated record player I had bought. The sound quality was a bit tinny, and the rhythms were jumpy, skittering syncopations. There was none of the heavy, well-recorded rumbles of *Catch a Fire* or *Burnin'*, the major-label follow-up to *Catch a Fire*.

But the voices grabbed me, blending in high, feathery harmonies that reminded me of the Impressions, Curtis Mayfield's group, whose music I had come to love when I was in my early teens. The bobbing and weaving voice of Bob Marley transfixed me. It was thin and reedy, sinuous but insistent as he sang bursts of melody like a bird fluttering from tree branch to tree branch. At times he scatted and improvised off the rhythm like a jazz soloist. I did not know then that this miraculous music had been produced by the mad genius, Lee "Scratch" Perry. Nor did I know that the Wailers were really a group of three great singers and songwriters—Peter Tosh, Bunny Wailer, and Bob Marley—Jamaica's Beatles, in fact. But as wonderful as the harmonies and rhythms and songs of *African Herbsman* were, including a couple of songs on which Peter Tosh sang lead, it was Bob Marley's singing that mesmerized me. Bob sang like a man possessed by some otherworldly spirit as he sang wrapped in the spectral wails of his comrades. Sometimes there was an atmosphere of impending doom or menace: "If you are a big, big tree / I am a small axe / ready to cut you down / cut you down."[2] There in Africa I played the LP over and over again, wearing down the grooves already encrusted with fine Sahelian grit blown through my hotel window by the desert winds.

Each succeeding year brought a new Bob Marley and the Wailers album, sometimes two. *Natty Dread* was a revelation. The sound of the music had changed again; Bob's comrades, Peter Tosh and Bunny Wailer, had left to pursue solo careers. In their place, three female vocalists—Rita Marley, Marcia Griffiths, and Judy Mowatt, known collectively as the I-Three—provided warm, soulful, gospel-like harmonies. Lyrically, the songs grew harder and deeper, delivering in-your-face proclamations about poverty ("Dem Belly Full," "No Woman No Cry"), oppression ("Revolution," "Rebel Music [Three O' Clock Roadblock]"), and Rastafari ("So Jah Say"), the apocalyptic back-to-Africa spiritual movement that melded Old Testament prescriptions with Afrocentric perspectives. Many Rastafarians wore their hair in dreadlocks, uncombed, uncut locks meant to inspire dread in the unrighteous who would be obliterated on Judgment Day.

Bob Marley, at this point, had just started to grow dreadlocks. As he toured Europe and North America, the word spread: This was no ordinary artist, no ordinary man. A live concert recording of a Wailers performance at London's Lyceum Theatre fanned the flames. Prior to this recording, a relatively small number of people had experienced Bob Marley and the Wailers in live performance. But the *Live* album enabled millions around the world to experience the propulsive, transcendent mass séance that was a Bob Marley concert. Suddenly, Marley was a global star, particularly in the so-called Third World, where his songs of oppression, faith, struggle, and revolutionary change resonated mightily. He toured far-flung capitals, playing for huge crowds in Europe, Asia, North America, Australia, and New Zealand, where the Maoris began referring to a joint as a "Marley" in honor of the prodigious herb smoking that Bob, as a follower of Rastafari, regarded as a spiritual accessory. Marley rapidly became one of the most recognized and revered people on Earth.

Bob Marley had been considered "different" since birth.[3] Many who knew him felt that Bob Marley had always been destined for something special. He was born in 1945, in a country district called Nine Mile, a lush, sparsely populated part of north central Jamaica where most people scratched out a subsistence living by farming, fishing, or hunting. Nine Mile had few roads, no electricity, and no plumbing. And, although Jamaica is a place of many ethnic strains—European, Asian, African, Indian, and Arab—almost everyone in Nine Mile, other than a handful of plantation owners' families, was of African stock. Bob's father was white, a British colonial officer, while his mother was black, the daughter of one of the more prosperous black men in the district. So Bob had a unique background for that area. In Kingston, he would not have stood out so much. Even though his parents had married, Bob grew up fatherless, as his father disappeared from his life early on. From a young age, neighbors and relatives thought Bob had special powers, what in other times and places has been called "second sight."[4]

You see it in Bob's face, this specialness. A small, pursed mouth; narrow, straight nose; hooded, piercing, almost Asiatic eyes arched by thick, black brows and flanked by prominent cheekbones. Even his complexion was unique, an indefinable nut-brown. Adding to the effect was Marley's animated spirit. Even as a young boy that spirit had manifested itself in his precociously serious mouth and through a penetrating stare that made even grown-ups flinch. Although Bob had an infectious, spontaneous grin, his face could flip instantly into a mask of judgment.

I met his mother once and got a sense of at least one source of Bob's vibrant spirit. It was in the early eighties, and I had been invited to a party at a small farm in southern New Jersey. Bob's mother, Cedella Booker, had been living in nearby Wilmington, Delaware, since the mid-sixties when she had remarried. Bob had endured a brief sojourn there in his early twenties, working at a Chrysler plant. As I walked into the farmhouse, the pungent aroma of curry filled the air. I had to pass through the kitchen to get to the party out back. and I found Cedella Booker standing at the stove, stirring a huge pot of goat stew. She looked up as I came into the room, a robust, dark-skinned woman of middle age. She had a scarf wrapped around her head and her hearty smile filled her eyes with light. She had the healthy, radiant vitality of a country woman who, like so many country people, encountered all she met with a forthright, open-hearted mien.

At ten Bob moved with his mother to live in a "government yard" in Trench Town, a daunting cauldron of new experience for any country boy. All around him, young men were becoming hard, scuffling for scraps, fighting for dominance in a city that was growing helter-skelter. Bob's toughness made up for his slight stature. He was short but wiry, with spidery arms and tree-trunk thighs. He hung with the "rude boys" in the ghetto, but his mind was on music. Bob began to sing with like-minded youths such as his boyhood friend Bunny Livingstone, later to be known as Bunny Wailer, and tall, cool, guitar-playing Peter McIntosh, who became known as Peter Tosh. By age sixteen, Bob was writing songs and looking for a chance to record. After a couple of false starts, he, Peter, and Bunny, along with three other chums, got their chance, recording as the Wailers. Their second release was "Simmer Down," a song addressing the rude boys who had such an impact on ghetto life. "Simmer Down" became a ghetto anthem. Even then, Bob was the leader of the group. Years later, Peter Tosh would become bitter about Bob being singled out by Island Records as the front man for the Wailers, suggesting it was because Bob's lighter complexion and less African features made him more palatable to white audiences. But even in the Wailers' early days Bob had sung the most leads and had written most of the songs, although Peter and Bunny were gifted singers and writers too. People viscerally responded to Bob's urgent intensity, in contrast to Bunny's more reserved spirit and Peter's laconic, often acerbic public persona. And Bob was always writing, always thinking about developing his music. He had a burning desire to reach the world.

By 1974, Bob was on the verge of international stardom. At that time he was in many ways living an ideal life. He would rise early in the morning, meet up with a group of mates, and go for a long run, sometimes out to the beach, or sometimes into the hills. At the end of the run, Gilly, Bob's personal cook, would prepare a breakfast of fresh fish, fish tea, ital (vegetarian) stew, bammy (fried cassava bread), plantains, and all manner of fresh fruit and steamed vegetables. Then, it was back to his Tuff Gong headquarters at 56 Hope Road in uptown Kingston where Bob would work on songs, sometimes by himself, sometimes with others. He seemed always to have a guitar in his hands. In the afternoon the band would rehearse, or, if there was no rehearsal, a soccer game would be organized; Bob was a soccer fanatic (and a pretty good player). Among his circle was the famed Rasta soccer star Allan "Skill" Cole. Evenings found Bob hitting the nightlife circuit, stopping in at sound-system dances or, more likely, hitting the cutting-edge nightspots in Kingston. Often, he would end his night in the wee hours at Tuff Gong, sleeping on a mattress on the floor in an upstairs room, sometimes with female companionship, sometimes not.

Bob's existence at that time was a tremendous balance of physical, emotional, social, creative, and spiritual activity. This was the calm before the storm: within a year, he was sucked into the whirlwind of global stardom. But maybe it is wrong to say that he was sucked into it. After all, Bob Marley wanted to take his music to the world. He willingly stepped onto the accelerating roller coaster of recording, performing, and promoting. He was willing to do what was necessary to achieve the success that he had been pursuing with single-minded focus for over a decade—far more willing than either Peter Tosh or Bunny Wailer.

"Bob was always the first one on the [tour] bus," the noted photographer Kate Simon once told me. She had traveled with Bob during those early European tours as a kind of official photographer. "He was the first one at rehearsal."

It was not fame or fortune that Marley was seeking. He wanted to be heard. He was on a mission to deliver his music and his message to the world, and the world was listening. Guerrilla fighters in Africa—especially in Rhodesia, Namibia, and South Africa—passed around tapes of his songs (and those of Peter Tosh) among one another as though they were valuable weapons. In Europe and the United States, Bob became a lightning rod for all those countercultural forces that had emerged in the sixties but dissipated in the seventies. At home in Jamaica, the two main political parties courted him, knowing that his endorsement might sway an election. The ghetto bad men who had known Bob as a youth expected him to give them a cut of his good fortune. The CIA opened a file on him. Some people wanted him dead, and indeed, they almost got their wish when gunmen ambushed the singer at his headquarters and shot up his entourage; Bob was wounded in the arm and Rita Marley had a bullet graze her head. Marley's manager, Don Taylor, was badly wounded in the groin. It had been a straight-up assassination attempt. Nonetheless, Marley appeared at the much-ballyhooed Smile Jamaica concert. The show was ostensibly intended to defuse tensions surrounding the impending elections, but in reality it fit a PNP party agenda. Most likely, the would-be assassins had not wanted him to play that concert, though some have suggested other theories for the attack. Indeed, immediately after the attack no one knew for sure if he would play it.

On the afternoon of the concert, a crowd of fifty thousand, which some say swelled to eighty thousand,[5] crowded Kingston's National Heroes Park to hear some of the most popular reggae groups in Jamaica. Ultimately, though, the people were there to hear Bob Marley who, after the shooting, had retreated to a secluded location in the hills. Toward evening, hearing via walkie-talkie how the crowd responded to his name when members of the band Third World saluted him during their performance, Marley decided to risk his life again and perform. As he descended by car from the hills, he was cheered on by throngs in the streets. A clear path to the stage opened up. Onstage, the mood was tense; it was like a combat scene in a war movie. Dozens of people—some say two hundred[6]—crowded the stage. It was difficult to distinguish performers from bodyguards, friends, and sympathizers. The darkness was lit by flashes of light; conventional stage lighting was absent. Some of the Wailers had not dared to come, so members of Third World substituted. Rita Marley, wearing a nightdress, her head still bandaged from the bullet wound she had suffered in the attack, was on stage with fellow I-Three backing vocalist Judy Mowatt.

"I was told there would be no politics," Bob intoned, his bandaged shoulder a testimony to the danger he faced. His trusty guitar was absent because his shoulder injury made it impossible to play. "I'll play one song."

He launched into "War," an all-too-appropriate selection. His bodyguards scanned the crowd for possible attackers; his supporters clustered around him to make a clear shot difficult. "War" evolved into ninety minutes of intense music. Bob was triumphant, miming people shooting, acting out the assassination attempt, whirling and pointing his finger as he danced his way off the stage, the Lone Ranger riding off into the sunset. The next day, though, he left the island and did not return for fourteen months.

In 1977, I returned from my sojourn in Nigeria and found Bob

Marley's latest album, *Rastaman Vibration*, in the stores. Each new release was received by millions around the world as the next chapter of a story, in the same way that new albums by Bob Dylan and the Beatles had been. Each new Marley album was scrutinized eagerly for clues about the course of human history, as though it contained prophecies. *Rastaman Vibration* was undeniably catchy but a lighter, less substantial sounding album than *Natty Dread*, Bob's previous studio recording. Pop radio stations gave some play to the song "Roots, Rock, Reggae," which became Bob's first single to hit the American charts. Many fans were vaguely disappointed. Looking back, this disappointment seems ridiculous; the album had propulsive anthems such as "War" and "Crazy Baldhead," as well as such classic message songs as "Who the Cap Fit," "Johnny Was," and "Rat Race." But fans were measuring the album against the pristine diamond that was *Natty Dread*. Many Bob Marley fans at this point wanted pure greatness and uncompromising "rebel music" every time out. Already, for countless people, Bob Marley represented much more than just music.

Any disappointment occasioned by *Rastaman Vibration* was immediately eclipsed by the news that Bob was coming to the States on tour and by the release of his next album, *Exodus*. In Philadelphia the Wailers' concert was held at the Spectrum, an indoor sports arena of medium size. The acoustics were not especially good, but a midpriced ticket still put a fan within a reasonable distance of a big stage that stretched across one end of the oval building.

On the night of the concert the Spectrum was packed, and the air was filled with feverish anticipation. The band ranged across the stage: Family Man Barrett, a dark, short, husky figure on bass, wearing shades and a red, green, and gold knit tam; his younger brother Carly behind the drums; the young but precocious Tyrone Downie on keyboards stage right; the bearded elder, Seeco Patterson, on hand percussion; lean, hyperactive, Afroed Junior Marvin on guitar; and the I-Three, resplendent in colorful African wraps, blouses, and red, green, and gold scarves, stepping and swinging their hips in unison.

The band hit the jaunty opening groove to "Trench Town Rock" and Bob Marley strode onstage, his guitar slung over his shoulder, and sashayed up to the microphone. He wore a blue denim work shirt, open slightly at the chest to reveal a red T-shirt underneath, blue jeans, and stylish black boots. His dreadlocks cascaded down below his shoulders. He let the groove build for a minute before he slid his guitar off his shoulder and chopped out a rhythm pattern. Then he stepped up to the mike and—eyes clenched closed in concentration—sang an invocation: "one good thing about music . . . when it hits you, you feel OK! Hit me with music! Hit me with music, now!"[7] Marley looked older than his thirty-three years. His skin was taut over his face and frown lines were etched between his brows; there were lines around his mouth. "Trench Town Rock" climaxed, and, without a word Marley kicked the band into "Dem Belly Full," as if to remind everyone that the concert was more than just a good time. The I-Three chanted the chorus line like a Greek chorus: "A hungry man is an angry man!" Little time was wasted between songs and Bob did not have much be-tween-songs patter. As the band hit the opening fanfare of "I Shot the Sheriff," which Eric Clapton had made a familiar staple on rock radio with his version, the crown roared, and Bob strode around the stage in little circles, whipping his head in around circular motions almost like a Sufi dervish beginning a trance-inducing dance. He spread his arms wide, fluttering them like wings, as if drawing on cosmic energy. The audience was already on its feet, swaying in place and raising their arms.

More often than not, Bob sang with his eyes closed, sometimes tap-ping his forehead or patting his chest to amplify or illustrate what he was singing about. On the portentous "Crazy Baldhead," when the band broke down into a sparse "dub" section, Bob held his hands straight out from his shoulders, fists clenched, forming a cross. He swayed in place, eyes closed, and riffed on the refrain: "you're running away but . . . you can't run away from yourself,"[8] singing the line differ-ently each time, relentlessly improvising phrases, repeating the phrase "you're running away."

The band shifted gears and kicked the groove up a notch into a driving, hypnotic version of "War," a song with lyrics from Emperor Haile Selassie's 1963 address to the United Nations. (Selassie is regard-ed by followers of Rastafari as an earthly incarnation of God.) Only Bob Marley could make a song out of a speech; he sang the words to a sinuous, minor-key melody: "Until there's no longer / first and second class citizens / There will be war / Until the color of a man's skin is no more significance / Than the color of his eyes / There will be war."[9]

The arena was a sea of motion as the crowd was on its feet, moving with Bob. The show climaxed with the relentless urgency of "Exodus," an ecstatic, full-throttle chant of liberation, escape, and triumph. It used the biblical tale of the Jews' escape from Egypt as a template not just for black liberation but for human liberation. As the song peaked on the refrain "Exodus / movement of Jah people / set the captives free!"[10] Bob was hopping and running in place as though he was running to Africa, to freedom, a captive set free. The I-Three echoed him with rapid, circular movements of arms and hips, until Bob danced offstage, as the Wailers jammed away and the crowd exploded in cheers. In roughly two hours, Bob Marley had taken his audience on a journey, sketched a state-of-the-world message, and pointed the way to a better future.

Bob Marley opened the floodgates. Reggae albums began showing up in American stores on a regular basis, a development that coincided with the peak of reggae's golden age of "roots" music. Dreadlocked, robed Rastamen, like incarnations of Old Testament prophets, were delivering, via song, denunciations of corruption, exploitation, racism, and poverty as well as visions of spiritual transcendence replete with biblical imagery. Bunny Wailer, Burning Spear, Peter Tosh, Culture, the Mighty Diamonds, the Abyssinians, the Gladiators, Lee "Scratch" Perry, and others were a welcome antidote to the hedonistic disco and overblown rock music that was flooding the world. Reggae provided much-needed nutrients for spiritual sustenance as well as a reminder of the urgent needs of the dispossessed and oppressed peoples of the world.

Meanwhile, in 1978 Bob Marley returned to Jamaica for the first time in fourteen months and headlined a concert as dramatic and significant as Smile Jamaica had been. Despite the bravado of his theatrics at the earlier concert, Bob was keenly aware that his life was still in danger. He had no desire to be a martyr. In his absence, the violence in Jamaica had continued to escalate. Rival gangs, funded and armed by the rival political parties (one of which was supported by the CIA), were murdering one another and anyone else they did not like, as well as innocent bystanders caught in the crossfire. The murders were happening almost daily. Even the murderers realized that such a level of violence was untenable; they, too, had children, wives, mothers, fathers, brothers, sisters, brothers, cousins. The gang leaders broached the idea of a truce and conceived of a peace concert to seal it. They approached Bob Marley while he was in England and asked him to headline the concert. It was an appeal that he could not refuse. At least this time he would not be a pawn of politicians.

The One Love Peace Concert, as it was billed, was held at the National Stadium in Kingston on April 21, 1978. A blockbuster array of sixteen top reggae artists were lined up to perform, including Jacob Miller, Dennis Brown, the Mighty Diamonds, Culture, Big Youth, Peter Tosh, and, of course, Bob Marley. Jacob Miller invited the rival gang leaders onstage and got them to sing and dance. Peter Tosh used his performance to directly confront the government officials present regarding the legalization of ganja. He lit up a spliff onstage and taunted the police who glowered at him from the aisles. In the weeks following the concert, Tosh was arrested and brutally beaten by the police.

The crowd was at a fever pitch by the time Bob Marley stepped onstage—and he soon took it to a higher level. Dancing across the stage, he attained a trancelike state. As he and the Wailers played "War," Marley took the song into a transition that became the celebratory "Jamming"; he and the Wailers were acting out the mission of the concert, moving the doleful meditation of "War" to a song that united the crowd in spiritual joy. Then Marley did the unthinkable. Speaking into his microphone, he invited Prime Minister Michael Manley and opposition leader Edward Seaga to join him onstage.

"Could we have up onstage," Bob intoned, "the presence of Mr. Michael Manley and Mr. Edward Seaga? Just wanna shake hands and show the people that we can be friends."

He then sang: "We gonna unite . . . we gonna make it right!" while dancing in an ecstatic little circle.

Seaga arrived first, looking stiff and tentative. After a long delay, Michael Manley also appeared onstage, the two men flanking Bob. They avoided one another's gaze, staring off above the crowd, their mouths compressed into tense lines of disapproval. But they were trapped, shamed into a show of unity. It was, after all, a peace concert that had clearly captured the imagination of the people. Neither Seaga nor

Manley made any move to embrace or shake hands. Their expressions indicated that shaking hands was the last thing that they wanted to do. But Bob seized their hands, clasping them together with his. Then he raised their hands triumphantly overhead, physically uniting the two men physically and grinning euphorically. Who but Bob Marley could have done it? He had a power that did not emanate from guns, that did not stem from fear or coercion or money. His power was rooted in the people's love for him, his righteous spirit, his transcendent music, and his faith in a higher power. He was bigger than all of them.

Exodus was a masterful album. It was anchored by the propulsive title track that spoke of the diaspora of Africans and their pending return to the Motherland. In short order the mellow *Kaya* album was released, promoting some reviewers to suggest that Bob Marley was taking the edge off his music in order to reach wider audiences. That thought was blown away in 1979 by the release of *Survival*, whose inner sleeve featured period illustrations of Africans stacked like cordwood on slave ships. The images starkly captured the brutal essence of the transatlantic slave trade. The songs on the album were an uncompromising look at the physical and spiritual survival of black people since the slave trade's inception four hundred years previously. The album was also a call to arms. On one track, "Zimbabwe," Bob sang of the liberation of the country known to the world by its colonial name, Rhodesia. The song would inspire the Africans rebelling against the white, racist government of that country, which had banned Bob's music. Bob Marley and the Wailers were soon to be invited by the new government of Zimbabwe to headline the concert celebrating Zimbabwe's independence. How many artists could say that their music helped to liberate a nation? As important and meaningful as that event was to Bob, he maintained a humble perspective. Later recalling the concert, he described how some of the soldiers who had fought for the country's liberation had been unable to gain admittance to the show. Soon they were storming the gates, only to be repelled by tear gas from the new government's forces. The tear gas drifted over the stage and the Wailers panicked, running for safety. "Well," Bob chuckled when recounting this event, "I guess we know now who the REAL revolutionaries are!"

The release of *Survival* heralded yet another Bob Marley tour. My radio show gave me an opportunity to meet him. I arranged an interview through the publicity department of Island Records. One sunny afternoon I found myself walking up Walnut Street in Philadelphia to the Warwick Hotel, where Bob and his entourage were staying. The Warwick was an old, slightly frayed hotel that had once been elegant. On the elevator up to the floor where Bob was staying, I primed myself for the interview, going over in my mind the topics I wanted to broach. When I reached the room to which I had been sent, I knocked on the heavy, wooden door. The door swung slowly open and a slight, dreadlocked man gazed at me impassively.

"I'm here to interview Bob Marley," I said.

He nodded, motioned me in, and led me through the entry hall to the living room of a suite. Rounding the corner I was startled to find a roomful of people, a polyglot mix sitting on chairs or on the floor, leaning against the walls, and perching on window sills. They all faced a slight figure sitting in the center of the room: Bob Marley. Evidently, it was not going to be a private interview. At first glance it resembled a college dorm bull session, but the atmosphere was more portentous. My next thought was of Socrates sitting under a tree discoursing with students. A little later I thought of Jesus conversing with his disciples. I threaded my way through some bodies and found a spot on the floor about ten feet from Bob, slightly to his left. Bob was talking, holding forth on the concept of Rastafari.

"There are groups who say they are Rasta . . . You can't just say you are Rasta. You have to have authority to be Rasta! You have to believe it." He was speaking in an oddly flat yet assertive near monotone. "Some groups may use it for their own purpose. That *cyaan* [can't] work! It is not our own . . . It's God's own! What we deal with is not just an individual thing, yuh know . . . What we deal with is the *survival* of a people! Seen? When you know the truth, you *cyaan* compromise. You just deal with it!"

He paused and took a draw from the prodigious spliff he held between his fingers.

"How many Rastas are there?" a young African American woman asked. She was the only female in the room.

Bob picked up a Bible that was on the small table next to him, opened it and flipped to a page. Clearly, he knew his Bible.

"Chapter 7 . . . Revelations," he declared. "No man could number the multitude."

A young man asked what Bob thought of the MOVE organization, a Philadelphia-based back-to-nature cult whose members wore dreadlocks. MOVE had clashed with the authorities. Surprisingly, Bob was familiar with MOVE. His was an open and curious mind that absorbed the currents of every new place that he visited.

"I hear a lot about the MOVE," he said. "I met some who say they are Rasta. The police here, they tell me, they come just like the police in Jamaica."

"Beast is beast!" a low, male Jamaican voice hissed from the back of the room "Beast" was a term used to refer to police in Jamaica.

Someone I could not see spoke up, telling Bob about police attacks against the MOVE organization's house.

"Wha?" Bob exhaled in amazement. "Blood *claat*!"

I ventured an ironic comment: "There is no shortage of suffering!"

Bob laughed delightedly, ending in a smothered giggle and repeating my words. "No shortage of suffering!"

When he caught his breath, he turned serious. "But when you check it out, it's not really that. The problem is the law that govern the country. Newspaper say Russia and America going to war . . . so people keep quiet. The president change and the people suffer. And the president change again and still the people suffer . . . *Fuck!* Them naw do anyt'ing . . . They enjoy themselves!" He shook his head. "Terrible t'ing, you know, terrible t'ing." He gave a bitter laugh and shook his head again.

There was a brief, melancholy silence. I tried to change the mood.

"Do you have control of your music now?" I asked. "There was a time when you didn't have control and you had to record some songs you didn't want to record like . . . 'What's New Pussycat?'"

Bob broke into a hearty chuckle, amazed that an American knew an obscure version of a Tom Jones hit that he had recorded nearly fifteen years previously. "'What's New Pussycat!" he repeated, cackling.

An earnest young African American man, smooth-faced and impeccably dressed, notebook in hand, followed up on the theme.

"It would seem that it would be the business of enemies to infiltrate the music, to bastardize it, and twist it around," he said. "Are you guarding against this?"

His question reflected a widely shared assumption: Namely, that Bob Marley was a threat to the established order and, therefore, was a target for repression, or, at the very least, attempts at neutralization.

"Well, let 'em try!" Bob said. "Sometimes, I see thing . . . like having a naked girl on a Third World album jacket."

"What about Tosh and Mick Jagger?" somebody else asked. Bob's old bandmate had recently recorded a song with the lead singer of the Rolling Stones, a move many decried as a sellout.

"Who?" Bob asked, a little too innocently. There was general laughter. When the laughter died down, he groped for words. "What can I say? You have to say something!" He laughed.

The same young man asked, "But would you let Mick Jagger sit in with you?"

"With . . . *me*?" Bob asked. Then quickly, decisively: "I don't think so."

A white man of about thirty with shaggy brown hair, mentioned that the English reggae bands such as Steel Pulse had made some alliances with punk rock and new wave groups. His voice was a thick, gorgeous Anglo/Jamaican brogue. I had heard that Jamaica had colonies of white Jamaicans whose families had lived on the island for many years in certain locales, Manchester on the south coast and also a few miles down the coast from Kingston.

"You know," he continued, "it kind of remind me of reggae ten years ago . . . like rudies, before Rasta come out . . . They like . . . re*bel*!"

"Yes," Bob said, nodding approvingly. "Re*bel*!"

"Most people here don't know any other reggae artists," I said. "They think reggae is Bob Marley."

"I'll tell you the reason," Bob replied matter-of-factly. "The reason is that I've come out here and played. If other artists come out and play, as long as their music is in tune, people would know them."

"Name some!" I said. I wanted to hear whom Bob would single out.

"Burning Spear! Bunny Livingstone!" he proclaimed. "Give me some more!"

"Earth Disciples!" someone interjected.

"More!" Bob said.

"Dennis Brown," another guy proclaimed.

"*Cha*! Dennis Brown!" Bob exclaimed. "More! Give me more!"

"Israel Vibration!" another voice rang out.

"*Is*rael Vibes!" Bob echoed.

"Culture!" another one called out.

"Kul-tchah!" Bob squeezed out the name as if stricken by a heavenly thunderbolt. "Ah, Culture!"

He had turned the little gathering into a reggae church, a call-and-response celebration of artists delivering revelatory music. The hubbub of voices died down and there was silence for a moment.

Someone asked if reggae could conquer America.

"Well," Bob said, "you have the funk, the disco. I don't really know if it's really black music . . . 'cause it kind of . . . upset the thinking. 'Cause I feel black music is a higher *ras claat* form or thing . . . if reggae is music, if the potential is just music and nothing else, if you want to dance, then the dance music is disco 'caw disco is the speed of dancing. But if it's something more for the benefit musically, then you're gonna listen to reggae . . . 'cause you have to listen to it, that's how God make it. It make you have to have interest . . . It naw going to trick you, like 'pap pana pana pana,'" he said, imitating a hyperactive disco beat. The room erupted in laughter, Bob included.

"In Jamaica, the more reggae you play, the more Rasta you have. But the more disco you play, then you'll have more eyebrow pencils and lipstick."

Laughter bubbled around the room.

"Nothing is wrong with music to me. What I figure might be wrong sometimes is . . . the lyrics! The message! It can be too vain sometimes. The good things have to be there.

"The more reggae you play the more Rastas you have. The more disco you play, the more fantasy you get!" The laughter intensified. "They want you to think of that glass of wine . . . and that pretty girl and that car in the car park. You listen to that, you just dead, you'll never get it. You listen to reggae and live the *ras-claat* life!"

Murmurs of assent followed his words.

"You have to check the psychology behind everything. Why is

this and why is that? We ask questions!" He gave a self-deprecating chuckle.

Another brief silence ensued.

"Are you going to play in Africa?" I asked. I related an anecdote about Jimmy Cliff coming to Nigeria when I was there. An irate promoter had him arrested and Jimmy left the country as soon as he was bailed out. "Jimmy wrote a song about it," I said. "He sang 'I went to Africa . . . down to Nigeria . . . they put wme in *jail*!'"

"Well, for instance," Bob said," the Nigeria black doesn't deal with Haile Selassie but deals with English, or French, or German t'ing . . . Some of these states are run from France. I don't see them as African."

A general murmur ensued, and several small discussions broke out.

"African man is a Rasta man," Bob proclaimed. "If Africa is united"—he sighed in wonder at the vision—"anything could happen! The next day . . . everything clean! Water washed everything . . . pure!"

"A new race of men . . ." a man intoned.

"That's true," Bob said.

Another silence ensued, the kind of meditative moment that occurs when a group of people is seated around a campfire, staring at the dancing flames.

After awhile, I broke the silence.

"Aren't you tired of all the interviews yet?"

"No," Bob answered without hesitation, "'cause what we're talking about is food . . . food for the spirit . . . So the more we talk about it, is the stronger we get! If you don't talk about it, you getting weak!" He chuckled.

"Some people thought *Kaya* (the album from two years previous) was a move away from your past lyrics," I offered.

"It's my war!" Bob said evenly but emphatically. "It's not their war. They can't tell me how to fight it!"

General approving laughter ensued.

"Seen? So you can't trick me! I have to fight my war, my way. If you watch me fall down, they say, 'Yes, him fall down, fall down . . . Lord, Lord, him fall down!' It's *me* fall down, yuh *blood claat*!" The room erupted in laughter again.

"Time shall record the judgment. Not one shall escape the judgment, not even the dog that piss against the wall of Babylon shall escape the judgment," he continued.

"But I really love when they say 'Kaya, Bob, Kaya, boy, why Kaya, Bob? Me no like Kaya, Bob . . . You should be more stronger now.' Yes, you want me to be stronger now . . . but if they shot me and kill me can you *ras claat* help me? If me get too strong then I want action . . . back me up with a shotgun!"

He paused.

"I have to take it easy and . . . get my timing *right*!" He paused again and then, with the timing of a comedian, continued, "So long as we have some guns on our side!" He laughed heartily.

"But," he continued, in a serious tone, "I like how dem go down 'pon it because I realize that . . . they listen, they're interested. I love them for that. I love them more than ras here. True, I thought it was a joke but I come to find that they really are serious. They are all together. I find that out 'cause they say 'No, Bob, no, no *ras cleat* soft tune . . . stay tough!

"But, same time, you can't stay in my life and protect my being, 'cause you know dem lick [kill] Marcus Garvey, dem lick Malcolm X, dem lick Luther King . . . dem even say dem overthrow His Majesty! So you have to take a time to cool it down 'cause they could overthrow me, too. You don't need me to tell you more things now. You have to think now. Look, now, look to yourself!"

"Meditate . . . " someone in the group intoned.

It seemed like time to leave. I had been there a couple hours, though many in the room had been there long before me. For how long? I wondered: how long would they stay? Give the man some rest, some space. Let him breathe!

During this time period Bob rarely had time to himself, hardly ever was allowed to be alone. For starters, there was the whole Wailers entourage—the band, the I-Three, the cook, the assistants, and the hangers-on. Bob was captain of that ship, so the weight of all those people's needs and problems fell on him. He had to keep the ship sailing, and everyone looked to him. Many called him "Skipper" or "Skip." Besides the Wailers' extended family, there were the hordes of fans, supplicants, worshippers, would-be helpers, and activists who materialized in every city at the hotel, backstage, and at the sound check. They were ubiquitous, sometimes just gathering, wordlessly, to be in the same room as Bob.

Bob tolerated it. He rarely—if ever—pushed anyone away. I witnessed a rare exception during the session in the hotel room, when a beautiful African American woman, dressed in decidedly un-cultural style, had entered and knelt by his chair in the hotel room in the midst of the reasoning session. She had gazed at him as though hypnotized. In the middle of the conversation she put her hand on his thigh and began rubbing it. Without pausing in his talk, Bob looked down at her, lifted her hand gently off his leg, and pushed it away. But, generally, he heard everyone out. It was as if he was offering up his being, his soul, to the multitude, as though fulfilling his destiny. Sometimes he would just disappear, melting away into whatever sanctuary he had managed to secure—a bedroom, a car, a woman's room. Yet it often happened that someone would knock on the door where he had been resting and once the door was open, people would begin to drift in, like the tide. The man could hardly get any rest. I was determined not to contribute to his exhaustion. I got up as unobtrusively as I could and stepped gingerly out of the room, as though to avoid waking a sleeping infant, and walked out the door.

That night, Bob and the Wailers brought a relentless, raw energy to the Philadelphia Convention Center, which was then a nondescript hall holding maybe three thousand people. It was large and boxlike, with a feeling similar to an oversized school gymnasium. It was packed with a standing-room-only crowd. There were no seats. The lighting was basic too—flashes of white illuminating the stage also lit the faces in the crowd like flares in a war zone. The crowd heaved and swayed in the darkness, in thrall to the Wailers' pulse, swept up in Bob's chanting. Bob did his sorcerer's jig, eyes closed and clenched fist raised, his guitar slung over his back when he was not playing it. The songs of the *Survival* album sounded stark and indomitable.

I had an all-access pass, so after the show I went backstage to see Bob. It was bedlam back there, the hallways thick with humanity, smoke, and zones of light and dark. I came to a dressing room door and, just as I arrived, the door swung open and there was Bob. I was struck by how short he seemed in contrast to his large persona. The room behind him was so crowded it was as though he were trapped in a closet. It was unclear whether he had opened the door in hope of escaping or to welcome yet more visitors. I looked at him, and he gazed at me. I do not know if he recognized me from earlier. But some sort of understanding passed between us. "You see me here? See what I deal with?" his expression seemed to say. The fact that I did not speak, my calm, I think let him know that I understood his situation, that I was not going to ask anything of him. He stepped back into the room, slowly closed the door and was gone from view.

That was the last time I saw Bob Marley. The next year was an accelerating rush of events. In 1980, *Uprising*, his next album, was released. Of course, Bob's fans around the world immediately began listening to it for clues, signs, directions. In contrast to the focused militancy of *Survival*, *Uprising* was darker, more emotional, more spiritual. Songs such as "Coming In from the Cold" and "Bad Card" conveyed a consciousness of evil and death hovering in the air, ensnaring the unwary. "Zion Train" and "Forever Loving Jah" spoke to salvation. "Could You Be Loved," on the surface a catchy ditty seemingly aimed at popular appeal, rode over a crackling Afrobeat-inflected rhythm track; it made a musical connection with Africa, and it was a homage to the revolutionary Afrobeat of Fela. But the high point of *Uprising* was a track unlike anything Bob had ever done. Over a stark, strummed acoustic guitar, Bob sang the passionate, elegiac "Redemption Song," which seemed to sum up the essence of his being, when evil forces were out to get him and fate was inescapable: "singing these songs of freedom . . . they're all I ever had . . . redemption songs."[11] Its mood was reminiscent of Sam Cooke's "A Change Is Gonna Come" or Otis Redding's "Dock of the Bay." Both of those seemingly prophetic songs recorded shortly before their deaths were radical departures from anything they had previously done. Indeed, death was waiting for Bob, too, around the corner.

Late in 1980, another U.S. tour was announced. Bob Marley and the Wailers seemed permanently on worldwide tour. Thus it was a complete shock when someone told me they had heard that Bob had collapsed in New York. He had played a concert and afterward had gone to Central Park to play soccer, where he had collapsed. Rumors swirled: Bob had a terminal illness; Bob had been poisoned; the government was deliberately spreading false rumors of his death. Even through my contacts, it was impossible to get reliable information. I was reassured, though, when I heard that Bob had played the next show on the tour in Pittsburgh. Maybe it was all a false alarm. That hope was shattered when the next news came: The tour was cancelled. Bob Marley had cancer. Many refused to believe it. After all, Bob was only thirty-five years old, seemingly at the peak of his powers. The amount of energy he generated through his performances, his recordings, and his spirit was astonishing. How could he have cancer? But as each news bulletin arrived, the reality became inescapable. It was not simply cancer; the cancer had metastasized and spread throughout his body. He had injured his toe years before, playing soccer, and it had never healed properly. In treating that injury, the cancer had been discovered. Doctors had recommended that the toe be amputated, but Bob refused to do that. The word circulated that he had been taken to Sloan-Kettering for treatment, but that the prognosis was not good. Surely if anyone could beat cancer, it was Bob Marley! Hopes were raised when Bob got out of Sloan-Kettering, but then we heard that he was in Europe for treatment. Finally he went to Miami, where he died. The news of his death was a heavy blow. Millions mourned around the world. A photo taken shortly before his passing shows a shrunken Bob Marley, shorn of dreadlocks, with a bewildered expression on his face. Death had ambushed him in a way that he had never anticipated.

There are those who say Bob had predicted that he would die at a young age. That is why he had always been in a hurry; he had so much work to do before he left the earthly realm. A friend of mine had obtained a tape of Bob's final concert in Pittsburgh. Despite having collapsed only days earlier, Bob had run a two-hour sound check prior to the show and then delivered a high-energy performance that was almost inconceivable given his physical state. I played the concert tape on my radio show as a memorial and a testament to the indomitable spirit that was Bob Marley.

In the years that followed, Bob's worldwide popularity increased. *Legend*, a posthumous collection of his catchiest, most pop-oriented tunes, became the best-selling "catalogue" album (a term for records that were not new) in the world for many years. His song "One Love" was appropriated for television commercials by the Jamaican tourist board, an arm of the same government that only a decade earlier had reviled Bob, his Rasta "bredrin," and his ghetto comrades. The image of Bob as a jaunty, spliff-smoking, dreadlocked, free-spirited Pied Piper fueled the popularity of his music, which became a soundtrack for collegiate beach parties. This was not the Bob Marley I had encountered, nor was it a legacy he would have wanted. No, the man I encountered was serious—deadly serious—and his grin was a means of warding off the evil forces out to get him. I remember him in the trenches, determined yet gentle, open-minded yet devoted to his faith, laughing in the face of guns and inviting all of us to join the battle for spiritual salvation.

If his spirit had gazed down upon the Earth it had departed, it would have been disappointed to see the in-fighting and scheming that went on in pursuit of the empire he had built. During his life he had his shared his wealth, paying his band and those who worked for him freely, with no written agreement. I thought of this as I quietly entered the back of a New York City courtroom a year or two after I had seen Rita Marley in Kingston. The occasion was yet another legal action connected with Bob's estate. Rita and her accountants were the defendants, and they faced allegations of malfeasance and misappropriation of estate funds. I had no way of judging the validity of the charges. I was simply there as moral support for an artist with whom I, by that time, had had a decade-long association. Rita and her assistant sat by themselves on one of the court's long, wooden benches about five rows back from the phalanxes of legal folk shuffling papers and droning on about legal minutiae. No hangers-on were with her that day. As I reached her row, she turned and smiled, obviously surprised to see me. I embraced her and sat down. Rita laughed softly, and said: "People must be wondering who is this white man coming into court and giving me a kiss!" I sensed a double meaning in her comment. She may have been implying that my mysterious appearance might in some small way have tilted the balance of power a little less in favor of the system and a little more in favor of a solitary woman born of the ghetto. It was, after all, a long way from Trench Town.

Augustus Pablo, photo courtesy of Shanachie Entertainment

Augustus Pablo

Composer of Dreams

"East of the River Nile": it is a short, simple phrase, yet it evokes an entire world—distant, exotic, mysterious. What *is* east of the River Nile? Arabia, most obviously, and further east, the Orient. But immediately east of the Nile's ascent into Africa, south of Egypt, lies Ethiopia. Indeed the Blue Nile veers off and plunges into Ethiopia's heart. Ethiopia in the early 1970s was an ancient land whose emperor, Haile Selassie I, known as Ras Tafari, according to tradition could trace his royal lineage back to King Solomon and the Queen of Sheba, the Ethiopian queen known as Makeda. Haile Selassie had been on the throne for forty years and, unbeknownst to him until late in life, was venerated as the living presence of God on Earth by Rastafarian believers in Jamaica.

Ethiopia is also the site of one of the oldest branches of Christianity. In its mountains you can find churches carved out of solid rock. In some parts of Ethiopia people still live in a manner essentially unchanged for a millennium or two. The land was also home to ancient Jewish sects. Some say that the Ark of the Covenant had been brought to Ethiopia for safekeeping.

These sorts of thoughts were occasioned by the appearance in 1977 of a Jamaican 45 r.p.m. single entitled "East of the River Nile." The name of the artist—Augustus Pablo—was no less mysterious. Copies turned up in America and it was even officially released by a small label, Hawkeye Records, in England. The music on this obscure little record lives up to its exotic title. A minor-key, vaguely oriental ascending line, played on what sounds like a breathy accordion or harmonica, guitar, and bass, punctuated by rimshots, creates an invocatory fanfare. Then comes a rat-a-tat-tat on the snare drum and bass and guitar kick in with a hypnotic, loping figure, like a slow, swaying parade of elephants. The accordion-like instrument plays a melody and the guitarist flares off jazzy filigrees. The melody is simple, just a few notes, yet instantly memorable. Washes of reverb and echo leave notes trailing into space, giving the feeling of distance to the music. The overall effect is cinematic. Something is happening. But what? It is an utterly unique musical concoction.

Only two years previously, another Jamaican single by Augustus Pablo had hit Jamaica and England with even greater force. "King Tubby Meets Rockers Uptown" is an epochal record, a sonic thunderstorm in comparison to the subtle and spaced-out "East of the River Nile." An invocatory set of rimshots and snare flourishes from the drummer kick the record off and a thunderous, titanic bass figure rumbles into action topped by a bit of melodica echoed by a disembodied voice. Scraping, ratcheting, electric guitar chords chop through the mix, whirl around spectral snatches of a male vocalist cut off in mid-phrase: "Baby I . . ." and then "doo doo doo doo . . ." Every so often there is a chuckle echoing off into space. The record is an ever-shifting kaleidoscope of sound and rhythm, never repetitive or static. It was far from the first example of what had become known as dub music but was widely accepted as the ultimate expression of the style.

Dub music is a sub-genre of reggae that has had great impact on music around the world. It was originated as simply a version of another piece of music, a remixed creation that reimagined a piece of music in rhythmic and spatial terms. If the original recording had singing, only bits and pieces of the singing remained on the dub mix. By dropping out instruments and adding echo, reverb, and other sonic effects, different aspects of the musical piece would be highlighted in ever-changing relationships, which made for a largely instrumental tour-de-force created completely in the recording studio from pre-existing recordings. More than one pundit has asserted that dub music was the most important development in popular music in the latter half of the twentieth century, a crucial catalyst in the development of hip-hop, dance music, and electronica. This is an ambitious assertion, but the fact that it is even arguable measures the impact of dub, a music created by, in the beginning at least, relatively obscure, even anonymous, people. Thanks to "King Tubby Meets Rockers Uptown," Augustus

Pablo became known around the world as a "dub master." But like so many things about him—including his name—that designation was misleading. It was just one aspect of his musical artistry and probably not even the most significant.

Who, then, was Augustus Pablo? Not a few people around the world posed this question as "King Tubby Meets Rockers Uptown" bubbled up from the reggae underground. It was not the man's real name. His birth name was Horace Swaby. Herman Chin-Loy, a music entrepreneur in Kingston, Jamaica, discovered the teenaged Swaby holding a melodica outside his Aquarius recording studio and record shop. As it happened, Chin-Loy was looking for a fresh sound to put on the reggae instrumentals he was releasing. Swaby, by coincidence, had just been given the melodica a short time prior by the girlfriend of a pal. Seeing the instrument, Swaby had asked the girl if he could try it out; the girl said he could have it as she had no use for it. Swaby, fascinated, began exploring the sonic and musical possibilities of a device generally regarded as a child's toy, an instrument of seemingly limited possibilities whose main function was to allow young people to easily acquire a bit of musical facility before they learned a real instrument.[1] The harmonica-like sounds heard on "East of the River Nile" and "King Tubby Meets Rockers Uptown" were in fact this very melodica. Chin-Loy was using the name Augustus Pablo as a nom-de-music for various musicians who played the instrumental solos on his reggae instrumentals. Session musicians such as Winston Wright, Glen Adams, and Lloyd Charmers had been "Augustus Pablo" on recordings. Chin-Loy thought the name sounded like some kind of exotic Western outlaw. But when Horace Swaby entered Chin-Loy's studio to blow his melodica and play keyboard on a couple of tunes, the line of Augustus Pablos stopped with him. He owned the name thereafter, laying claim to it through sheer brilliance.

Young Swaby was not supposed to be standing in front of Aquarius Studios that day in 1971. At sixteen he had pretty much abandoned school, much to the consternation of his middle-class parents. Growing up in the Havendale sector of West Kingston, amid the gently rolling foothills rising above the hustle and bustle of the lower city, Pablo heard the siren sounds of reggae early on. From his home he could hear the waves of sound from outdoor sound systems blasting music from a ghetto neighborhood far below. From the fifties on and up to the present time, outdoor sound systems have been part of the landscape in Jamaica. Huge stacks of speakers and powerful amplifiers are set up anywhere—in someone's yard, on a street corner, in an open-air nightclub. The music might start cranking in early evening and continue into early morning. It was cheap, most often free, entertainment for poor people. Competition between different sound system operators was fierce, sometimes even violent. Some people would follow their favorite "sound" wherever it went. Following the "sound" became a way of life. Folks would argue the relative merits of one "sound" against the other and there would be "sound clashes," whereby two, or even three, sound systems would set up in proximity and compete for the favor of the assembled multitude, doing sets in turn. The "sound" with the greatest selection of records, the craftiest programming by the record "selector," the greatest audio power, the most entertaining deejays/rappers, would win. Reggae music is uniquely suited for this high-volume sonic combat because reggae is a musical style with a lot of space in it. There is room for the sound to expand at high volume and fill the empty spaces. Anyone who has not heard reggae music played over a premier sound system has not truly experienced one of ultimate expressions of the music.

This then was the siren call that entranced young Horace Swaby. "I used to just go there and listen to sound," he told Lol Bell-Brown and Rootsman in an interview in 1993, "becaw from my house I could hear the big roun' steel 'orn they use to 'ave in those days and that use to draw me, from I 'ear the music deh I couldn't stay in my house! Nuttin' could hold me, I'd sneak out. I got a lotta beatin' for them thing there but, y'know, for the love of music."[2]

By age fourteen Horace was in secondary school, the prestigious Kings College. But he had little use for school. In fact, beyond instruction in such skills as reading and writing, he subconsciously resisted what he instinctively felt was a kind of indoctrination. In any case, he was interested only in music and spent much of his time cutting class to play the organ in the school chapel, along with his buddies, Junior Boyd and a future member of the Wailers, Tyrone Downie. The boys were inspired by top reggae organist Jackie Mittoo who had played on, written, or arranged hundreds of hits. This led to disciplinary action, and soon Horace was roaming downtown Kingston, haunting the record shops down by Parade and turning up at recording studios to watch and learn.

So it was not an accident that the sixteen-year-old found himself in front of Aquarius that day in 1971. The location of Aquarius was convenient, in Halfway Tree, a relatively benign, neutral part of the city between the Havendale neighborhood, downtown Kingston, and the Trench Town ghetto.

Interestingly enough, Swaby's first recorded effort was an early version of "East of the River Nile." Herman Chin-Loy had purchased the rhythm track from producer extraordinaire Lee "Scratch" Perry. He hired Pablo to create and blow a melody over it with the melodica. Aside from the melody itself and the overall structure of the rhythm track, the resulting recording is nothing like the expansive, cinematic version that Pablo reshaped as auteur six years later. The original "East of the River Nile" is unique and interesting, with the same quirky rhythm track of its successor, but a prosaic saxophone doubles the bass line and repeater percussion clatters in the midrange. Very little echo or reverb is used so the overall effect is somewhat claustrophobic and two-dimensional, rather than the three-dimensional spaciousness of the subsequent version. If you never heard the later version of "East of the River Nile" you would think the original was impressive. But the later version is transcendent, as the fully mature Augustus Pablo took it to another level. In any case, it was at this moment that young Horace Swaby became Augustus Pablo. In time, everyone who knew him called him Pablo.

"East of the River Nile" did not come out immediately; instead Chin-Loy released another instrumental Swaby had played on, under the name of Augustus Pablo. Introduced by a bit of nonsensical double-talk by Chin-Loy, "Higgy Higgy" is a languorous, breezy reggae instrumental topped by a Pablo melodica melody that utilizes thirds or other two-note clusters as much as single notes. It is quite pretty and definitely induces a summery mood. It was Pablo's first release and, though it was no big seller, it attracted attention by its uniqueness.

Pablo was always quite reticent about his relatively privileged upbringing, which is understandable since he was entering the world of ghetto sufferers who were not only the core audience for reggae but also the vast majority of performers, deejays, and selectors. He was a middle-class kid navigating realms filled with hangers-on, hustlers, badmen, and the desperately needy. Nonetheless his background afforded him some advantages. One obvious advantage was that one of his classmates, Clive Chin, had parents who owned Randy's Records, Kingston's biggest record retailer, and a recording studio attached to it. His chum had access to the studio and certain rhythm tracks that had been recorded there. Clive gave Pablo a demo of one rhythm track and told him to practice playing over it. Clive liked what Pablo came up with and arranged for him to record it.

In the cramped studio, Pablo stood up to the mic and blew his melodica. Listening to the playback, he sat on the edge of the mixing board, taking in everything Errol Thompson, the engineer, was doing. He wore an untucked striped dress shirt, jeans, and a billed cap, into which were stuffed whatever incipient dreadlocks he may have had. Perhaps because of the endless hours he had spent hanging around studios, Pablo was not overawed by the studio setting. He was relaxed, focused, in his element, the hint of a confident smile leavening his serious expression, the look of a young man who had found his milieu. He had an air of casual authority, as though he could have been running the session.

"Java," as the recording was called, opened with a stock Middle Eastern–inflected riff on guitar, reminiscent of the so-called "hootchy-cootchy" melody—dah-dah-DAH . . . DAH . . . DAH . . . .dah-dah-DAH-dah-dah-dah DAH—as what sounded like a female voice shimmering in reverb and echo intoned: "from the East of the Rio Cobre, to the West of the Rio Cobre . . . . .here's the hottest . . .*java!*" Pablo blew sinuous melodica solos over a minor-key, two chord reggae vamp with a distinctive bass line consisting of two descending nine-note figures, as jazzy octave accents on electric guitar and backing vocals singing "Java" fleshed out the mood. "Java," with its unique "far east" sound, was an immediate hit and Pablo took full ownership of the Augustus Pablo nom de plume. He was then in demand as a session musician, playing piano, organ, or melodica for any number of producers, quite a feat for a completely self-taught teenage musician.

At the same time that he was venturing into the world of recording studios, Pablo established, with his brother Dougie, a sound system, Rockers International. Though never one of the most popular sound systems, Rockers emphasized cultural music and gained respect within that niche. Running the sound system put Pablo in direct touch with the grassroots reggae audience. More importantly, it led to a relationship with King Tubby, who had one of the most popular sound systems on the island. Tubby was something of an electronic genius; he built and reconstructed electronic equipment not only for the sound systems but also for recording studios. He had built his own studio from scratch and was at the center of the sound system business, cutting "dubs," acetates of recordings that had not been commercially released, for anyone who wanted them. "Dub plates" were a key part of the sound system scene because they made it possible for a sound system operator to play a piece of music that no one else had. Pablo, like other sound system operators, went to Tubby to buy dub plates and began to pick the brain of the man who had "the greatest sound in the world," as Pablo told me years later. At the same time, Tubby, who had a keen appreciation of unique talent, encouraged the precocious teenager. It was not long before Pablo was recording exclusive musical pieces for Tubby to play on his sound system. It was a crucial connection for Pablo as Tubby was also the man who had created "version"— a remixed version of a song that dropped the vocals and various instruments in and out for dramatic effect—in short the essence of what came to be called dub. A close, simpatico, working relationship was established between Pablo and the older doyen of the dancehall scene.

Pablo was also given free access to Randy's studio. Together he and Clive Chin created a series of recordings that were released as *This Is Augustus Pablo*, Pablo's first album as an artist. Working with the highly creative engineer Errol Thompson and such musicians as Robbie Shakespeare (at that time a young bass player looking for a break), "Family Man" Barrett of the Wailers, and others who regularly played sessions at Randy's, Pablo was able to create a debut album that was a true reflection of his artistry. One track, "Pablo in Dub," produced by Clive's uncle Leonard Chin, was an early example of what later would be called dub-wise production, with echoed drum accents and spacey in-and-out arrangement behind Pablo's sprightly melodica melody;

Pablo also used the melodica to play at certain points the rhythm-chord "skank" normally played by a guitar in reggae music. "Pablo in Dub" was a local hit.

"You see," Pablo explained to Lol Bell-Brown and Rootsman during their interview, "at that time I was about seventeen years old, goin' on eighteen, an' I mix that album, y'know, yeah so you must 'ave to un-nerstan', you see, come when I was younger I use' to deal with studio work, two track an' everyt'ing, so my knowledge was like likkle bit in-crease from very early. So when I reach eighteen it come like I'm doin' some forty year old man work. That's why for years, people see me an' them say 'boy, can't believe say it innit Pablo' . . . dem t'ink it a big man . . . the man them think say I'm older than them, believe me. 'Caw the works we are doin', people imagine all kinds of things about you."[3]

The experience of recording *This Is Augustus Pablo* emboldened Pab-lo to form his own labels Hot Stuff, Yard, Message, and Rockers, the latter so named in honor of his sound system. The name also referred to an emerging style of reggae, harder, deeper, more powerful, driven by rhythmic innovations and an apocalyptic Rasta sensibility. Accord-ing to Robbie Shakespeare, Pablo originated the term.[4] Pablo him-self embraced Rastafari and, typically, committed himself completely. Many years later a British interviewer, who corralled Pablo at London's the Dub Club during a rare visit to the U.K., asked him what made his music so special. Pablo, clad in a yellow jacket over gray sweater and dress shirt, a black tam containing his locks, stood somewhat stiffly in front of a colorful mural on the club wall. As he answered, an uneasy smile flickered around his lips while he stood next to his interviewer in front of the eye of the video camera: "Well, I put my whole heart into it, you know. Some people come to follow the work but I just come heartically to do the work for the Most High and for the people of the world, you know. I put my whole heart into everything I do . . . other-wise I don't bother going into it, you know."[5]

Just as he had focused his energy and time as a youth toward music, he now focused solely on devoting himself to music that he felt was an expression of spirituality, of the essence of Jah Rastafari. Nothing else was of interest. So, although he still occasionally played sessions for other musicians or producers if he felt the music was worthy, to a large extent he curtailed his session work in order to devote himself completely to composing, arranging, and producing music for his own label. He had no interest in becoming a star or making money, except as a means to fund his various musical projects. Nor was he interested in making music to fit any commercial purpose. He was a classic example of an "all or nothing" personality. What followed was an outpouring of creativity that led to some of the most distinctive, influential, and magnificent music ever created.

One of the most important of the early works was "Cassava Piece," released in 1973 on his Hot Stuff label. Featuring an original, rumbling bass line propelling a hypnotic two-chord, minor-key chord vamp, "Cassava Piece" highlights Pablo's atmospheric melody on the melodica. In the second half of the piece, the mix breaks down to just bass and drums underneath Pablo's melodica; then the bass and drums drop out and the guitar and keyboard skank carries the groove. That is a common dub-style move, but Pablo plays the melody continuously, unlike most dubs that feature only snatches of melody.

Years later Robbie Shakespeare, who played bass on "Cassava Piece" before going on to fame as one half of the premier rhythm section of Sly & Robbie, told me he considered the piece as a high point. "The way Pablo and Tubby mixed that was very special," he noted. "There never was another song like it."[6]

Indeed "Cassava Piece" served as the source for the epochal "King Tubby Meets Rockers Uptown" as well as Jacob Miller's vocal hit "Baby I Love You So."

Characteristically, Pablo went completely against the grain of the tried and true practices of the reggae business. Most producers made sure to cut tracks on the latest popular singer or deejay who was creating excitement, as well as recording established stars whenever possible. Pablo rarely recorded established artists or those who were currently "hot." Instead, he recorded young, unproven talent. He felt an explicit imperative to encourage, nurture, and develop "the youth."

"Yeah, well, everyone should give a helping hand [to the youth] still," Pablo once explained to me, "because we started from nothing, really, and we had a lot of people teach us along the way. I feel that each one can set a path that the youth can follow. All the while they can take up an instrument, rather than waste their time firing guns and all these things. It's not necessary in this time . . . 'caw Jah will take care of it still."

In Jacob Miller's case, Pablo's outreach led to him actually taking the teenager in. Miller was an "uptown" youth who had started singing as young as six years old, hanging around studios and sound systems. He was a precocious lad with an impressive voice. He had recorded a couple of pieces for Coxsone Dodd's pre-eminent Studio One label but nothing much came from them. He was perhaps thirteen when Pablo encountered him.

"He used to stay at my home," Pablo told me, "I used to look after him. True, his parents had left him alone. His mother worked in America. His parents just left him alone, I don't know why. They just left him in Jamaica. So I just take care of him and help the youth out. And I start producing him."

Pablo's first recordings with young Jacob, "A Girl Name Pat" and "Each One Teach One," attracted a little attention, but "Keep On Knocking" was a hit as Jacob's rapidly maturing voice was coming into its own. "Baby I Love You So," followed in 1975 and was released on the flip side of "King Tubby Meets Rockers Uptown" in the U.K. Then came Miller's epochal "Who Say Jah No Dread," also known as "Too Much Commercialization of Rasta." It featured Miller's powerful chanting vocal over one of the heaviest rhythm tracks created by Pablo—or anyone else, for that matter. Originally recorded as "555 Crown St.," an instrumental, the rhythm track features an explosive bass line that starts with an ascending three-note phrase high on the neck of the bass and then plunges to a deep four-note phrase. It repeats this call-and-response throughout the track. The textures of each phrase set up uncanny sonic vibrations that penetrate to the marrow and hit deep in the gut. The overall effect is spooky, as if referencing the spirit world.

After recording this cut, Miller was recruited by the band Inner Circle. By 1980 he was one of Jamaica's most popular vocalists, known for his flamboyant stage antics, irrepressible spirit, and magnificent voice. Inner Circle was one of the first Jamaican bands to get an international recording contract but their progress was stopped short by Miller's untimely death in an auto accident in 1980.

Another youth with whom Pablo had even more impact was Hugh

Mundell. Like Pablo, Mundell was from an affluent family; his father was a lawyer. But just like Pablo, at a young age Mundell was captivated by reggae. Pablo encountered Mundell, when he was around age twelve, at Joe Gibbs's recording studio. Mundell was looking for a break. Although he did record something for Gibbs, it was never released. Pablo felt the urge to help the youth when he saw him next at Aquarius Studio.

"I just saw him at a studio one day, at Joe Gibbs's, with some musicians," Pablo recalled when I asked him how he met Mundell. "And we started reasoning and 'im say he wanted to do some music. So one day I saw him at Aquarius—he never to go school that day, you know—and I just carry him to my home and give him a rehearsal. When I hear him at rehearsal, I just say, bwoy, I must carry him to a studio! So I take him to Lee Perry's studio. True, I used to move around Lee Perry's studio at that time and I just asked Lee Perry for some free time, you know. So we get some musicians together and we did "Let's All Unite." That's the first track we laid. Then we did "Africans Must Be Free.""

Mundell's reedy, hypnotic, chanting style made an immediate impact when Pablo released "Africa Must Be Free (By the Year 1983)" in 1976. The release of the song coincided with a rising consciousness of the anti-apartheid struggle in South Africa and Zimbabwe, and the song's title became a catch phrase that resounded internationally when Mundell's debut album of the same name was released the following year.

Though Pablo was making exceptional music and a number of releases created a stir, he was not having many true hits. Given his single-minded focus on his own productions, there was not a lot of ancillary income from session work or backing other artists. And he was not particularly oriented toward live performing—there were not many opportunities for that in Jamaica in any case, and his reputation abroad had not yet reached critical mass. As a result, money was always in short supply. Pablo tended to put any money he had into his work or to his circle of protégés, hangers-on, and supplicants. As a result, Pablo turned to his father for financial assistance, requests that were not well received. Claude Swaby, an accountant, took a dim view of his son's musical ambitions. Nonetheless, he did advance funds to him on occasion, though he insisted on designating them as loans with interest due rather than outright donations, in hopes of instilling a sense of financial responsibility in his son. He also insisted that Pablo set up his business in a proper way. So early on Pablo had a publishing company, Pablo Music Ltd, as well as his labels.[7] Having access to this information was an advantage that most other reggae artists from less affluent backgrounds did not have. From nearly the beginning of his career, Pablo adopted a practice of retaining control of his productions, by publishing his compositions through his own company and only licensing the music for limited terms to companies who wanted to release it abroad. At the same time, Pablo adopted the principle of reinvesting any income into the company, which usually meant funding more productions, buying studio equipment or instruments, and otherwise advancing the music—to the point of neglecting personal needs.

He opened a record shop in downtown Kingston at 135 Orange Street, not far from Parade, that served as both a retail outlet and distribution center for his productions. It was not far from Studio One's headquarters and Randy's retail and studio operations, as well as numerous other notable music business outlets. Still, money problems were frequent and Pablo continued to seek assistance from his father until finally the elder Swaby refused to give any more money. For awhile, Pablo sent his compatriot Gichy Dan to his father's accounting offices to try to wheedle some funds and, later, he sent Joan Higgins, who had become part of his circle, on the theory that his father would find it harder to refuse an attractive girl. Pablo became estranged from his father, to the point that the elder Swaby would walk by his son without speaking or acknowledging him if they encountered one another in public. Eventually, however, they reconciled.[8]

Around this time a deal was struck with fledgling U.K. reggae label Greensleeves to put out compilation of early Pablo productions called *Original Rockers*. Pablo had heard about Greensleeves, and when Joan Higgins went to England for schooling, he instructed her to contact Greensleeves. Aside from a formidable track listing that included "Cassava Piece," "Wareika Hill," "A.P. Special," and more, the album was notable for the photo of Pablo that appeared on the cover. A seemingly out-of-focus snapshot captures Pablo, seated, smoking herb from a huge hand-carved chillum. The out-of-focus effect may have actually been the result of the large clouds of smoke wafting around Pablo, who was captured just after inhaling. Wearing sandals, untucked dress shirt, and slacks, as usual, Pablo's dreadlocks, just shoulder length at this point, are uncovered. Pablo's slightly Oriental eyes, set in his narrow face, are unfocused. For many outside the Jamaican reggae world, this was the first image they saw of Augustus Pablo. Reggae was already strongly identified with herb-smoking in the minds of non-Jamaican fans, and this image resonated strongly with those for whom the freewheeling, drug-fueled countercultural sixties never ended.

A year or so later, with the international release by Shanachie Records in the United States of a new Augustus Pablo album titled *Rockers Meets King Tubby Ina Firehouse*, an even more striking image of Pablo was widely exposed. Pablo was photographed looking directly at the camera from between thick branches of a tree. His features are unique and ethnically unclassifiable. His face is narrow, deltoid in shape, with a high forehead and long nose. His complexion is beige. He looks at the camera unsmiling, his dark brown, almost black eyes locked in a penetrating stare, accented by short, dark eyebrows slanting down toward his nose. A wispy mustache and goatee set off a compact mouth. His locks now fall past his shoulders; his arms are crossed in front of him as he leans forward, and he holds a spliff between the fingers of his left hand. The photograph accurately captures Pablo's serious mien, as he was not given to frequent smiles. When he did smile, his lips parted only slightly. He appears enormously self-possessed in the photograph.

It is especially notable that this striking image of Pablo is on the back of the album jacket. The reason for this is simple; Pablo did not want his photograph to be on the front of the album. Instead, the front cover is a collage of photographs of various musicians who played on the album, including Pablo, as well as King Tubby and an illustration of Emperor Haile Selassie I. On the back, above the credits, was a statement: "(give thanks to King Selassie I) for health, strength and energy, life for I & I to create this album . . . .selah!" All of this was evidence of Pablo's strong desire to avoid self-promotion, as he believed his music was divinely inspired.

With the release of *Original Rockers* and *Rockers Meets King Tubby Ina Firehouse* into the wider market, Pablo found an audience beyond the Jamaican reggae market. Although he was widely respected as a musician, Pablo's records, with a handful of exceptions, were not particularly big sellers in Jamaica. Singers such as Dennis Brown, Gregory Isaacs and Johnny Clarke, along with deejays such as U-Roy, Big Youth, and Dillinger ruled the roost in Jamaica during the seventies. So the release of his recordings in the larger international market was an important development.

After hearing *East of the River Nile*, *King Tubby Meets Rockers Uptown*, and the *Original Rockers* collection I was inspired to spread the word about Pablo, and wrote the first significant article about him in the U.S., for the *Village Voice*. He was still a mysterious figure to any but the most hard-core reggae fan. Coincidentally, I joined the staff of Shanachie Records several months after they had released Pablo's *Rockers Meets King Tubby Ina Firehouse* album. The deal had been struck after an emissary from Shanachie had gone to Jamaica for a meeting with Pablo to discuss the deal. After five days of waiting in a hotel room for Pablo to show up, the Shanachie man was about to return to the States when Pablo finally arrived, and a deal was struck. Later it was suggested by one of Pablo's compatriots that the waiting game had been a kind of test, designed to weigh the Shanachie man's seriousness and sincerity.[9]

With Pablo's albums released on Greensleeves in the U.K. and Shanachie in the States, Pablo's music was no longer confined to the grassroots reggae market. His music found a much more enthusiastic audience internationally. Pablo's worldwide cult of admirers dates from this time. Before long, major critics were hailing the originality and evocative power of his music. A *New York Times* critic's declaration set the tone: "Pablo is more than a gifted instrumentalist, he is a masterful pop composer whose recordings are possessed by a reflective, almost mystical sadness."[10] Even such a mainstream publication as *Newsweek* devoted an entire page to Pablo; the magazine's music critic opined, "his rhythmic originality and uncanny melodic sense set the highest standards; the improvisation that he creates with his evocative melodies are worthy of the best jazz improvisers."[11] Yet those writing knew very little about Pablo and related only the sketchiest details of his life. This only added to his mystique.

At this point in his life, Pablo's existence revolved completely around music. Always reclusive, he lived in different dwellings, moving rather frequently, generally in the Havendale vicinity of Kingston. He also at times lived up in the hills, in the countryside behind Kingston, and during one period lived in the rural precincts of St. James Parish, adjacent to Montego Bay, far from the intense environment of Kingston. He might have remained there but people made their way to find him, often entreating him to come to Kingston to do a session. Pablo himself explained his propensity for country living by saying that his parents had come from the country, so it was in him.[12] But it also served the purpose of making it difficult for people to get to him. They had to be very highly motivated to find out where he was staying and then travel a distance to see him. Wherever he lived, he had an array of instruments and some means of recording. His residences in Kingston were stuffed with recording equipment and all manner of instruments, including some from India, Japan, and Africa, as well as synthesizers.

He typically would head for his record shop in downtown Kingston around 11:00 a.m., earlier if he was staying out in the country. He had a driver take him downtown and on to whatever stops he had later in the day. The shop on Orange Street was where he met the world. He was not one to give out his personal phone number or let more than a few select associates know where he was staying. Anyone who wanted to get in touch with him had to call or come to the shop. When Pablo arrived he would see who was looking for him, return phone calls to record distributors, the pressing plant, recording studio, or anyone else who had left a legitimate business message. People would see his car and come. This is what Joan Higgins described to me as his "outreach program."[13] People would come to ask for money for various purposes or for assistance. Pablo made a note of every request.

Many who only knew Pablo from his public persona might have been surprised at his businesslike approach. He kept a notebook to keep track of his expenditures, something his father had instilled in him, as well as lists of things he needed to do. It may be difficult for those who have never lived in or spent much time in a desperately poor environment to understand the constant demands faced by anyone of means who lives in or has business in those areas. A well-known reggae artist, for instance, when visiting his old neighborhood had to carry a large roll of currency to dispense more or less continuously to all who approached him. It would be incomprehensible to the ghetto dwellers that the artist might be experiencing financial challenges. To them, a recording artist was wealthy and it was mandatory to share the wealth.

After taking care of business at the shop, Pablo would head off to get some food and make a stop at his herbsman, the "bush doctor" Bagga, who dispensed not only ganja but also herbal remedies for a variety of ailments. For years Pablo had suffered from a problem with his leg, reportedly stemming from diabetes, which a conventional doctor had unsuccessfully attempted to treat. The problems worsened and Pablo developed a mistrust of conventional doctors. He took herbal treatments thereafter. Bagga had an office in his home, a modern, neatly kept house in one of the nicer neighborhoods of the city. There was a small waiting room, similar to that of any doctor's office. Bagga would listen to his patient's description of the ailment, do some basic examination, and tell the patient to return the next day. When the patient returned, Bagga would dispense the appropriate herbal remedy.

At Pablo's urging, I went to Bagga on one of my visits to Jamaica in order to get a remedy for arthritis for acquaintances of mine, twin sisters from Nigeria who, when they heard I was going to Jamaica, requested that I seek out an herbal remedy for them there. Bagga had listened to my description of their ailment and bid me return the next day. On my return, he gave me four bottles filled with a special liquid preparation—two with dark brown liquid and two with a sienna-colored liquid—along with some elaborate instructions. He said they must stand in a certain posture and drink the sienna-colored liquid first, then raise their arms and drink the dark brown liquid. According to the sisters, the preparation did help ease their arthritic condition.

After visiting Bagga, Pablo would proceed to whatever appointments he had set up for that day, meeting people, going to the printer, the pressing plant, and the like. The night tended to be reserved for studio work, which often went into the early morning. Indeed his recording "Rising Sun" was named because of the time it was recorded.

"'Rising Sun,' that title now," Pablo confided to me, "how I came up with that name, I was in the studio one night from about 11 o'clock. The sun came up the next morning and I went to play for Chinna

Smith. But when I finished creating the song I went out and I saw the sun rising up. It was just a vibes that make me create the song so I just named it 'Rising Sun' to create a little vibes around the vision, you no see it?"

Doing business with Pablo was sometimes unpredictable. Though Joan Higgins handled much of his business abroad capably and aggressively, Pablo did from time to time make forays to the United States, usually when he had a new recording to license or wanted to make available earlier recordings that had not been released there. That meant coming to Shanachie's offices, at that to time located in Ho-Ho-Kus, New Jersey, a small town about twenty-five miles northwest of New York City. The locals were not used to followers of Rastafari. If a Rasta arrived by bus from New York and attempted to make the walk from the bus stop to Shanachie, they were liable to be picked up by the police. A call would come from the local police station: "We have some Indian-looking guy here, says he's coming to Shanachie." Pablo, fortunately, never experienced that indignity, and on later visits a car would be sent to pick him up. Often accompanied by Miko McKenzie, one of the Rockers inner circle, Pablo would arrive with master tapes and newly pressed 12-inch singles from Jamaica. After the release of *Rockers Meets King Tubby Ina Firehouse*, Pablo insisted that his productions be released by Shanachie on his own Message label rather than Shanachie, even though that tended to lead to lower sales because Message was not familiar to American retailers. He also was resolute in pushing for the release of new young talent such as Delroy Williams and Norris Reid. He approached business from an artistic, cultural, and spiritual point of view. When he made a deal for the release of *King Tubby Meets Rockers Uptown*, it was pointed out to him that the artwork only listed eleven song titles even though twelve songs were on the album.

"What would people think when they saw the extra track? Would they not be confused?" he was asked.

"They will give thanks," Pablo said with equanimity.

He also strongly resisted putting his own picture on album covers. The album *Earth's Rightful Ruler* featured an illustration of Haile Selassie I on its cover, but for the American version he agreed, after much argument, to allow his own picture on the front of the album. He insisted, however, that Selassie be listed as the producer of the album and himself as co-producer. His message on the back of the album was a simple statement of his rationale for music-making:

> This album was created through the powers of his Majesty Emperor Haile Selassie I for He inspired I and taught I to play I harps unto him and his sons and daughters over the creation. Oh, Jah, all I ask for is life, health and strength, wisdom and understanding. Some see this music as Lovers Rock or Dub Music, well I and I see it as Jah Rastafari Haile Selassie I. Work to call I and I brothers and sisters from the four corners of the earth; so you see no matter how long it takes all have to bow and give praise unto I father who rules creation in righteousness.

Those who only knew his quiet, reserved public persona would have been surprised to learn that on occasion he could be quite voluble and forceful if he felt strongly about something. One time, after we had not done any licensing deals for a while, he came for a visit. He looked a bit frail and indicated that his leg had been bothering him. Despite rather lackluster sales of his recent releases, we agreed to license Pablo's latest production, a beautiful new collection of music entitled *Blowing with the Wind*. After a brief negotiation, we sat around chatting amiably, basking in the glow of a business meeting with a happy ending. Pablo mentioned that he also had a compilation of various new artists available, and would we be interested in that as well? "Sure, why not?" he was told, but we suggested to him that maybe some established artists might be added to the compilation to help make the collection more salesworthy. The happy glow vanished immediately and Pablo's countenance darkened.

"You are exploiters!" he cried. "You do not support new talent. You only want to make money from artists who are already known!"

His tirade lasted a few minutes and the idea of releasing the collection was dropped.

By the early eighties Pablo had a worldwide cult following, but few of his fans had ever seen him perform. Pablo had rarely performed live in Jamaica, let alone internationally. His lack of visibility, in conjunction with his exotic name, only added to his mysterious, even mystical image. So when tour dates were announced in 1985, it was for many a highly anticipated opportunity to at last see the man who created such mesmerizing music.

The American portion of Pablo's touring was not large, a handful of dates on the East and West Coasts, mainly. In Philadelphia, Pablo was booked into the Chestnut Cabaret, a clean, well-run, somewhat anonymous midsize venue that could hold perhaps seven or eight hundred people packed in like sardines. It was the premier midlevel showcase venue in Philadelphia, and thus presented all sorts of music. On the night of Pablo's performance, excitement ran high among the packed crowd. The announced showtime of 9:00 p.m. had come and gone, but reggae concerts typically did not start on time and so the people waiting—a multicultural mix of Americans of various ethnicities, as well as a significant quotient of Jamaicans—were unfazed. The people might have been less relaxed if they had known that Pablo had not yet arrived in town and no one had heard from him. The Chestnut Cabaret booker informed me of this rather pointedly, since I represented Pablo's record company in the United States. I could not tell him anything reassuring since I had heard nothing. I was worried that something truly unfortunate had happened.

By 10:00 p.m. the mood was growing more restive. Just then word came that Pablo's van had pulled up outside the club. I rushed out to learn what was going on. I spied Pablo, dressed in an indigo-and-white-striped dashiki with white embroidery around the neck, a light blue dress shirt underneath, black slacks, and a black tam with a button featuring the visage of Haile Selassie on it. The pattern of the shirt, which I recognized as based on a type of Fulani traditional dress, was highly familiar, as it had made its way out of West Africa to African cultural shops around the world. Pablo's expression was phlegmatic, as usual, as he watched the musicians unloaded their instruments.

"Hey, Pablo," I greeted him. "Everything all right?"

"Yeah," he replied, betraying no sense of anxiety.

"We were worried 'cause you were supposed to be here four hours ago for the sound check."

"Oh," he replied with equanimity. "We had to stop along the way to do some laundry."

A little while later, the house lights went down and the dark shapes of the musicians moved onto the stage. The crowd surged forward.

"Ladies and gentleman," came the announcement, "without any further delay, please put your hands together for Augustus Pablo!"

The lights came up and the band kicked into "Frozen Dub," one of Pablo's signature songs, based on a classic Studio One rhythm. I recognized Chinna Smith on lead guitar; there was also a drummer, bass player, rhythm guitarist, two percussionists (one playing a shaker, the other a tambourine), and a keyboard player. After a few moments Pablo entered from stage right, striding purposefully to the center of the stage where keyboards were set up for him. He picked up a melodica, gestured to the band to lower the volume, and leaned forward to speak into a microphone.

"Yes, greetings! In the name of my father Haile Selassie I in creation . . . There are times when Jah directs us to take the music to the four corners of the earth . . . Have no fear, my father Ras Tafari lives!"

With that he brought the melodica, painted red, gold, and green on its sides, up to his mouth and began blowing sinuous lines over the groove, his head bobbing forward and backward to the rhythm. Now and then he jigged from side to side as he played. The familiar haunting melodica melody streamed out of the speakers and at key points he skirled his fingers up the melodica keyboard to create a climactic accent. Contrary to what many may have assumed, Pablo in performance was intense, compressed, focused, at times almost jerky in his movements. He did not look at the audience; instead his entire being seemed focused on his instrument as he squeezed his eyes shut, cheeks puffing, and blew. His mien was an interesting contrast to the mellow, often pastoral mood of much of his music.

"Frozen Dub" came to a climax and rapturous applause greeted it. The audience had witnessed something special and knew it. Without a word, Pablo turned toward his musicians and nodded. The band then launched into "Rockers Rock," another Pablo instrumental based on the classic Studio One "Real Rock" rhythm, which had been popularized worldwide by a vocal version of the song entitled "Armagideon Time." Pablo was intent, eyes focused down in front of him, bending forward, turning now and then to signal the band with a gesture or look. One of these gestures caused the band to break down into a dub section, and Chinna Smith, one of the finest guitarists ever to emerge from Jamaica, took a jazzy guitar solo. As Chinna soloed, Pablo continued to move in place, looking down, completely absorbed in the music. He signaled to the band and the musicians slowly faded the music out. As the song ended, Pablo intoned: "Yes, that is Rockers Rock." Again Pablo turned and signaled the band, and they launched into a distinctive original groove. Pablo moved to a xylophone and began playing a pentatonic, oriental-sounding melody with two mallets. After a while, Chinna took a solo based almost entirely on octaves, in the manner of Wes Montgomery, and Pablo answered him with xylophone improvisations off the melody. The crowd responded with extra-intense applause as the unnamed song ended.

"Like that one?" Pablo asked. "You don't hear nothing yet! This one is called 'African Frontline,' 'caw Africa struggle right now!" The show proceeded in the same vein. Pablo's evocative music came to life on-stage with extraordinary presence. Pablo only occasionally spoke to the audience between songs, making just two or three statements. There was no "show" or showmanship, just sparkling musicianship and the majesty of the music itself. When the last song unwound and faded, Pablo quickly gave a slight bow, clasping his hands in front of him with palms together in quasi-oriental style, abruptly turned, and quickly walked offstage. In spite of sustained, rapturous applause interspersed with shouts, there was no encore.

The day after the Chestnut Cabaret show, Pablo came by the radio station to be interviewed by me during my weekly reggae show. In my mind was the day a little less than two years previous when Pablo had called from Jamaica to deliver a shocking message: "Dem shot Mundell." he had said, somberly yet with the matter-of-fact tone of someone who lives in a place where murders are common. Hugh Mundell had been shot, at the age of twenty, by a man who had come up on his car and fired point-blank, hitting him in the neck. There were varying accounts of the motive. Pablo said it was the result of Mundell having confronted the man about a stolen video recorder. Others said it was a dispute over a malfunctioning refrigerator that Mundell had sold the man. Seemingly Pablo was fatalistic and as a Rasta he did not believe a Rastaman could die. Still, he had delivered the news in slightly lower tones than usual, and it was easy to sense his sadness. He had probably had a closer association with Mundell and had more success with him than any other singer. Ironically, Mundell did not live long enough to see the end of the prophetic year of his song, "Africa Must Be Free (By the Year 1983)." Mundell's murder was a reminder of how volatile the streets of Kingston could be. It made clear the wisdom of Pablo's low profile and his conscious inaccessibility.

These thoughts swirled through my mind as Pablo made his way into the studio, his locks tucked into a crocheted gray tam. I gave him a pair of headphones, which he put on without comment. He betrayed neither nervousness nor the slightest bit of anticipation as I sat him down in the guest booth that faced the control panel where I would sit. A soundproof glass window would separate us. Pablo had no real interest in being interviewed and so it was a small miracle that he was there in front of me. I tried to loosen him up a bit as I sat down on the other side of the glass and spoke into my microphone.

"So, how long have we been talking about you coming on this show?" I asked him in a jocular tone. "It's been years, right?"

"Yeah," Pablo replied. He gave a soft chuckle, a good sign; in all the years I had known Pablo I had never once heard him laugh out loud.

I asked him to explain the difference between instrumental and dub music in light of the fact that he was most often referred to as a "dub master."

"Well," Pablo began, "the word 'dub' just come from the early days when we just draw out the rhythm section, just try an experiment. And we have a bredrin name Philip Smart, and Errol Thompson also [both engineers] . . . and Tubby more time have a dub-plate on his sound. But it wasn't commercial; just for the sound. They play dub plates. And true the name 'dub' comes from that. They play dub plate, they play otherwise. I just play instrumentation but just because they use this name 'dub' . . . lots of time they start to commercialize on the name, calling me 'dubmaster' and all these things.

"But I really don't come up with the names and t'ing. It's just the people who come up with these things. I don't really like it still . . . 'cause I check it as just instrumental, just doing Jah works, you know, within that form, you know . . . because you have in Jah chambers all different ways to control the people and bring the people to him, you understand? And that's the way I see the works still."

I pointed out that not as much "cultural" music was being recorded in Jamaica at that time as previously.

"True," Pablo agreed. "Everyone put away their creative thing and try to follow traditions that are already created, you understand? They're just followers, you understand?"

"Many are just recycling Studio One rhythms," I noted.

"Well," Pablo said, "all those Studio One rhythms still rule, you know." He began speaking more rapidly, more animatedly in insistent cadences, as he did when something close to his heart was being discussed. "I don't care what they try to do, what them try to create . . . no one knows if someone will respect them for that rhythm they create, you understand?"

I noted that Leroy Sibbles, The Heptones' lead singer, had created the bass line for Pablo's production of Jacob Miller's "False Rasta" and that he had created many of the classic Studio One bass lines as well.

"Yeah," Pablo said, "he play a lot of songs for me . . . a lot of them! 'Cause I asked a lot of people about [Studio One producer] Coxsone's music, who plays the bass line and they say 'Leroy.' Though he wasn't an original bass man, he has a different feel. 'im have a 'singer' feel and it was a different thing than the original bass man. He see it differently than them."

It was a great example of Pablo's knowledge of the history of the music and his single-minded focus. He researched who had played the bass lines of his favorite recordings and went out and hired that man to play bass on his recordings, regardless of who the top session bass players might be. Pablo went for an original feel and sound.

I played an obscure Pablo recording from the early seventies called "Feeling Moody" and asked him how he came up with such creative melodies.

"Where does it all come from?" Pablo asked rhetorically. "His Majesty, still. 'Cause he's the one who inspired me with the feelings in me that I have to play out. It just comes through 'cause he's the teacher of all teachers, you know. He plays the most beautiful harps in creation. So he's the one who teaches us to play all these beautiful songs to his people."

"Pure inspiration, huh?" I asked.

"Yeah, mon!" Pablo responded emphatically. His entire rationale for creating music was divine inspiration. If not specifically inspired, he was not motivated to create. If he was inspired, then he felt compelled to bring the music forth.

I then asked about the tour, whether he felt it was a satisfying experience in light of the fact that it was his first real multi-city tour in the United States.

"It was not *irie*," Pablo said without hesitation, using the patois word for "good." He was not given to platitudes. "But it was a good experience still. Some of the shows, the promoters didn't have things right and if things not right then I have to get miserable and I really don't have to do that. I could just stick to recording. I can just do the works in JA."

"But what about the larger festivals?" I asked, since I had heard they were wonderful concerts. "How was that?"

"Yeah," Pablo said, "in California, that was better."

"So you're comfortable in front of large or small crowds?"

Pablo gave a soft laugh. "It really doesn't matter to me . . . whether it's one or a thousand."

I then asked him about a song that Pablo himself had sung on his *Earth's Rightful Ruler* album, the title track in fact. The wispy but oddly affecting vocal was his first on record, and I wondered what inspired him to sing.

"Well," Pablo replied, "dem times I seat up in the hills, St. James, and I wasn't really thinking about doing traveling and these things. I used to go to this spring on the land where I lived and every day I used to hear this melody come to my mind and I sing the song. So I just have to do it, 'cause Jah did inspire me personally to sing that song. And I went straight to town and . . . I'm kind of shy about singing. I love singing but I don't like to be upfront . . . and you have to be to sing. I sing by myself, practice on cassette but no one hears that still."

I pulled out a copy of his recording "AP Special" from 1974. It featured a simple but beguiling melody played on what sounds like a xylophone over a sparse arrangement anchored by thick, deep bass line.

"It really has an interesting keyboard sound," I said.

"It really is a small xylophone, a *tszuki*," Pablo explained. "King Tubby buy this for me."

Tubby's relationship with Pablo was more than that of a mentor. Pablo himself had said that Tubby was like a father to him.

I asked Pablo about the growing prevalence of electronic instruments in reggae. Pablo had never been shy about experimenting. He would have Joan Higgins seek out and buy all manner of new electronic instruments that he had heard about or read about. By the mid-eighties he was creating some rhythm tracks with currently fashionable drum machines, synth basses, and synthesizers. Indeed he had first experimented with a rhythm box on "Hot Milk," a recording from 1977. But many of his international fans felt the organic feel of his great early recordings was being lost. King Tubby was also releasing new music with synthesized rhythm tracks, such as the popular rhythm called "Tempo." Meanwhile, King Jammy, another major producer who had begun as a protégé' of Tubby, created a sensation with the release of "Under Mi Sleng Teng," a recording whose completely unique, hypnotic rhythm track was created on a cheap Casio synthesizer.

"So what about 'Sleng Teng'?" I asked. "Is it good or bad? Have we had enough of it?"

"Well," Pablo answered, "the vibes of that music is *irie*, still. But it's computerized music still . . . only thing is, it run a little too hot. Too many versions. People stop creating. It just keep the music stagnant-like, instead of creating now they're just depending on the synthesizer to create for them instead of using natural inspiration. 'Cause no one really play that song, you know. It's just a rhythm box. What is programmed into it . . . .in a Casio machine, they're already set. They just pass it down."

After nearly two hours, the end of my show was approaching. Pablo had been far more forthcoming than I had expected. But he had never been short of ideas or opinions about the subjects he considered important: music and Jah Rastafari.

"Well, we could talk all night, even wait for the rising sun," I joked in reference to the title of his upcoming album, which he had already shared with me. Pablo laughed, a slightly more animated chuckle than before.

"It's been a pleasure having you," I said.

"Give thanks," Pablo answered. He accepted my handshake and disappeared down the stairs outside the studio door.

Reggae styles were changing rapidly at the time I interviewed Pablo; soon the digital revolution of the late eighties, engendered notably by the productions of King Jammy, was turning reggae away from the organic pulse favored by Pablo and other roots reggae masters. The new wave of hard-core dancehall "ragga" styles, heavily influenced by

American hip-hop (which, of course, had been—and continued to be—influenced by reggae), posed a challenge for Pablo. Never afraid to experiment, he incorporated heavily synthesized rhythms into his work. *Blowing with the Wind*, released in 1990, presented some beguiling new pastiches of old and new textures. "Drums to the King," for instance, integrated traditional nyabinghi hand percussion, a staple of Rastafarian spiritual music, with echoed melodica melody and acoustic guitar flourishes, at times creating a mood reminiscent of gypsy music. The intriguingly named "Zion UFO" used an eerie synthesizer sound with heavy tremolo for the main melody, while "Twinkling Stars" offered a sprightly melodica melody over synthetic drum sound. Many of his fans welcomed *Blowing with the Wind* as Pablo's best album in ages.

"This music," wrote Pablo in the liner notes, "which is sometimes misunderstood, has been called many different names. This music is strictly spiritually orientated by inspiration received through the Most High Jah Rastafari Selassie. It is then translated as reggae music—the music from Creation."[14]

In 1999, shortly after he completed work on his album *The Valley of Jehosaphat*, shocking news came from Kingston. Pablo had been rushed to the hospital with a mysterious ailment and had suddenly died. He was only forty-six years of age. The official cause of death was a cessation of breath due to myasthenia gravis, a somewhat rare autoimmune disorder that could suddenly cause muscular weakness that in some cases affected the ability to breathe. Given Pablo's distrust of conventional doctors, it is questionable whether he would have accepted the Western medical treatment that could have saved him. But he never had the chance to make that choice; the disease can manifest suddenly and is notoriously difficult to diagnose. Ironically, *Valley of Jehosaphat* refers to what many interpret as the biblically described valley of judgment, a place where people would be gathered to face divine judgment.

The noted producer known as the Mad Professor had worked with Pablo in London on parts of *Valley of Jehosaphat*, in the good Professor's studio. "My last memory of Pablo was being in Ariwa studios with smoke so thick that we could not see the desk!" he noted, smiling at the memory. "One thing I clearly remember . . . when Pablo came to the studio, for the first three hours he had this piece of board and he was mixing up ganja on it, along with all kinds of herbs and liquids. He had ten bottles or more of different liquids . . . .he would be mixing and pouring . . . and pack it into a pipe and smoke it . . . and then cough like it was going out of style! Like it was going down too fast! I don't know if that affected his health. He was another mystical character but nowhere near as talkative as Yabby You. He would talk almost mumbling . . . he moved mysteriously."[15]

Pablo's working methods never changed and neither did his view of music-making. He created a special, self-contained world with his music—magical, surprising, and evocative, cosmic yet subatomic in its elemental rhythmic and melodic brilliance. As such, he succeeded in his mission, which was simply to be a vessel for higher forces, for spiritual energy. Since Pablo had never sought to be in the pubic eye, the dissemination of his music had never been dependent on him. A decade after his passing from this earthly realm, Pablo's music continues to captivate and inspire multitudes around the world, the continuing legacy of the quiet, determined messenger of the Most High.

The Neville Brothers, photo by Paul Natkin/WireImage, © Getty Images, Inc. All rights reserved.

The Neville Brothers

First Family of Groove

New Orleans is laid out like a giant spider web suspended from a huge, lazy coil of the Mississippi, with parallel avenues replicating the river's snakelike curves and cross streets radiating from some mythical center. The river loops around so far that at some points the west bank of the river is actually east of the east bank. Much of the city is actually below the level of the river and, as is well known in the wake of Hurricane Katrina, most of New Orleans is below sea level, leading some to speculate that subtle differences in atmospheric pressure explain why ordinary rules of logic do not seem to apply to New Orleanian thinking. In this town a straight line is not always the shortest distance between two points—and that is part of its beauty. Some would say that is also a source of its problems.

Despite its cultural riches and seemingly fortuitous position as one of America's busiest ports, with proximity to the offshore oil operations in the Gulf of Mexico, New Orleans has been a backwater for many years. It is a city with a long and deep history and fiercely clings to its past; its legal system is still based on the Napoleonic code, for instance. The city has historically been run by an oligarchy of business and political interests that cornered the wealth and left much of the population scuffling in poverty. While racism has been a powerful force in most of the United States, in New Orleans race took on its own perverse twists, giving rise to Creole culture, and the cult of the quadroons, as well as the oldest community of free people of color in the nation. Though hardly the only American city with a diverse multicultural mix, New Orleans is unique in the way French, Spanish, Irish, Italian, and African cultures shaped the city's life rather than being homogenized into the expeditious American amalgam of other cities. Some people describe it as America's only European city; others call it a Third World city.

All of this is manifested in the city's music. Stereotyped as the birthplace of jazz, New Orleans has been fertile ground for distinctive and seminal blues, rhythm 'n' blues, and rock 'n' roll, as well as jazz—a musical wellspring for American music. Underlying all of these musical styles is the essence of New Orleans music, a certain unique groove and feeling that taps into very deep currents of the human psyche. Tapping into that essence references a different way of walking, a different way of talking, a different sort of sort of consciousness—something magical and transcendent. It all emanates from the groove, a particular life-rhythm that is definitely not in 4/4 time.

Some of these thoughts were on my mind one fine spring day in 1981 as the plane carrying me swooped low over the Gulf of Mexico and made its approach to the New Orleans airport. It was dusk and I got a glimpse of the city sprawled to the left as the plane wheeled over the vastness of Lake Pontchartrain which borders the city to the north. As I emerged into the airport walkway, I inhaled the warm, thick, moist, fecund New Orleans air. Bouncing along toward town in a cab down Highway 61—the same mystical Highway 61, memorialized by Bob Dylan that stretches from New Orleans to Memphis and ultimately all the way to Minneapolis—I took in a procession of frayed pawnshops, bars, cheap motels, gun shops, and assorted roadside retail effluvia. It was here that Jerry Lee Lewis's cousin, the Reverend Jimmy Swaggart, famously lost his soul. My mind was focused solely on getting as quickly as possible to an Uptown club known as Tipitina's where The Neville Brothers were playing that evening. The Neville Brothers were the holy grail of groove, the authentic successors to the Meters, who had been second only to James Brown's band as America's preeminent groove band. Ironically, there is some evidence that essential elements of James Brown's revolutionary funk actually originated with New Orleans drummers.[1] Groove and rhythm have been underappreciated musical elements in Western culture. Melody and harmony carry more prestige; indeed for publishing purposes a song is generally considered to consist of melody, harmony, and lyrics (if any)—with no recognition of rhythm structure. In Jamaica, by contrast, songwriting credit is routinely accorded to the creator of a rhythm pattern as well as the creators of the melody and lyrics. In Africa and the Caribbean, rhythm is considered an integral part of a composition. New Orleans is more or less a Caribbean city.

The four Neville brothers had come together definitively as a band only four years previously, but their musical history was long and deep. Art Neville scored his first hit with "Mardi Gras Mambo," which became a New Orleans standard, with his teenage group The Hawkettes in 1954, and had sung or played on a number of early rock 'n' roll hits. In the late sixties Art formed the Meters, who lasted a decade playing innovative funk and stretching its boundaries. Aaron Neville is a singer with the voice of an angel who broke through to national recognition with the indelible R&B ballad "Tell It Like It Is" and then faded from national prominence. Charles Neville is a jazz and blues saxophonist who played with the likes of B.B. King and Bobby Bland, and had gigged on the New York scene for years. Cyril Neville was vocalist and percussionist with the Meters during the seventies. The word on the Neville Brothers was that their performances were a peak musical experience. It was supposed to be the next best thing to experiencing the live, boundary-stretching funk-based magic of the Meters. Stopping only briefly to drop my bags at the cheap motel on Tulane Avenue where I was lodging, I grabbed another cab and headed uptown.

The cab had no air-conditioning, so when we pulled up to Tipitina's I could hear the music, a deep, viscous throb, pulsing out of the club through the cab's open window. Tip's, as the locals called it, is a large two-story frame building, standing at the end of Napoleon Avenue, a wide uptown thoroughfare ending at the corner of Tchoupitoulas Street, just a stone's throw from the river. A levee loomed in the dark and I could feel the presence of the mighty river barely contained by the grassy bank. At one time Tip's had been a venue for boxing matches, and further in its past had been a storage building of some sort. People were lounging in the cool of the wide grassy median strip bisecting Napoleon Avenue. The club was not air-conditioned in those days, and the side and front doors of the club were usually open, leaving just louvered half doors, so you could listen to the music from outside. As I walked up to the front door the music hit me: the bass deep and fat, right in the belly where it should be.

I paid the few dollars admission, stepped through the door past a bust of Professor Longhair, a legendary New Orleans piano player who had died just a year previous, past the long bar that ran along walls festooned with faded posters of classic R&B shows from the sixties and seventies, and onto the packed concrete dance floor in front of the stage. The club had been opened specifically to give Professor Longhair a place to play after he was rediscovered in virtual retirement, sweeping out a shop to hustle a few bucks. A backdrop bearing Longhair's likeness loomed from behind the stage. People swayed like undersea plants in an ocean of rhythm, sweating in the soupy steam bath. Dead ahead was the Neville Brothers.

Dominating the stage was Aaron Neville, a hulking figure in short pants and a muscle shirt that showed off his fullback's build. He stepped in place to the beat, turning this way and that to the rhythm, playing a cowbell and staring fixedly over the heads of the audience to some distant spot. A sword was tattooed on his left cheek and other tattoos marked his bicep and forearm. A large mole over his right eyebrow blemished an otherwise handsome countenance. An earring with a circular medallion dangled from his left ear; I later learned that it was a medallion of St. Jude—the patron saint of hopeless causes. Some said that Frank Sinatra had wanted to put Aaron on national television if he would agree to have the sword tattoo removed but that Aaron had declined to do so; Aaron himself has said that story was nonsense, but it is a part of the lore that hovered about him as a singer everyone thought should be famous. At that moment he seemed in a trance. Playing a cowbell is not inconsequential; if not done correctly it could seriously disrupt the groove. In West African music, the rhythm played on the *agogo* (a traditional instrument made of two cowbells) is often the central beat.

On stage left, peering phlegmatically over a stack of keyboards, sat Art Neville, prime mover in three generations of music. Broad-shouldered but not as big as Aaron, he gazed out at the crowd as he sang, with an understated yet amiable expression. He wore a denim jacket with the sleeves cut off over a t-shirt; a bushy Afro swelled from under his cap. Art has been present at the creation more than once, first at the birth of rock 'n' roll and then at the dawn of funk with the Meters, but somehow that one national smash hit eluded him. As he sang with laconic soulfulness, it was easy to imagine that his cool was just stoic acceptance of too many disappointments.

The rhythm kicked into a wrenching, metallic funk groove behind Cyril Neville's singing on "Africa," an old Meters tune. Cyril Neville, a whirlwind of jabbing hands and darting head on congas, looked like he might just fly over his percussion arsenal of congas, timbales, cymbal, and cowbell. At thirty-six he was a decade younger than his brothers, a jitterbuggy sixties child with none of his siblings' dignified stoicism. He looked different as well: bold black eyebrows jutted over fierce brown eyes, and his small, thin-lipped mouth added to the impression of compressed energy.

Near Cyril toward center stage, Charles Neville amiably tapped out a counter-rhythm on cowbell as he too danced in place but with a more freewheeling exuberance than Aaron. He looked like the bebopper he had once been, with a black beret set at a rakish angle. Slight of figure but wiry, he was wearing a green and purple tie-dyed shirt or tunic that hung below his waist, gathered there by a multicolored sash. He had done three years' hard time in Angola, the notorious upcountry Louisiana prison, after being busted for the possession of a couple of joints. The fact that he survived Angola was testimony to his strength.

The brothers were backed by their young rhythm section. Guitarist Brian Stolz, the lone white member of the group, ambled around the stage chopping out funky chords on guitar, a beatific expression on his face. Now and then he strolled up to one of the players as if to present the lick he was playing or perhaps to just share the moment. Daryl Johnson, a tall, lean, youthful figure with shaggy hair on bass, was plucking the deep, wall-rattling bass lines that had plenty of space in them, in the style of African bass lines. Behind the drum kit, "Mean" Willie Green was churning out polyrhythms, looking out over his drums with gleaming eyes and a close-mouthed smile. He looked like he was in heaven. I noticed that a medallion earring was dangling from the left ear of everyone onstage.

The group-chant of "Africa" shifted into a loping second-line rhythm, the rhythm of New Orleans parades from funerals to Mardi Gras, a propulsive yet easy-rolling groove with space for endless rhythmic accents. The rhythm is an African-rooted rhythm related to the clave rhythm of Latin music that informs people's walk, talk, and dance moves in the city. Art began to sing what had become a New Orleans anthem rooted in the traditional chants of the Mardi Gras Indians, a variation of which had been recorded by Jelly Roll Morton in 1939: "Little bitty boy / with a heart of steel / he won't boogie now / but his sister sure will / feel good music / in your soul / makes your body / do a slow boogie roll / everybody say hey! hey, hey, hey / hey pocky way!"[2] The crowd shouted along with the chorus harmony, which was supercharged by Aaron's high, sweet near-falsetto. People danced in a loose frenzy, caught up in the groove.

Then the rhythm shifted again into a stomping rock 'n' roll rhythm as the Neville Brothers ripped into "Johnny B. Goode" and "Short Fat Fanny," like bar bands the world over. But Art, Charles, and Aaron had come of age in the original rock 'n' roll era; Art had sung background on one of Little Richard's hits, and all the brothers had at one time or another played with Larry Williams, who originated "Short Fat Fanny." So they could play rock 'n' roll with an authority most bar bands could only dream of. The song built to a screaming climax amid soaring arena rock squalls from Brian Stolz's guitar as the sweating throng stomped, cheered, and whistled. At a Neville Brothers performance you hear funk, rock 'n' roll, R&B of all types, ballads, blues, reggae, jazz, gospel, and all manner of indigenous New Orleans music. Aaron might even sing "Home on the Range." Their musical universe knew no bounds.

The crowd spilled out Tipitina's louvered half-doors and sprawled on the grassy median strip of Napoleon Avenue. I stood outside enjoying the cooler outside air when I saw Art Neville emerge from the side doorway of the club. I said hello and asked him when the world might be blessed by a new Neville Brothers record. Up until then they had had only had two album releases, an eponymous album on Capitol that had failed to sell and a second, critically acclaimed album on A&M that had sold only marginally better. Art related, with bemused bitterness, what one record company executive had told him.

"They said we weren't *black* enough!" Art snorted.

It was a ridiculous statement. The Neville Brothers were deeply rooted in not one but many African American traditions and were probably "blacker," in the sense of cultural authenticity, than 99 percent of the black artists on the scene. But to record companies, "black music" was what was being played on black radio stations. On the other hand, rock radio stations did not typically play many black artists. So the Neville Brothers found themselves too black for rock radio and not black enough for black radio stations.

"What we need to do is get on AM radio," Art remarked. This was a revealing statement: AM radio had not been a factor on the popular music landscape for a number of years at that point. It was a very New Orleanian kind of lapse. I knew he meant pop or Top Forty radio. Still, the reflexive use by him of the term "AM radio" underscored how far out of touch with the mainstream scene the Neville Brothers were at that time, a problem common to the New Orleans music scene in general.

Just a couple of blocks away from Tip's was Valence Street, where three out of four Neville Brothers were born, and where all of them had spent substantial portions of their youth. When Aaron was one year old, the family had moved to the Calliope housing projects; in the forties, housing projects were actually considered a step up for working people. The family moved back to Valence a decade later, but not before the brothers formed lifetime friendships with others they met in the densely populated projects, including a number of brilliant musicians. Valence Street was—and is—a quiet, gravelly street defined by rows of modest "shotgun" cottages inhabited by working people, a black neighborhood a short distance from the larger, more imposing homes of Uptown New Orleans. As is often the case in New Orleans, much of the Nevilles' extended family had lived in close proximity to them on and near Valence Street. Strong, deep family and neighborhood relationships define New Orleans culture, and the special character of New Orleans music owes much to notable musical families with names such as Neville, Batiste, Marsalis, French, and many others.

Just as important are the many nonprofessionals who play an instrument; someone in the neighborhood who may work as a cab driver or carpenter may be a wonderful piano player or trumpeter or singer who is never heard by the larger world but who inspires and influences those around him. Playing music in New Orleans is something lots of people have traditionally done for the sheer joy of it with no thought of making money. Lee Dorsey, who had a number of national R&B hits in the sixties and seventies, never stopped working in a local body and fender shop. That is just another of the ways that New Orleans is an old culture. Many of the city's greatest musicians never left the city, content to make their living where they were comfortable. Masterful piano player Tuts Washington, who grew up in the Storyville era of "piano professors," was playing hotel gigs in town in the early eighties without even an album to his name. Snooks Eaglin, an absolute guitar wizard, rarely has left New Orleans. Despite Tipitina's growing fame as one of the greatest music clubs in the world, playing Tip's was for the Neville Brothers like playing a neighborhood club, the same thing they had done when growing up. The flipside was that, for all their brushes with national success, they found themselves without a record deal following the failure of two albums and playing local gigs to survive.

A year or two later I was walking up the 1000 block of Valence Street on a hot afternoon, headed to Art Neville's house. I had an assignment to do a piece on the Neville Brothers for *Spin*. When I came to 1015 Valence Street, a narrow, two-story twin shotgun home, I saw Art, the elder statesman of rock 'n' roll and funk, supervising the sanding of a door. The front of the right side of the shotgun had been opened up and renovations were in progress. He walked over, goggles dangling from his neck, and extended a hand. His movements were easy and unhurried yet undeniably authoritative, while his eyes, squinting out from under a navy baseball cap, were mildly skeptical.

Of all the Nevilles, Art had been on the verge of success the longest, scoring the first hit and the most hits in the family. When the Rolling Stones chose the Meters as the opening act for their 1975 world tour, it seemed as though the Meters would break through to a pop audience, just as other Stones opening acts such as Ike and Tina Turner, B.B. King, and Stevie Wonder had done. But the Meters had been at odds internally, squabbling over money, management, and business decisions, and so had dissolved amid rampant ego, money disputes, and too many fast-lane indulgences. Some have suggested that if the others, who were younger and less experienced in the business, had listened to Art they would have made it. Art is often portrayed as the wise old head who avoided the traps of drugs, crime, and street life that his brothers got caught up in. Art himself has often dispelled that concept.

"I did many of same things those guys did," he has said. "I just never got caught."[3]

Art led the way into the midst of the partly renovated side of the building. I thought maybe it was being converted into a garage; It turned out he was making it into a rehearsal studio. Huge cases, amplifiers, and keyboards, some with NEVILLE BROTHERS stenciled on them, were stacked in the bare room. An upright piano stood against the wall. Art straddled the piano bench and waited for my questions; he had been down the interview road many times. Maybe this time the Nevilles would beat the New Orleans jinx. He noted that the band had been getting rave reviews without the benefit of rehearsals.

"We haven't rehearsed in two years," he noted ruefully. "We had no place to rehearse. The sound that is keeping us working is the old sound. We got some new things and now there's no staying away from it. I don't know whether to say 'to get a deal.' Kinda scared to say *anything* about it. We just tried to do something good that sounded different.

"As soon as I finish this place here, I'll be doing some *serious* writing, anytime of day, anytime of night. I ain't got no clock running. I'm gonna have a couple of tape recorders, just a four–track, a couple of boards. All of the things we grew up with and that's a part of our lives up until this point that we haven't been using, we'll come in this room and put the shit down *so* serious and *so* tight."

"Serious" in Art-speak is the ultimate expression of substance, just as he uses "treacherous" as an ultimate accolade. He speaks in a grainy, molasses-thick baritone, the words coming in an understated rhythmic bop—a classic New Orleans voice. His particular genius as a musician is hard to recognize because it also is understated and subtle. Art likes to leave a lot of space in his music, to let the groove breathe. He has an uncanny ability to play just a note or two or perhaps a single perfectly placed chord that accentuates and embellishes the groove. This is the aesthetic of funk, which Art finds most satisfying; as a result, musicians who know him call him Poppa Funk.

"Like I always tell cats," he said in the Nevilles autobiography, "nobody don't care if you can play a thousand notes in one bar. You have to play the *right* note at the right time. Silence is also a part of music."[4]

New Orleans is so much a part of who the Neville Brothers are, as musicians and as people, that any thought of moving to a more strategic locale—say, New York or L.A., as they all had done at various points individually—is resisted. They would rather be real people, part of a workaday world of families and community, connected to New Orleans's nurturing soil.

"I don't go for it," he said, his eyes half closed. "I ain't goin' nowhere. I figure you can commute back and forth if you have to. Everything we do is a part of New Orleans. The fact that we're still together on the street we grew up on proves it. Through that door there I can see my parents' house and all my brothers' houses. All of my great-aunts, my uncles, my mother's people, my daddy's people, all of them lived right around here."

I asked him about their touring plans, but he did not answer. His eyes were closed. Suddenly they blinked open.

"Excuse me, what did you ask? Obviously I suffer from narcolepsy; it's related to hypoglycemia. Nothing I can do about it; I've had it all my life. I even fell out once over my keyboards onstage. So, if I fall asleep, just wake me up."

He turned to the piano and began pensively playing a series of rolling arpeggios, lush at the beginning but soon slipping into slurred little twists that added a rhythmic lift, something as natural as breathing for a New Orleans musician.

"Let's go inside if you don't mind, where it's cooler," he said. "I need to walk around."

We went around to the kitchen, where his young, pretty new wife was doling out sandwiches and cold drinks to a couple of workmen. His cute little curly-haired son Ian toddled around the floor as we stepped into the living room, which was filled with artifacts of his musical life. For years he had tried to create music here, amidst the clutter of family life. Against one wall stood shelves holding turntables, tape decks, a VCR, stacks of records, and master tapes. A sepia portrait of the Meters, looking very young, peered out from another wall. A tiny drum set was in the corner and battery-operated toy airplanes dangled from the ceiling. Since childhood Art had loved gadgets and toys and science fiction.

"These are Ian's and my toys," he chuckled. "I'm a sucker for anything with batteries in it. If it moves, I'll buy it! This is what keeps me going. I just try to keep some happy shit going; there's a lot of heartache in music."

Those words came back to me when I heard a year or two later that his wife had died, another piece of hard luck for someone who did not deserve bad luck. Art popped a tape of some demo tracks cut in Nashville at the Castle, a studio owned by Nevilles fans who had made studio time available. That was the Nevilles' ace in the hole—they had a lot of fans in strategic places, insiders in the business as well as other artists.

"We got all types of things," Art said, "things nobody's heard. We can do anything, man. It's just a question of what we'll be allowed to do."

A slick, midtempo slice of pop-rock came on, a demo of a song written for them by a New York songwriter—another fan. Aaron's inimitable warble was wrapped around some subtle lyrics about lovers meeting on a foggy night; the chorus was a catchy fifties-ish singalong based on the irresistible nonsense refrain "sheck a na na." Next up was a hard rock love song written by Aaron, then a loping midtempo tune with a gritty vocal from Cyril that harked back to classic sixties soul. Art continued to rummage bemusedly through tapes as if to say, "What do you want? Whatever it is, we got it."

The demos were catchy and sounded like they would fit right in on pop radio playlists; but they lacked the Nevilles' organic groove, that special thing that was uniquely their own. The question they were wrestling with was how to translate that groove into a contemporary commercial sound.

"But how do you do that?" Art asked. "That's the trick, 'cause nobody knows how to do that. We're working on it. We strike it now and then on gigs. I write stuff about M.I.A.'s (soldiers missing in action), nuclear war, stuff like that, but nobody wants to hear that. I think people want to know but they *don't* want to know."

He put another tape on, a Japanese group playing an astonishingly faithful version of "Hey Pocky Way." Art shook his head, gratified by how far his music had spread yet bemused by their inability to get more recognition.

"They can't even speak English!" he noted. "This is a good group. Some of the shit we can't get away with, they can get away with. They got a Neville Brothers fan club in Japan but they ain't got one in New Orleans."

Valence Street was ground zero for the Neville family, their spiritual center. The church where Art first touched a keyboard was right up the street. If Tip's was the Nevilles' neighborhood club to which the world made pilgrimages, Benny's was their corner bar, only a block from their homes. When they were kids, they knew it as Jake Callahan's, a center of adult good times that they could only glimpse. In its new incarnation it was a nondescript frame house set back from the gravelly street. As I approached, the throbbing funk of an old Meters tune pulsed through its flimsy walls. I pushed through the screen door—no one was collecting any cover charge—into a knot of outsiders gleefully leaping up and down as a score of middle-aged regulars sat stoically along the wall. Through the skeletal remains of a knocked-out wall, the jammers in the next room were visible, crammed helter-skelter in what was once someone's parlor. Willie Green and Daryl Johnson anchored the proceedings on drums and bass respectively. Cyril Neville conducted from behind his timbales and congas, punctuating the changes with a jungle-cat screech. Art Neville hunched over a little beat-up electric piano. In short, most of the band that had been hailed as conquering heroes in New York and Los Angeles, fresh off a national tour opening for Huey Lewis and the News, was playing for about fifty people in a corner bar—for free.

A version of the Meters classic "People Say" crashed to a halt amidst scattered claps and delighted yelps from the outlanders in town for JazzFest, people who probably would tell their grandchildren about seeing such legendary characters in this cool little neighborhood joint. Art got up and strolled outside, as if to say "let me leave this raggedy jam to the younger folks," and a young woman, hair trailing down her back, took his place at the electric piano. Local blues rocker J. D. Hill, a dark harp player in shades, kicked off the classic blues shuffle "Dust

My Broom" and the group romped through the previous forty years of popular music, hitting blues, standards, Neville Brothers faves, reggae, and Sixties rockers like the Hendrix/Buddy Miles classic "Them Changes." Cyril called a break and everyone streamed outside to dry their sweat in the cool night air.

The following day I met Cyril Neville in the afternoon at Benny's, where there were just a few locals drinking beer. He had particularly wanted to talk there.

"Let's rap," Cyril said as he hustled over to where I was sitting at the bar. With his button-festooned black tam, cut off black tee-shirt, gold chains and single medallion dangling from his left ear, Cyril projected an irrepressible street vibe, accentuated by his black, exclamatory eyebrows, darting dark eyes and hyper-activity, which I learned was in part the result of a blood sugar imbalance, perhaps the flip side of Art's narcolepsy. Cyril was darker by a couple of shades than his brothers, with an intense look in his eyes that contrasted with the slightly dreamy look they often had. However, when he did smile, his smile flashed the brightest of all of them. His singing was the group's most powerful, a soul/gospel shout that reflected his childhood decision to attend a Baptist church rather than the Catholic or Methodist churches his family attended. A question flipped him into interview mode, his eyes focused, and he was all business, succinct and messianically serious about social issues and the musical traditions of black people in general and New Orleans in particular.

"I try to keep a certain energy level going," he began. "I don't know if I should say this but when I'm not working I *gotta* do this. I got the idea from John Belushi. A long time ago, when we played in New York at a place called the Bottom Line, the Blues Brothers had a club with instruments set up where they could jam anytime. I can't stop playing; I feel it makes new things happen. The problem in New Orleans now, there's nowhere to play. That's why we started these sessions. We had a group called Endangered Species 'cause they were closing up all the small bars and we wanted to keep the local stars and local bars together. Plus black males in America *are* an endangered species. So is black music. We got to take control of it or it will die out. So we started this scene and now people are coming to it from all over the world, just like Harlem, to check out the cultural thing we got going on right here.

"We could start doing things together that could save the New Orleans musician, who is the endangered species that this movement speaks about," he elaborated in a later interview for *Wavelength* magazine. "We as musicians, and to be honest about it, as black men in America, are an endangered species, and we have to do something for ourselves and our children. What we have to do it with is our talents. What we're going to do is make a stand right now, so the next generation will be a little better off than we were. I'm not just speaking about music. I'm talking about culturally, and as a people, period."[5]

"The neighborhood's just full of musicians," Cyril continued at Benny's, dispassionately machine-gunning information over the blaring jukebox. "Most of the guys in the Meters came from this neighborhood. The rhythms come from Mardi Gras Indians; the ones from our neighborhood played the beats we use. Every kind of rhythm that there is at some time passed through New Orleans. And there's something about the longitude and latitude, something about the forces working here on people. My brother Charles came up with that. Sometimes me and Willie Green and the rest of the fellows, I'll just start a rhythm on cowbell and it'll develop through the drums and everything else.

"You know," Cyril said, shifting gears, "I got this wild reputation but there's other sides of me that people don't see. For instance, I've been with the same woman for many years. I'm not a womanizer."

A couple days later I was having lunch downtown with Barbara Hawkins and Rosa Hawkins of The Dixie Kups, who as a popular early-sixties "girl group" scored a national hit with their version of the traditional Mardi Gras Indian chant "Iko Iko," probably the first time that New Orleans Indian culture popped into national consciousness. They were from the neighborhood too, and were family friends of the Nevilles; in fact a Neville sister, Athelgra, had sung with the group. We talked about the uniqueness of the Neville Brothers and why they had not had a popular breakthrough.

"You know," Barbara said, "some people are put off by the way they look and dress. Sometimes they look like they might mug you or something!"

I thought at the time that she was exaggerating. But the Neville Brothers street-tough reputation was rooted in reality. All had had serious drug problems at one time or another. Aaron, Charles, and Cyril had all spent time in jail. The crimes they committed to feed their drug habits—robbery and burglary, mostly, but not exclusively—had been part of their lives. Cyril's run-ins with the law had tended to be related more to street brawling, confrontations with the police, or political activity. But all of them had been involved with the kind of violence that comes with living the street life. All had witnessed violent deaths of people close to them. Art tells of being taken as a teenager to the Dew Drop Inn by an older acquaintance, Art's first time in a nightclub, and seeing the man murdered in front of his eyes by a jealous woman.[6] Cyril wrote a signature song, "Brother John," about John "Scarface" Williams, a vocalist and member of an Indian gang who was stabbed to death on Rampart Street. And all had had searing experiences of racism. Each handled it in a different way, according to their personality. Art's way seemed to be bitter fatalism; Aaron took a wider spiritual view. Charles early on rationalized his criminal exploits as justifiable revenge against a racist system. Cyril's way was direct confrontation.

"Some people have a high consciousness of racism at a young age," Cyril told biographer David Ritz. "I was one of those people."[7]

It is no surprise, then, that Cyril wrote such socially conscious songs as "My Blood" and "Sister Rosa," the latter about Rosa Parks, heroine of the civil rights movement. He tends to analyze events through the lens of class conflict, economic exploitation of the poor by the powerful, and racism.

At the annual New Orleans Jazz and Heritage Festival, popularly known as JazzFest, a large area is set aside for craftspeople and artisans, many representing crafts and art native to Louisiana. For a number of years in the eighties, Charles Neville had a booth in this area. Aside from his work as a painter, he carved distinctive walking sticks. Charles is an interesting study in contrasts. Onstage, he is the beatific one, radiating beneficent joy. He looks like a bebopper, a Beat era survivor who transitioned into the hippie era, which after all was a sixties transmutation of the beatniks. Yet he had that criminal past, had done the hardest time imaginable, was tougher than he looked, and had been in thrall to a heroin habit for more than two decades. His brothers single him out as the intellectually gifted one, who turned away from school when he was told that his science project would never win the contest he entered because a winner would never be picked from "a colored school." When he went to New York City in the late sixties, shortly after getting out of prison, he embraced the hippie culture he found in the East Village and elsewhere. On the road, while Aaron lifted weights in his spare time, Charles did Tai Chi, a part of his embrace of Eastern spirituality. As a musician his roots are as deep as Art's. They played together as teenagers in their first band. As the "Boy Wonder of Saxophone," Charles even went on the road at age fifteen as part of the Rabbit Foot Minstrel Show, the last of the storied traveling entertainment troupes that crisscrossed the South entertaining the black populace in rural areas beginning in the nineteenth century. He later traveled as a sideman with blues legend B.B. King and hung on the jazz scene in New York. I found him in his craft tent filled with walking sticks, many with carved human faces erupting out of them, and other smaller artifacts he had carved.

"The walking sticks are African survivals," he explained. "Woodcarving is a highly developed art; it has something to do with the carving of a totem or talisman. That's how I feel about the one I have. The faces are like ancestral spirits—they all have a family look—but I didn't copy them."

He is also the family member who has an affinity for the paranormal. He has had some paranormal experiences himself. The brothers' mother, Amelia Landry Neville, came from a Creole family that had some spiritualist ability and involvement with the New Orleans variant of voodoo.

"The second line rhythm is the same as one of the voodoo rhythms," Charles noted. "That's the rhythm that's been basic to New Orleans music. One of the mainstays [of the Neville's music] is the interaction of the rhythms . . . the drums, the rhythm section. We each have our weave in the fabric. The changes can weave around the central pulse, often with some suggestion of these voodoo rhythms. The main one is one that has an effect on everyone. It makes you have to dance!"

I did not have the opportunity to meet Aaron Neville while I was in New Orleans. I did see him perform a concert on the riverboat *President* with Irma Thomas, dubbed the Soul Queen of New Orleans, who had known Aaron since the fifties. For that concert, Aaron had dressed in a white suit, in contrast to his usual streetwise performing attire. At one point, Irma had remarked about the tough times they had had coming up.

"Oh, it wasn't so bad," Aaron said in a soothing tone, his expression placid. He stood next to her with a quiet dignity, holding himself erect until it was his turn to sing. Then he hunched forward, gripped the microphone tightly in one hand and inclined his head as he poured himself into the song.

I caught up with Aaron in Philadelphia when the Nevilles came to perform. He suggested I come by his hotel room one afternoon. Aaron would admit to having a shrine to St. Jude in his home but not to voodoo. A deeply religious man, he speaks as though he has walked amidst the fires of hell and laughed with the devil himself. When he opened his hotel room door, I was struck, as most are, by his physical presence, which is an interesting mix—imposing, even intimidating, given his hulking physique and unsmiling mien. Yet he is soft-spoken, easy in his movements, and has a benign look in his eyes. He looms silent, contemplative, and gentle—a man apart. In the Neville Brothers he found himself in a strange position, that of a ballad singer in a groove band, which meant that one of the finest, most distinctive singers in the nation often got only a couple of lead vocal showcases per set. That was a sacrifice he made to maintain the family band. His high, sweet voice contrasts with his physique; imagine a bodybuilder crooning "Mona Lisa" in a smoky club.

He stretched out on the bed on his side and propped himself up with his elbow. I saw a pair of hand-grip exercisers lying on the dresser. I asked him about his wilder years that led to him spending time in jail. His heroin habit had started when he was in junior high school, and in his teens he got into stealing cars, joy-riding, and petty theft.

"I don't really want to talk about that," he said quietly. "Those are negative things that are in the past."

But he will talk about his vocal style, a totally unique amalgam of Sam Cooke's soulful lyricism, the delicate tenor of Pookie Hudson (lead vocalist of seminal R&B harmony group the Spaniels), and the yodeling he heard from cowboy singers.

"I was a cowboy as a kid," he said. "I had the fastest mop stick in the projects. I used to listen to all the cowboy stuff like the Sons of the Pioneers, Roy Rogers, and Gene Autry. I'd listen to the yodeling. When I started singing I guess it just kind of stuck."

He spoke reverently of the nuns in Catholic school and how deeply moved he had been by the singing of "Ave Maria" in church.

"I've been spiritual all my life," he said. "I feel like I got a dozen guardian angels." He gave his peculiar choked giggle; he laughed gently, with a wry expression, a kind of laugh I have often encountered from American Indians. Aaron mentioned that he thought there was Indian blood in the family line. His spirituality had sustained him through many disappointments, not least of which was the collapse of the record company that released his hit "Tell It Like It Is," stopping his career momentum dead just as he seemed to be breaking through, and the nominal remuneration he had received from the national hit. He ended up back in New Orleans working on the docks.

"I'd be workin' on the waterfront," he continued, "and the longshoremen sitting there would say 'man you ain't got no business here; you ought to be singing someplace.' I'd tell 'em, 'I'm supposed to be here right now.' I look at life like on a higher plane. Sometimes I just leave my body and look down on me and the rest of the people and realize that we're all just humans struggling. What keeps me going is people tell me that my voice means something special to them. I feel I have a gift."

He pulled out a notebook of neatly typed poems, with titles like "Street World," "In The Family," and "With God's Love." As I read a spiritual poem, he began to sing the words in a soft vibrato: "steer me right, sweet Jesus, keep me goin' straight. When you see me slippin', please don't let me fall." I asked about another one called "The Owl Hoot Trail."

"Well, that's something from the cowboy movies," he said. "You know, The Owl Hoot Trail is like going down the wrong road."

To help young people stay on the right road, he had recently founded the Uptown Youth Center near his Valence Street neighborhood. When not on the road, it was not uncommon to find him there, sweeping up or otherwise keeping things going.

For Aaron, the right road has a lot to do with tradition, like his uncle Big Chief Jolly's tradition—that of the Mardi Gras Indians.

"To those people," he says, "it's real, like a ritual. It don't just happen on Mardi Gras day, it's a year-round thing, and they lived it. Sewin' those suits together, you know he might stay inside for three or four months, but when he comes out with it, it was worth it. Yeah, it's an attitude, just like Mardi Gras. We bring the attitude with us every time we go on a gig. It's all a mixture of the second line, jazz, and the feel of Mardi Gras and the Indian rhythms."

"Music today seems like it's more a brainwash thing, you know, a pattern thing. It's gotta sound a certain way and have the drum machines. Sometimes you might be listening to a song and you don't know if it's humans or what. But, the old doowops, it was *humans*. That's where it's at. The music goes in a circle. It's coming back to that. It ain't got no other place to go."

Considering the wide differences between Art, Charles, Aaron, and Cyril—in their personalities, their musical inclinations, and even their life experiences—it is somewhat surprising that they have been able to come together as a cohesive entity. The catalyst for that has been family, first and foremost their own strong sense of commitment to one another, but also more specifically the influence of their uncle, George Landry, Big Chief Jolly. Although Art has said that he had had the vision of a family band since the sixties, and in fact did briefly have all the brothers together in Art Neville and the Neville Sounds, events spun them away from one another for many years. Their father and mother, who they had respected and loved deeply, had both died relatively young by 1975, their father from a heart attack at the age of fifty-two and their mother from a random accident when she was hit by an out-of-control truck while walking. Their mother's brother George brought the brothers together because he wanted to record an album of Mardi Gras Indian music.

Uncle George loomed large in the brothers' eyes all their life. He and their mother had a dance act that they performed together in local clubs. He and the brothers' father were so close—shipping out in the merchant marine together—that the boys thought their father and uncle were brothers.[8] George was a man about town with a lot of style. Cyril and Aaron in particular speak of emulating his style of dress. He played piano quite well at family gatherings and parties—but never professionally. At a certain point he became very serious about "masking" as a Mardi Gras Indian and soon was chief of the Wild Tchoupitoulas. The Indian "gangs" had been masking for over a century, possibly a homage to the Indians who had harbored runaway slaves. Semi-secret societies, they had their own language, code, and music. A couple of years previously, local piano player and recording artist Willie Tee had masterminded the national release of an album by the Wild Magnolias tribe, a highly effective marriage of the Indians' songs and chants with funk rhythms. It was the first recording of Mardi Gras Indian music to reach national attention. Uncle Jolly wanted to do the same thing with the Wild Tchoupitoulas.

The resulting album brought together all four Neville Brothers, the Meters, and the Wild Tchoupitoulas. The music of the Mardi Gras Indians, normally just voices and percussion, is loosely structured. Drummers and tambourine players get a groove going, then the Chief starts singing while the other members of the tribe answer him with a refrain. On this album the songs, many of which are adapted from traditional Indian chants, were developed melodically so that they were much more than chants, and then fleshed out harmonically with keyboards, guitars, and bass. The vocal choruses opened up as well into full harmonies with all the Nevilles singing, as well as a couple of other local singers, rather than the usual unison chants. The combination of catchy rhythms, singalong melodies, and full harmonies made for an irresistible listening experience that was critically acclaimed on release in 1976.

"Your mother and father would have wanted this," Uncle Jolly told the brothers.[9] He had reconnected them as a musical unit but also immersed them more deeply in the Mardi Gras Indians tradition. As a result, The Neville Brothers band was born the following year. Cyril in particular, who as a young boy had spent much time in the company of Jolly and his fellow Indians as they worked on their costumes, actively studied the Indian culture and its relation to the culture of Native Americans.

Many years later, he talked about Indian culture and his uncle on video for the Living Folklore Center. He stood outdoors, wearing a red cap, cutoff red sweatshirt, brown slacks and several long necklaces of beads, some of which appeared to be African trade beads. He held up a beaded panel from his uncle's Mardi Gras Indian costume, fringed with red feathers, the beads illustrating an Indian encampment: brown tepees in a green meadow by a turquoise lake with a golden sun peeking over purple peaks in a pale blue sky.

"This is my uncle's—Big Chief Jolly—the last suit he wore," Cyril began. "This patch alone is maybe ten pounds. With the whole suit on it must have weighed a hundred and fifty pounds. He did this one mostly in rhinestones.

"To be a Mardi Gras Indian you have to know how to sew. And sewing is something that brings patience. Usually while my uncle and some other guys were sewing, I'd be helping by threading needles and things. They'd be talking. In the conversations would be something about what work was going on, but more times it would be about Native American culture and history. 'Cause my uncle's spirit warrior was Colorado. One of the other chief's spirit warrior was Cochise. Another spirit warrior was Geronimo. And they knew the true history of these people and what they stood for amongst their people. And that is the essence of what Mardi Gras Indians were. If you get to be a big chief of the Mardi Gars Indians in the neighborhood you come from, this is basically a social aid and pleasure club. If something happens to one of the guys and his rent needs to be paid, the other guys will kick in to help him out. So it's not just on Mardi Gras day that you are a Mardi Indian. . . . it's a badge of honor to be, not just chief, but to be a part of Mardi Gras Indian culture. Because everybody knows that this is our link to our African heritage as well as our own Native American heritage, because a lot of us in New Orleans have Native American blood. This happens in whole neighborhoods. Whole generations of families are involved. It's passed from one generation to the next."

Cyril again looked down at the panel he was holding.

"This is my uncle's dream on canvas."[10]

Four years after I spoke with the Neville brothers, they got another shot, signing with EMI, which released their album *Uptown* six long years after *Fiyo on the Bayou.* It included some of the songs that Art had played me in demo form at his home. For longtime fans it was a major disappointment. The material, including "Sheck-A-Na-Na," was mostly highly structured pop songs that were catchy enough. But the production and arrangements were an attempt to shoehorn the Nevilles into a highly synthetic sound in tune with what was happening on pop radio at the time. There was none of the Nevilles' trademark organic feel and flow in the grooves—the essential element of their artistry. Such big-name guests as Jerry Garcia of the Grateful Dead, Carlos Santana, Keith Richards, and others were featured on various tracks but their contribution sounded like window dressing rather than any true meeting of musical minds. Since none of the singles broke through on mainstream radio, the album won few new fans and garnered dismal sales.

The failure of *Uptown* would have been devastating to the group were it not for the steadily growing fan base they were developing through widespread touring. Legendary concert promoter and impresario Bill Graham had taken on management of the group and he was able to leverage high-profile concert dates and opening act slots for them. The Nevilles (and the Meters before them) have always benefited from the support of celebrity fans. Paul McCartney had hired the Meters to play his birthday party aboard the Queen Mary back in 1974, prompting the Rolling Stones to add the group as opening act on their worldwide tour. Bette Midler had midwifed their deal with A&M Records for the *Fiyo on the Bayou* album. The Stones tapped the Neville Brothers to open for their 1986 worldwide tour. Aaron's solo career had at last taken off when Linda Ronstadt, enthralled with his voice, invited him to sing with her and ultimately record with her in 1989. All of a sudden Aaron Neville's voice was being heard on the radio again and he was having hits. Most fortuitous were a series of shows where the Neville Brothers opened for the Grateful Dead. The Dead's huge audience, accustomed to sprawling groove-oriented jams, was perfectly suited to appreciate the Nevilles' live magic. Better yet, the Dead's army of fans had strong word-of-mouth networks, a multicultural bent, and an appreciation of socially conscious material. Before long, word had spread that a Neville Brothers concert was a special experience not to be missed. Suddenly an exponentially larger number of people were experiencing the power of the groove delivered by the Neville Brothers.

By 1988 the Neville Brothers were established as the traditional closing act at the annual New Orleans Jazz and Heritage Festival, making their set the climactic event of what for tens of thousands of people had been a blissful, often transcendent experience spread over two week-ends. It was the Tipitina's experience on a huge scale. Closing the 1988 Fest, The Nevilles attacked Professor Longhair's Mardi Gras Indian anthem "Big Chief," playing a hard-kicking, very funky fast version. Charles' daughter Charmaine, a singer and dancer in her own right who had reconnected with her father a couple of years before, danced up a storm onstage, long braids cascading down her back and flying wildly as she executed spins, kicking her leg high above her head like a Rockette to accentuate certain rhythm parts. (Unlike the Rockettes, however, she was not holding on to anyone's shoulder when she did it.) Charles danced exuberantly alongside her in a white beret, playing a cowbell. Cyril sang with his usual passion and energy. Suddenly members of the Golden Eagles Mardi Gras Indian tribe came onstage in full regalia, brilliant costumes of turquoise, red, and white feathers and beads, dancing, playing percussion, and shaking tambourines. It was 360 degrees of the Neville experience. How could it be captured in the recording studio? It was the same question Art Neville had raised when we had spoken in his home. New Orleans provided the answer.

By 1988 French-Canadian producer Daniel Lanois had become a New Orleans resident. Fresh off major successes producing acclaimed albums by U2 and Peter Gabriel, he, like so many others, had fallen under the city's spell and had established a combination residence and recording studio in a massive old mansion on St. Charles Avenue at General Taylor Street. Superficially, Lanois might not have seemed to be the right producer for the Nevilles: he had been a protégé of ambient auteur Brian Eno, and both the U2 and Gabriel albums boasted big, highly produced sounds. Lanois, however, approached recording the Nevilles in an organic way deriving from the artists' personalities and histories as they recorded what would become the album *Yellow Moon*.

"It was a five-story house," Charles Neville explained in an interview for *Wavelength*. "The second floor was set up as a studio, where on one side we had two big rooms joined together by one of those big New Orleans arch doors. We set up all the equipment there so that we could play just like we were playing onstage. Daniel lived on the fifth floor and his assistants lived on the third and fourth floors. I lived on the first floor!"

The setup allowed the group to develop the songs organically.

"A lot of the collaboration occurs in the actual musical arrangements," Charles explained, "as we are putting the music together. In 'Yellow Moon,' Aaron wrote the song, then it evolved. He might say 'we'll do it like this' but for something he's heard in his head and just played on keyboard, if we tried to do that with the whole band it doesn't quite come out like that. Nobody tells me: 'here's the horn part, play like this.' It's more like, we play and I'll come up with something and we try something and by the fifth, sixth, or eighth time we play it, it'll evolve in the final version that come out on the record. The same with everyone else, like the bass player . . . so when people contribute something to a tune or an arrangement we give them some of the credit because everyone does contribute to making the tune what it is."[11]

Cyril Neville delivered some of his strongest songwriting efforts with the hypnotic "My Blood," the Mardi Gras Indian–inspired "Wild Injuns," and "Wake Up," as well as the rap-inflected "Sister Rosa," which Cyril wrote specifically to make a new generation aware of the contribution of Rosa Parks to the civil rights movement. Lanois suggested an obscure Link Wray gem entitled "Fire and Brimstone" for Art Neville to sing, along with Art's composition "Voodoo." Charles got a showcase on the instrumental "Healing Chant." Virtually all sides of the Neville Brothers were presented on the album, and the few musical guests are there for musical reasons, not name value.

Lanois's other crucial contribution was finding a common ground in the production and arrangements to bring together the disparate songs written by different members of the band into a cohesive musical statement. This was most salient for Aaron's ballads. Where on earlier Neville Brothers records Aaron delivered beautiful renditions of such ballads as "Mona Lisa," "Ariane," or "The Ten Commandments of Love," they sounded like departures in the midst of the more groove-oriented fare. On *Yellow Moon* Aaron's moving versions of Sam Cooke's "A Change Is Gonna Come" and two Bob Dylan songs, "With God on Our Side" and "The Ballad of Hollis Brown," fit right in with the flow of the album. This was accomplished by a discrete thread of ambient keyboards and atmospheric guitar textures and other elements played by Lanois and Brian Eno.

Yellow Moon was the Neville Brothers album everyone had been waiting for. Its 1989 release dovetailed perfectly with the momentum the band had established on the live front. For once, an aesthetic triumph was a commercial success. The album went gold and suddenly the band was in demand worldwide. The success of *Yellow Moon,* and the broadened fan base that resulted from the album's sales and ever more widespread touring around the world, definitively established their future viability, no matter what the sales of their future albums might be. They continued to tour and record throughout the nineties and into the new millennium.

In 2005 Hurricane Katrina shattered the city that was as much an anchor for the Neville Brothers as was their family. It was not immediately clear whether the old and intricate relationships and neighborhoods that fed New Orleans's unique culture would ever be reestablished. Too many people were displaced, too many neighborhoods devastated, and the organic nature of the neighborhood milieu, a centuries-long development, could not be replicated by any rebuilding effort.

Typically, the brothers, who were on the road when the hurricane hit, each reacted in their own way. Art's house was not irretrievably damaged and he remained on Valence Street. Aaron found refuge in Nashville; because of a throat condition, doctors advised him not to return too quickly due to the poor quality of the air in the city, and initially he said he was not sure he would return. But within a year, he said in interviews that he hoped to return at some point. Cyril decamped to Austin, and issued bitter broadsides about the way various governmental agencies had failed ordinary people, which for him was simply a culmination of the decades of neglect and abuse of the city's poor, mostly black population. He vowed never to return. At the star-studded Concert for Hurricane Relief, televised nationally, Aaron sang Randy Newman's poignant song "Louisiana 1927," which memorialized devastating floods eighty years earlier. Wearing a black New Orleans baseball cap with gold lettering, blue jeans, and a simple dappled tee-shirt which barely contained his weightlifter's physique, Aaron sang with his eyes closed, his voice breaking at crucial moments, whether from his characteristic yodeled inflection or emotion it was hard to say at some points. He looked in tremendous shape for a sixty-five-year-old man.

At the Concert for New Orleans: From the Big Apple to the Big Easy, a packed Madison Square Garden witnessed a great lineup of New Orleans musicians and a few non-Orleanian fellow travelers such as Elvis Costello, who had recently recorded with Allen Toussaint; John Fogerty, whose brand of rock 'n' roll drew on Louisiana music in general and New Orleans music in particular; Bette Midler, the Nevilles' benefactor; Elton John, Diana Krall, Ry Cooder, the Nevilles' friend Jimmy Buffett, and Simon and Garfunkel.

The climax of the concert was given over to the Neville Brothers. Ed Bradley, the noted television journalist who had made no secret of his passion for New Orleans and especially its music, announced the Neville Brothers: "Now it is time to introduce the first musical family of New Orleans, including the next generation, Ian Neville and Ivan Neville; The Brothers: Art, Aaron, Charles, and Cyril." They took the stage and did a version of "Carry the Torch," from their latest album. Aaron's son Ivan was playing keyboards and Art's son Ian was playing guitar. Then Ed Bradley made an announcement: "for the first time playing together in New York City in twenty-five years, joining the Neville Brothers . . . the Meters!" And suddenly Zigaboo Modeliste was behind the drums and guitarist Leo Nocentelli and bassist George Porter were striding to the middle of the stage. Zigaboo kicked off the archetypal second-line intro to "Hey Pocky Way" and Art, hunched over a Hammond organ, began to sing the familiar, anthemic lines. It was a poignant moment, a reconciliation of all the tangled, often bitter interconnections between the Meters and the Neville Brothers. Amazingly, considering the large number of musicians on stage (the Nevilles' rhythm section had not left when the Meters came on), the music did not sound cluttered. Art's dictum of space in music was operative.

Aaron then stepped up to a microphone and took it from the stand. He wore a black baseball cap backwards on his head, black jeans and a black tee-shirt emblazoned with a dramatic, cosmic illustration of what looked like a tiger. Hunching forward, eyes closed, his left hand pressed against his left ear so he could hear himself properly, he sang an ethereal version of "Amazing Grace," his voice slipping in and out of falsetto, backed only by Art's organ.

"God bless y'all," Aaron said as he finished the song. "Joy to the world!" With that the band kicked into "When the Saints Go Marching In," and the Rebirth Brass Band, one of a new generation of brass bands that had revitalized the tradition of New Orleans brass bands at the root of jazz, strolled onstage, joining in. They were followed closely by everyone else who had performed that evening. New Orleans artists included the Dixie Kups, who once again counted Athelgra Neville as a member; Irma Thomas; Dave Bartholomew, the octogenarian trumpeter and bandleader who had cowritten, arranged, and produced most of Fats Domino's hits; Troy Andrews, who at twenty was probably the most talented new-generation jazz musician in New Orleans; and Kermit Ruffin, whose tradition-oriented band was one of the first to resume playing live music in New Orleans clubs after Katrina. Three generations of New Orleans music makers gathered onstage together, many of them related or connected by long association—a living, breathing representation of what made New Orleans music unique and special. Cyril Neville, wearing a tee-shirt emblazoned with the words ETHNIC CLEANSING IN NEW ORLEANS, stepped out front and sang the lead, taking everyone to church with his gospel voice, stepping out from behind his percussion to dance as he sang. At once a New Orleans cliché and an authentic piece of the city's tradition, "When the Saints Go Marching In" has been a staple of the famous jazz funerals: dirges were played on the way to the cemetery, but celebratory tunes were played on the way back as "second-liners" performed that distinctively New Orleanian freeform dance of cosmic liberation, the physical representation of New Orleans groove. At that moment, the song marked a symbolic funeral for the parts of the city—and the people—who would never return. It also marked a celebration of the survivors and an affirmation of the city's spirit.

The Neville Brothers are quintessential survivors. They have survived racism, drug addiction, prison, the tragic deaths of many loved ones, murderous street life, the vagaries of the music business, and, of course, the hurricane. Their sense of family and community, as well as that life-affirming New Orleans groove, has enabled them to do so, and now they are a key part of a dwindling number capable of bringing that groove to the world. That infinite, revitalizing, life-affirming groove is a carrier of some special essence of humanity. As Aaron Neville told me: "It's got to come back to that; it ain't got no other place to go."

Yabby You, photo courtesy of Shanachie Entertainment

Yabby You

The Jesus Dread

The bus, mercifully well air-conditioned, labored slowly over the crest of the mountain above the southern Jamaican town of Mandeville, and suddenly the spectacular vista of a lush valley came into view, sprawled two thousand feet below and glowing in the afternoon sun. Somewhere at the far end of that valley was the man I had come to see: Vivian Jackson, known as Yabby You. Marveling, I realized I had not seen him in at least fifteen years and had hardly spoken to him in ten years. It had been thirty years since I had first become aware of his existence.

A month earlier I had telephoned Yabby because I was coming to Negril on vacation and realized it would be a rare opportunity to see the man whose life had unexpectedly become intertwined with my own. A few days earlier, prior to my call, a friend had told me of some video clips posted on the Internet of a 2005 concert performance by Yabby You at the JASound Festival in France. His performances had always been rare and it had been years since I had heard of him performing anywhere, so naturally I was eager to see the videos.

The posting presented a description of the concert by French deejays named Nouns, Pady, and Slim Jay, who had attended the show. Yabby, looking frail, had been helped on stage and led over to kind of a high stool, since he had rarely in his adult life been able to walk or stand for long without crutches. His appearance at the show was greeted by the audience as the miraculous appearance of a fabled personage.

"Is he too ill to play onstage?" the commentators wrote, remembering the crowd's uncertainty. "Many doubts cross our minds until he is . . . here for real, onstage, deep emotion. After stepping forward on crutches, guided by two people, he sits painfully down on a stool."[1]

I barely recognized him as he appeared in the videos. He had aged significantly. His long dreadlocks had been cut off and, at sixty years of age, his beard had gone gray. He wore gray slacks and a dashiki with cross-hatched stripes of gold and gray. On his head was a red, gold, and green billed cap. His eyes were clouded by fatigue and pain. He resembled an old, sick lion.

In the first video clip, the French band kicks off, a bit tentatively, "Carnal Mind," a reggaefied church hymn that had been one of his earliest recordings. Yabby You turns in his chair toward the band and mouths an instruction. Then he begins to sing in a tremulous voice, his hands resting on his knees, his head tilted back slightly. He sings with fierce concentration, staring straight ahead then squeezing his eyes shut, singing directly into the microphone. As the drummer kicks into an instrumental section, Yabby tosses his head to the drum flourish. As the song proceeds, he gathers momentum and his voice strengthens, although the harmony singers in the band are off-key and that makes it more challenging for him to sing. He nods affirmatively as the band hits a climactic flourish.

"His voice is tired," the commentator notes. "Nevertheless Yabby You shows strong determination and sings his first melodies. Meanwhile there is still magic in the air. After the first moments, Yabby You's voice is warmer and brings us back to the mystical essence of his songs."[2]

In the clip for "Jah Vengeance," the band begins their introduction to the song but their playing is very ragged; Yabby You calls out "haul up!" and the band stops and kicks the song again as Yabby You intones "Jah Vengeance!" into the microphone. He gamely sings, at one point turning to gesture to the band, then nodding to the groove as the band comes together.

"We have the feeling we are taking in a historical event, maybe the last moments with Yabby You," the commentator notes. "After the last song, a car picks him up directly behind the stage. The man is exhausted, shaking, but he has given us so much joy and happiness."[3]

Yabby performed nine songs, over half of them from his first album, *Conquering Lion,* released more than thirty years previously.

Shortly after seeing the video clips I dialed the only telephone number I had for Yabby, hoping against the odds that I could still reach him at that number. A woman answered and I asked to speak to Yabby You. She asked me to hold and a minute later I heard his familiarly mellifluous tone.

"Greetings," he said.

I identified myself and he remembered me. I mentioned my reason for calling. His voice sounded weak as though he was in great pain or else had little strength, as one who has been fighting a debilitating illness. I had never heard him sounding that way and so was immediately concerned about his condition.

"How are you doing?" I asked.

"Well," he said haltingly, "great tribulation."

I was even more concerned when he said that. In all the years I had known him I had never heard Yabby express any negative feeling or complaint about his physical condition, no matter what challenge he might have been facing. And, true to form, he immediately qualified his answer.

"But we have to give thanks still," he said weakly, clearly in significant discomfort, "for it is all part of the plan."

I knew that during most of his adult life Yabby had suffered from severe rheumatoid arthritis and that he was no stranger to pain. But I had never heard him sound so debilitated. I explained that I was coming to Jamaica and would like to visit in order to hear directly from him some of his life history in order that I might include him in my book of "great spirits."

"Yes, that will be fine," he said. "Anything for the work."

I knew that when he said "the work" he was referring to his lifelong mission to elevate spiritual awareness and spread love through music. I mentioned that it did not seem as though much roots reggae was being recorded in Jamaica these days.

"Vampires. Vampires control the music," was his comment.

I told him I would call to set a time when I arrived in Jamaica. I knew that he lived out in the country, in Vere, a part of Clarendon in the south central region of Jamaica, an area not much visited by tourists. But I had only a vague idea of where Vere was. Knowing that at different times in his life Yabby had lived in very basic, even deprived circumstances, I wondered about his living conditions. I asked him if there was anything I could bring him from the States.

"Anything," Yabby answered without hesitation. "You know how we stay."

In truth, I did not know for certain, but I took his statement as a sign that his living conditions were somewhat desperate. All this was running through my mind as the bus wound its way down the mountainside via a two-lane road. At the end of the telephone conversation, I had felt it imperative that I see him. I wondered if I would find him in one of those small, tin-roofed wooden shacks so common in the Jamaican countryside. I wondered if he was getting the sustenance he needed. Not knowing what would be useful, I withdrew some money from my savings to give to him to use as he saw fit.

I had first seen Yabby You's name in 1977 in the British music magazine *Black Music*. The name had intrigued me; it reminded me of Fred Flintstone's trademark cry of jubilation: "yabba dabba doo!" I wondered what kind of music the owner of such a name would make. Appended to his name was the title of his album, *Deliver Me from Me Enemies*, which the reviewer proclaimed to be one of the most impressive recordings of inspirational roots reggae yet recorded. I had immediately ordered it from Daddy Kool Records, a small London shop that at the time was one of the few mail-order sources of reggae in the world. A couple of weeks later the album arrived, encased in a plain white sleeve with the label showing through the center hole of the sleeve. The pale blue label featured a ghost image of a dreadlocked face, locks falling forward down either side of his face, large, luminous dark eyes gazing out at me. The name Vivian Jackson was emblazoned across the top of the label as the artist name, with Yabby You written in parentheses. The company name was Prophets Records. The names of the songs were listed in black type on the label. It was not uncommon in the roots reggae world for a record to be sold in a plain white sleeve. When an entrepreneur ran out of album jackets but still had the records themselves, they were then sold "as is." If sales were to be made, a struggling producer would not let a lack of record sleeves stop him from making sales—especially when, as often was the case, the producer lacked the funds to print more sleeves. *Deliver Me from My Enemies*, I learned years later, had been pressed in extremely limited quantities. By luck, many years hence I obtained an original LP jacket for the album. On the back was a kind of manifesto in fractured

English, one of the strangest declarations ever to appear on any album jacket:

> The new roots phase of Vivian Jackson and his social role in public entertainment, the social role of Vivian Jackson popular known as Yabby You—writer, producer and director of V. Jackson Recording Co. Ltd . . . his music is introducing a new phase in the development of "Reggae Roots Songs". His phase has a natural organ of mass communication and strengthens the demand of "Reggae Roots" universally . . . note that we have not made exaggerated claims about the power of the reggae but the influence of "Yabby You" phase of the Reggae Roots is for both industrial and commercial mass communication to public understanding. Undoubtedly "Yabby You" phase will be the most vital area for future research. We do not know the exact nature of the influence of his music of the conditions under which the music is effective, but the practical limits to the power of his phase are mass entertained . . . .[4]

The notes went on in this vein for some four hundred words.

With great curiosity I put the album on. The title track was first; it began with a stately, purposeful, deep groove played on drums, bass, guitar, piano, and organ. A trumpet blew an heraldic line, reminiscent of those trumpets of antiquity that signaled the arrival of royalty or perhaps that moment "when the last trumpet sounds" referred to in the Bible. Yabby You began to sing in a resolute tenor:

Deliver me . . . from my enemies
Oh, my God, from my enemies
For I lift up my soul
Right up to thee
Teach me to do thy will
With all my heart, my God
For thy spirit . . . it is good
Lead me . . . in uprightness[5]

The entire song is a prayer, a declaration of faith, and a plea for divine intervention. Years later he told me that he had been inspired to write "Deliver Me from My Enemies" because he had been renting a room from a married couple who he had thought were Christians; one day he found in the washroom area some accouterments of *obeah,* an African-rooted spiritual practice similar to voodoo. Regardless of the specific inspiration for "Deliver Me from My Enemies," the combination of the powerful rhythm, an indelible melody, and deeply committed, heartfelt singing pulls you along in a tidal wave of feeling.

That stupendous opening track is followed by "Judgement Time," an even more propulsive groove topped by stinging, sparkling electric guitar lines as Yabby You and his chorus deliver lyrics straight out of the Book of Revelations, listing the signs of the impending time of judgment prophesized in that Biblical book.

The entire album is recorded with great definition and clarity, amplifying its impact. Other songs deal with such topics as the falling value of the British pound as a sign of corrupt Babylon's demise; a plea for God to remove obstructions from one's sight; and, on "One Love," a celebration of the essence of love shared by all humans—a hymn whose first verse is delivered in the Ethiopian language of Amharic. There are also a couple of wistful love songs interspersed amongst the fire and brimstone as well as a tuneful instrumental, a version of the classic reggae rhythm known as "Shenk-I-Shek" (probably a corruption of Chiang Kai-Shek) that is topped by jazzy guitar soloing from Earl "Chinna" Smith.

The beauty and power of the music on *Deliver Me from My Enemies* led me to seek out any and all recordings of Yabby You, no easy task since most of his music was manufactured in extremely small quantities that appeared momentarily in a few shops in the world, only until they sold out and became unavailable for a while. I had seen listings for a Yabby You album entitled *Conquering Lion* and another entitled *Ram A Dam.* I soon learned that they were different versions of Yabby's debut album, which predated *Deliver Me from My Enemies* by a couple of years. But all attempts to obtain either version were fruitless until one day I chanced upon a lone copy of *Conquering Lion* at Chin Randy's Records in the Crown Heights section of Brooklyn. The cover, which was entirely in pink, featured an illustration of a fire-breathing lion standing up on its haunches, overlaid by the album title, with Vivian Jackson and Yabby You in parentheses.

The centerpiece of *Conquering Lion* is the title track, one of the

THE JESUS DREAD   181

most unusual pieces of music ever created. I later learned that it had
been Yabby You's first recording. The track opens with a fanfare of
drums, bass, and guitar hitting staggered, dissonant chords followed
with low, massed voices droning out nonsense syllables: "be-you . . .
yabby, yabby you." Then it kicks into an insistent, ominous, minor-
key, one-chord vamp powered by bass and organ, a totally unique yet
hypnotic rhythm pattern. The singers chant out a "la-la-la" melody not
unrelated to "Hava Nagila" before switching into a verse: "The king of
kings, the Lord of Lords, the conquering Lion of Judah / Seventy-two
different nations, bow before Jah glory."[6]

Followers of Rastafari assumed the song was about Emperor Haile
Selassie, who was known as the Lion of Judah. The lyric was rooted in
a verse from the Book of Revelations: "weep not; behold the Lion of
the tribe of Judah, the root of David hath prevailed to open the book,
and to loose the seven seals thereof." In fact, Yabby You believed that
the Lion of Judah was Jesus Christ, but he was content to allow the
Rastas to embrace it. It was a hymn of sorts, one that demanded attention, even if it sounded like no other hymn ever created.

Much of the album was hymns. "Carnal Mind," for instance, was
derived from a hoary church hymn ("you can't get to Zion with a carnal mind"); "Run Come Rally," a stirring, minor-key anthem driv-
en by deep, strong reggae rhythms, was much beloved by Rastafarians. "Anti-Christ," set to an intense "flyers" reggae riddim driven by
a whooshing cymbal pattern, was a simple parable of good and evil:
"See dem dey, dem favor sheep, but dem a wolf; see dem dey, dem say
dem a Christ, but dem an anti-Christ."[7] The song "Jah Vengeance" is a
powerful, evocative tale of the coming retribution of God against the
wicked. In short, *Conquering Lion* was Yabby You's vision of a corrupt
world where righteous men were beset by evil even as the day of judgment prophesized in Revelations was approaching.

Most of the songs had been released as singles by Vivian Jackson
and the Prophets. Indeed the songs sounded like the declarations of
Biblical prophets. Yabby You's music had a raw, deep spiritual element
set off by powerful reggae rhythms that were on a par with such roots
reggae icons as Burning Spear and Culture. On my weekly reggae radio show I usually played at least one song by Yabby You every week.
One day, a Jamaican listener called in: "Why do you play Yabby You

all the time? No one listens to Yabby You in Jamaica!" I knew that in Jamaica such artists as Dennis Brown, Gregory Isaacs, Marcia Griffiths, the Heptones, and the Mighty Diamonds dominated the charts; in terms of overall popularity, the caller was not wrong. But those who really knew and loved the deepest roots reggae considered Yabby You a major artist, a key figure in the development of the music. Ironically, he got more recognition in England.

Yabby You was all the more mysterious because of the scarcity of his music and the fact that he was not known to perform in public at the time. There was confusion regarding his identity as well. Vivian Jackson was his given name but ever since "Conquering Lion" had created a grassroots sensation in 1972, he had been known as Yabby You, after the chanted nonsense syllables at the beginning of the song. Yabby had not wanted his name on the record initially; he figured that in the event that the record flopped, he would not be known as the producer of a failure.

When I first traveled to Jamaica in 1983, I had remarked in passing to the young singer Hugh Mundell, who was taking me around Kingston, that I admired Yabby You's music and wondered where he was. I extolled the uniqueness and power of his music, thinking of him as an impossibly obscure figure whom I would most likely never see. The next day I heard a knock on my hotel room door; when I answered it, Hugh was there grinning. He stepped into the room and said, "Meet Yabby You." Behind him a slight-figured, dreadlocked man hobbled in on metal crutches. He made his way over to a chair by the window and sat down, putting his crutches aside. I told him I was very glad to see him and that I had been playing his music Stateside. Yabby did not register any particular surprise or excitement. He simply began speaking in a matter-of-fact manner.

"Yes, yes," he said in his soft yet resonant voice, "give thanks for spreading the works."

Then he told me some of the events that had led to him recording. His mother was a dressmaker, his father a carpenter. Though his mother was from the country, Yabby had been born Vivian Jackson in Kingston in 1946. He was close to his mother and regularly accompanied her, a devout Christian, to church. Enthralled by the stories in the Bible and by the preaching about Jesus and the prophets, Yabby, at age seven, decided that the only way he could truly know the reality expressed in the Bible would be to experience it. He decided to emulate Jesus, who left his parents at about twelve years of age and discoursed with the learned men of his time and place.

"I was roughly about the age of seven," Yabby related, "mi plan when mi reached twelve, mi make them know that I'm going to roam and go around different kind of people that deal with doctrine and dem kind of things and try and live it and learn from the experience. But I never realize how rough it would be, living without parents."

So, at twelve he left home and began to stay with different religious sects in and around Kingston, Christians at first and then different Rasta sects such as the Ites people, the Ethiopian Orthodox Church, and the Bobo Ashanti.

"First I move among different kind of people, church people dem . . . but we never FEEL them . . . me never feel like them serious. They were much too sophisticated, you know? They much like the world, love vanity and all them kinda things. Then I come amongst the Rasta dem now . . . . see what it's like with them, it comes different. Dem caught my eye because dem live more nearer to what I'm looking for, you know? But I find out something about dem too . . . .just like with the church people, you have all different kinds of persons . . . you go to dis one and him say it is the wrong one you're trying; you go to that one and another one come and say that's the wrong one you're trying . . . they condemn one another . . . . .just like the church Rasta . . . you try the Bobo and he says the Ethiopian bredda is the right one . . . and then you go to that one and him say that the Orthodox is the right one . . . I realize that Jesus Christ was not a politician, his life was given by the Almighty . . . then me notice another thing about Jesus. He never write of himself. His people write 'bout him . . . So to me, I feel it's the highest form of righteousness, so I said to myself that I'm going to have to practice what he preach."

With this perspective Yabby attempted to live a completely pure life, living among the Ites people, who had extreme dietary restrictions; in observance of the commandment "thou shalt not kill," he did not eat meat. He lived in the outdoors because he felt that houses were manmade and not created by the Almighty, and often spoke in a kind of pig-Latin whereby the letter "I", representing the Almighty, was substituted for syllables, which caused some people he encountered to think he was a madman.

"I never realize that we are human beings and it's not like the animals that sleep outside," Yabby recalled ruefully. "But, you see, no one could really convince me, because what you are seeking after, you have to really experience it."

He also learned the trade of metalworking and worked at a foundry making dutch pots (cookware) in the Waterhouse section of Kingston, earning enough to sustain himself. From time to time he would stop work and wander around the country.

"I work six months and I'm sure to earn a certain amount of money," he related. "Now me just start walk around the island, carrying me bedding and every little t'ing, me cook pot and t'ing. And I get up in the morning and cook. I never used to have this beard and I had this long hair and people never know if I was woman or man. And I never talk to nobody and true I go barefooted. So everywhere I go people gather around and guess what I be like."

But at age seventeen he was experiencing weakness and shortness of breath during work at the foundry. He collapsed one day and was taken to the hospital, where he was diagnosed with a variety of ailments: pneumonia, malnutrition, an ulcerated stomach, and brain fever. The doctors decided surgery was in order. When he recovered from the surgery, he found that he could no longer walk. The doctors gave him two years to live. His arthritic condition dated from that time.

Up until that point, Yabby You's only involvement with music had been singing in church or at Rasta spiritual gatherings. I asked him how he happened to start making music.

"Awoah!" Yabby exclaimed. "Well, now you used to have these Rasta bredrin . . . they never like when I say Ras Tafari is just another man becaw I experience that the Almighty is like a spirit, which we in the eyes of flesh can't behold. But the Rasta people dem love when I'm amongst dem to ask me questions. Well, on this day me and dem were in this Rasta camp, it's a place now where all different type of people come and buy herb. Well, the whole of them worship Rastafari and I was the only one with another position. So each one a dem question and tell me things and I defend it. The sky black up and rain a fall and the whole of them start to leave when the rain come and me alone sit up . . . so dem a reason and try tell me say Rastafari is the King of Kings and the Lord of Lords but I say if he was the King of Kings, that would be Jesus and it's Christ that me preach. That would be the Lord of Lords. Well I hear, inside of my thoughts, all of a sudden this sound of thunder, you know, it start sound like music, so I tried to imitate that sound, but I no hear the words at all. So eventually, now, it's me alone, the sound weh I hear in my thoughts comes like a vision, me try and hum it and all of a sudden dem wake up and tell me say that I should try to put that thing inna record. That would be a new sound . . . a new kind of sound on a recording. So I say I should try and penetrate that now as a career in music."

Yabby had no idea what was involved in the process of making a recording, but he knew he needed musicians. He encountered an up-and-coming drummer named Horsemouth Wallace when Horsemouth came to the Gully Bank to buy herb.

"Horsemouth hear me sing dem tings and say show me that going to be a new set of music and it would be really good if I would do it."

With Horsemouth's help, a little group of musicians was gathered to give shape to the sound Yabby had heard in his vision. He began to save up money to make the recording, tossing any stray coin that he could find into a milk pan. When that was filled with coins, he then set about filling a gas can, then a paint can and other cans. This process went on for many months and still there was not enough money to pay more than three musicians, much less hire a recording studio. But the musicians, who included Horsemouth, guitarist Chinna Smith, and bass player Family Man Barrett of the Wailers, were committed. Horsemouth "borrowed" instruments from the band he played in, without their knowledge, and carried them down to Gully Bank. Electricity was obtained by running a wire from a light pole. They rehearsed the song right there in the Gully Bank.[8]

Finally Yabby had collected enough money to pay for a half hour of studio time. The musicians agreed to play for free, so strongly did they believe in the music. That was sufficient to record the rhythm track for the tune. Family Man played the unique organ part. Several more months went by and finally Yabby had collected another fifty Jamaican dollars. With that he went to King Tubby's studio in Waterhouse, of which Gully Bank was a part.

"Me carry the tape," Yabby recalled, "and when Tubbs hear it, 'im get fascinated by it. Him feel say it sound like it supposed to reach the earth and me is the one supposed to bring it."

So Tubby recorded Yabby's vocals, aided by a couple of harmony singers. But Yabby had no money to press any records up. Many more months of scrounging yielded enough to press a hundred copies of the song that would be known as "Conquering Lion," years after it had come to him in a vision. He took it around to sound systems and record shops, playing it for people, never telling them that it was his recording. He sold the first one hundred copies and used the money to press more. As he sold those, he pressed still more. It became a sensation. People were asking for the song as "Yabby You," since those were the words sung at the beginning of the record. Although he eventually began pressing the record with a label that listed Vivian Jackson and the Ralph Brothers as the artist, when people realized that it was he singing on the record, they started calling him Yabby You and he was known by that name ever after. The snowballing sales of "Conquering Lion" afforded Yabby funds to record more songs, and by 1975 he had recorded and released the songs that made up the *Conquering Lion* album. "Conquering Lion" was remixed in different versions, including a stark, powerful version by the popular chanting deejay (rapper) Big Youth that became a hit all over again.

Yabby broke off from his narrative, which he had delivered matter-of-factly, and looked at me meaningfully.

"Just like the ancient Israelites inscribed their praise on tablets with wax, so I would record my message with wax on record," he related.

This epiphany ushered in comparatively halcyon days for Yabby. Though unable to do physical work, he found that he had a knack for picking the winner of horse races. Since he believed it was wrong to use this power for his own personal gain, he passed the tips on to others, who usually would give him a portion of their winnings in appreciation. His recording efforts blossomed as he put the money from record sales into still more recordings. He began teaching aspiring singers how to sing and recorded such young artists as Michael Prophet, Wayne Wade, and Tony Tuff, all of whom went on to greater success. On his own recordings he used a vocal group he dubbed the Prophets to create ethereal harmonies behind his vocals. A photo from this period captures Yabby on a Honda motorcycle, wearing slacks and a simple knit shirt, a young woman perched on the back. He described it as a carefree time. However he soon became disillusioned by the music business. His music was being released in England and he was not receiving royalties. And unauthorized releases of his music were appearing.

"Pirates," Yabby told me. "Dem pirate my music and me can't accept that."

So he stopped recording new material himself and gradually his productions of other artists became infrequent. By the time we met in my hotel room, he had not recorded in several years and had been spending much of his time in the country.

Moved by his story, I asked him if he would be interested in having his music released in the United States by Shanachie. At that time none of his music had been officially released there. I proposed releasing a kind of "best of," drawing on all his works to date. I could not offer much advance money, only a few thousand dollars, since his music was little known in the States and there was no telling how it would sell. He did not hesitate or attempt to negotiate.

"Yes, that would be fine," he said.

We made a deal on the spot. We shook hands and he left soon thereafter. I returned to the United States and set about preparing the release of *One Love One Heart*, the collection we had spoken about. To my great surprise, when I called to let him know that we were sending down the advance payment, he told me that he was inspired to go back into the studio for the first time in years. A few months later tapes arrived of a new Yabby You album. I listened to it with a mixture of anticipation and apprehension. It is a rare artist who can match the depth and quality of his breakthrough work. Most simply create lesser versions of their best artistic moments. Yet Yabby You's new music sounded fresh. Only one or two songs followed the familiar patterns of previous songs. It opened, appropriately enough, with a hymn, "Praise Jahoviah," set to a sprightly, bass-driven rhythm and joyous horn lines set off by falsetto harmony choruses by Alrick Forbes and Da Da Smith of the original Prophets. The next track, "Fire Deh A Mus Mus Tail," sketched a stark portrait of a city embroiled in violence, over a strong, staccato rhythm, delivering lyrics that might as well have been from newspaper stories about random killing and clashes between police and gangs. The title of the song comes from a Jamaican proverb: "fire dey a mus mus tail, dem a t'ink it a cool breeze" which means, roughly, that a fool, feeling the wind from a fire burning by his backside, thinks it is a cool breeze, in other words, a foolish person does not see danger or evil forces for what they are. He sums up the effect of random violence on the ghetto dweller: "in dis ya time you can't skylark . . . you can't even laugh."[9]

"Fleeing from the City," the title track, is a pensive reggae ballad graced by the soaring harmony vocals of the Prophets. The song chronicles the ills of modern city life—violence, poverty, decadence—and declares that, like Sodom and Gomorrah, it is destined to be destroyed by fire. It is better, Yabby sings, to go to the country where you can still live a righteous life. On "Sat Up on the Gully Bank," drawing from his time living at Gully Bank, Yabby sings a poignant song about living at a subsistence level.

I sit up in my one room shack
and my small fire match rock
cooking some cornmeal porridge
in my little dutch pot
I hear Bongo George next door
come on over and have a seat
we sup together
and give thanks for what we have

The song's chorus then opens up with a full-throated declaration of love for God, which overwhelms the scene of material deprivation painted by the lyrics in the verse:

"Jah, Jah!
some call him Rastafari
but I know . . . Jah Jah is I guide[10]

One song, ironically titled "Hungry Belly Is the New Stylee," uses a popular hard-kicking dancehall groove to underpin an unflinching view of suffering and poverty. There are even two bittersweet love songs; since the release of *Deliver Me from My Enemies*, Yabby had been including one or two love songs per album, often tales of longing, unrequited love, or fleeting love. For long stretches of his life, due to the way he lived, Yabby had no female companion.

For Yabby, the message of *Fleeing from the City* was quite literal. The evil, corruption, and violence that many of the songs on the album depicted were literally the daily happenings anyone in Kingston—or many other cities around the world—could observe. Children having children, war and rumors of war, food shortages, disease, and other events conformed to the prophecies of the Book of Revelations in the Bible. As Yabby told U.K. reggae historian Steve Barrow in 1994, "It [Revelations] did prophesize, everything has to happen has been prophesized. It's just a repeating of history. He did prophesy the happening of the closing of the dispensation, and the beginning. Him say, 'when we hear of war and rumors of war, nation against nation, kingdom against kingdom, earthquake from one place to another, food shortage, plagues and pestilences, rejoice and look up for your redemption draweth nigh.'"[11] Since the time that song was recorded, the frequency of those sorts of events has hardly slackened; indeed they have increased in number and impact. Yabby himself had fled from the corrupt city and urged others to do the same.

Along with the tapes of the album, Yabby sent a photograph of himself to use on the album cover. It captures him on a grassy hillside, high above a city, silhouetted against the sky. He wears a rumpled, ill-fitting pair of beige corduroy pants, a light gray v-neck sweater over a green and yellow knit shirt, a pale green tam on his head, and black and white sandals. His dark dreadlocks fall past his shoulders down his back and his clothes hang loosely on his slight figure. His eyes are cast heavenward, his right hand extended in mid-wave, a spliff pinched between the thumb and finger of his left hand, which hangs limply by his side. He stands a bit awkwardly, somewhat rigidly, and only those who knew his physical condition would understand the triumphant aspect of the photo, which captures him standing without support. The most notable thing about his pose is the expression on his face; his eyes sparkle and he is smiling joyously. You could see the photo as a demonstration of the power of faith, which can empower even a disabled person to stand and walk. Or it could be viewed simply as proof that it is possible to smile despite serious infirmities.

The release of *One Love One Heart* and *Fleeing from the City* caused an immediate reaction among those who came in contact with them. A handful of salutary reviews appeared, reaction from reggae radio deejays was very positive and sales, though modest, were nonetheless more that would have been expected for a relatively unknown artist. Noted popular music critic Robert Christgau commented trenchantly, "The former Vivian Jackson could almost be a muezzin (or three) chanting nursery rhymes, most of which concern the end of the world as we know it, a prospect which cheers him considerably."[12]

Still, most people in the United States (and indeed the world) had never seen him perform. I suggested that it would be a good idea to tour in the States in order to assist in the promotion of the album, but I was well aware of the obstacles to booking an artist who was virtually unknown and only had a couple of modest selling releases to his credit. Yet, as is the case with so many events in Yabby You's life, the seemingly impossible came to pass due to the help of those who knew him or encountered him and were moved by his spirit to assist him. I received a phone call one day from Yabby You in Jamaica.

"I am coming on tour, "he informed me. "Albert and dem tell me say they have a tour in America and they will carry me with them."

I realized he was talking about Albert Griffiths and his group the Gladiators, one of the well-regarded reggae groups to have international releases in the second wave of reggae awareness in the late seventies. Albert and Clinton Fearon of the Gladiators were old acquaintances of Yabby and had played on many of his recordings, I knew, but how many times had I heard a reggae artist say the same thing? I called the Gladiators' booking agent and found that it was indeed happening; the tour was to be a substantial twenty-city tour across the United States. Yabby was to be the opening act, with the Gladiators band backing him.

In New York the group played at S.O.B.'s, a prime club outlet for reggae over the years. As the band took the stage, Yabby was announced and he came out on his crutches, ascended the stage and, to my surprise, put the crutches aside and stood up to the microphone to sing. His dreads, which trailed far down his back, had knotted together to form one long flat mat of hair, something you only see with those who have been dreads for many years; it's the mark of a very serious dreadlocks. His eyes seemed larger than ever, almost unnaturally big, and something about his look reminded me of the space alien in the film *ET*. He was joined by Alrick Forbes of the Prophets and Clinton Fearon sang the other harmony. In front of a packed crowd, Yabby began to sing, head tilted back, eyebrows raised with devotional spirit, in the manner of a choir member or a parishioner in church. As he brought the invocatory "Praise Jahoviah" to a close, spirited applause greeted him. A fair number of people in the audience understood what a rare event was taking place in front of them. Yabby did not say much between songs.

"Yes, yes, Yabby You loves you," he intoned placidly in a kind of singsongy voice as applause washed over him.

Then the band would kick into the next song and he would sing, nearly motionless, with great focus and determination. He sang some of his classics such as "Run Come Rally," "Deliver Me from My Enemies," and, of course, "Conquering Lion," but also a number of songs from *Fleeing from the City*.

After the show I went to the dressing room downstairs to greet Yabby. I mentioned my great surprise that he was able to perform without crutches.

"Yes," he said, "since I come on tour it come like I don't need to use the sticks again!"

Whether it was a better diet or the stimulation of moving around or simply divine providence, his ability to dispense with his crutches and walk a bit was a great blessing, a small miracle. Unfortunately it turned out to be only a temporary blessing, as he found it necessary to use them again some time after returning to Jamaica. So much about Yabby seems to defy normal expectations.

I considered him to be a spiritual person, one of the few people I ever met who I felt was truly spiritual. I was not the only one. Many people who met him, when asked to describe what he was like, would use the same word. Those few who have seemed truly spiritual to me have had a number of characteristics in common: They usually radiate an understated, benign aura. They also seem to possess a great calm at the center of their being. They tend not to be judgmental, although they certainly have strong convictions and express them as they feel appropriate. But there is no element of proselytizing with such people. Their manner of speaking from conviction is usually calm and matter-of-fact, like a wise parent who points out guideposts to his child yet knows the child will likely have to experience things himself. There is no sense of ego or superciliousness or excessive pride. Such people are not particularly enamored of or concerned with the trappings of the material world. Yabby You's manner fit this paradigm exactly.

"He's a very strong guy, very energetic," Neil Fraser, the producer known professionally as the Mad Professor, told me when I called him to ask about his work with Yabby. Neil put Yabby up in England for six months in the 1990s and recorded a couple of albums with him, one of them becoming the last Yabby You recording released to date. "He has always had his own sound even though he worked in many different studios because he is so spiritual that when he's in a room, the room embodies his spirit. He takes what he does very serious. He doesn't want people who don't truly believe in it. Musicians get something from playing with him. The musician receives something special so the money doesn't really bother him. He reads the Bible a lot, really believes a lot. He's one of the most spiritual people I've known."

Indeed, when word got around that Yabby was staying in a house in England, various people on the reggae scene began making pilgrimages to see him—singers, producers, sound system operators—some well-known, such as the producer Lee Perry, some less so.

When I asked Augustus Pablo what he thought of Yabby, his answer was simple yet profound. "Yabby You is an ancient Nyabinghi singer," Pablo stated succinctly.

In fact, there are many parallels between Pablo and Yabby You. Both regard their music as divinely inspired and have pure, uncompromising visions of music-making. Both have been somewhat mysterious, often reclusive figures, though Yabby You is far more outgoing than Pablo was and much more communicative. And both men had a knack for recording highly distinctive, powerful rhythms for their music. It is not surprising, then, that both worked closely with King Tubby and with him created some of the most powerful dub music ever created. "Tubbs," as Yabby affectionately called him, was involved with mixing most of his Yabby's classic works, and together they created dub versions of most of them.

Typically for Yabby, the dub albums that he created at Tubby's studio with Tubby and other engineers resident there appeared in very small numbers of copies—as few as three hundred—when initially released. *Prophesy of Dub* presented dub versions of most of the tracks on *Conquering Lion*. *Beware Dub* offered dub versions mainly of Yabby's productions of other artists, such as saxophonist Tommy McCook and singers Tony Tuff, Wayne Wade, and Patrick Andy. I had been fortunate to obtain a copy of *Beware Dub* in 1978; when an American company made a deal with Yabby to release the album on compact disc, my rare copy of the LP served as the master recording source because Yabby himself no longer had access to the master tape. Despite their scarcity, *Prophesy of Dub* and *Beware Dub* are two of the greatest collections of dub music ever made. The rhythms are deep and profound; *Beware Dub* is enhanced by copious hand percussion played by Sticky Thompson and sometimes Yabby himself. Echo and reverb, especially in conjunction with Yabby's spiritually oriented lyrics, lend an otherworldly quality. "Give Thanks and Praise," for instance, opens with a heavily reverbed vocal chorus: "give thanks and praise . . . .to the most high . . . . open your heart and let him in."[13] The track then embarks on a horn-led, hand percussion–driven excursion over a hypnotic, repeated bass figure.

All this ran through my mind as the bus plunged into the sunlit valley. We were moving past canefields now, great flat expanses of green and yellow. Now and then the two-lane strip of asphalt ran through a small town or village as we headed for the vicinity of Vere. We turned down a lane, passing a handful of houses on either side, until once again fields populated only by a stray cow or some goats filled the windows of the bus. I began to think we had lost our way.

Just then I saw the house Yabby had described coming up on the right-hand side, a modest but neat one-story bungalow with walls of white stucco and a maroon tile roof. The yard was surrounded by a white wrought-iron fence. A minivan was parked by the side of the house. Chickens, goats, hogs, and dogs roamed the scraggly yard, shaded here and there by a tree. There was a chicken coop out back. As we pulled up to the gate an attractive brown-skinned woman of middle years came out and opened the gate. We turned in and made our way slowly up the dirt driveway.

"Hello, I am Jean," the woman said, smiling in greeting as we disembarked. I recognized her voice from my phone calls and realized that she was Yabby's wife. I looked to the porch and saw him sitting in a wheelchair in the shade of the porch, his arms hanging slackly by his sides. I waved and he smiled as I made my way to the porch. It was a relief to see that he was living in reasonably comfortable circumstances after all. He was wearing a white shirt with blue and red stripes, black slacks, and sandals; a red, green, and gold knit cap was on his head. As I got closer I saw that, unlike the videos I had seen on the Internet, his face was simply an older version of the face I had first seen personally twenty-five years earlier, not unrecognizable and not unhealthy-looking. There was something feline, even leonine about his features (later in our stay we learned this his astrological sign is Leo).

"Ah, Yabby!" I said, grasping his hand. "It's been quite a long time!"

"Yes, yes," he said in his familiar melodious, syrupy tones. "Greetings!"

There was a little rasp in his voice that I had not heard before, and he coughed occasionally. I introduced my wife and Delton, the man who had driven us. My wife sat in a cushioned chair next to Jean and Delton sat on the chaise lounge at right angles to that chair. I sat in a chair to Yabby's left, close to him. It was pleasant on the porch, with a light breeze blowing in the shade.

"I said I'd bring something for you," I said, "but I wasn't sure what you needed so I just brought you something that you can use to get what you need."

I lay the envelope of cash on the little table next to him. He smiled and nodded with genuine appreciation.

"Give thanks," he said. Then, just as when I had first met him, without any preamble he launched into a pronouncement that set the stage for the theme of the day.

"'We don't know what death is," he began, "because no one living has experienced it. We only know what life it."

He paused as Jean brought out some fruit drinks on a tray for us.

"You want ice?" Yabby inquired solicitously.

Returning to his opening theme of people not knowing what death is, he related a story I had never heard him tell, about a pivotal moment in his life just before he had the revelation at Gully Bank. After his experience in the hospital, he had reconnected with his family and had been staying with his mother in Clarendon, going to a hospital three times a week for treatment. Now and then a Rastaman would make his way from Kingston looking for Yabby; his family would tell anyone who came that Yabby had died. As a result, word spread back in Kingston among the Rasta camps that Yabby You was dead. After some time his mother felt it would be better for him to stay with his father in Kingston.

"My father was what you call a rum-head," Yabby said. "'im cook 'im food and go 'im work but when it comes Friday, him drunk right back until Monday. Well I go for treatment every week but I want to go back to the herbsman at Waterhouse, where I can get herbs and be independent. I can walk now but I gwan like I can't walk. My father have a next friend, when him come in with his friend they just sleep 'til morning. So I realize if I'm gonna try and make it, I have to make it before daybreak. Well, when it reach about 11:00 o'clock when they're sound asleep, I put on my clothes and take time walk and go down to Waterhouse where they have Gully Bank. I go back to the place where I used to make pots, where you have other Rasta who practice certain work. So when I reach the door and I stop, eventually [I hear] them talk about my death."

"They were talking about your death when you came up?" I asked.

"Yes, they were talking about my death!" Yabby chuckled. "Well, you have one of them who was bigger than me, he was the person who took me to school. He said if me dead, then anyone could dead, 'caw I never used to believe in death, 'caw I always used to practice the truth, how we couldn't speak about death 'caw we never experience it, how we don't know anyone who experience it.

"So, when me try to open the door and go in, it come like dem seen a ghost!" Yabby smiled at the memory. "It come like a miracle. I try to tell dem what I go through and why they get false information but dem still hold on to their opinion. Well, I try to leave because I feel like I'm going to faint and I don't want to faint in front of them. Me have to siddown 'pon de groun' and crawl 'pon me bottom the whole way up Gully Bank. And it reach like two o'clock in the night and I just have to draw on my bottom, draw on my bottom, and when I reach 'pon me yard, I just sweat and wet and everything. So me change off me clothes—my father lay down his head sleep and his friend slept. When I lay down, I start now to revive. And me say, if a man who practices wickedness died and a man who practices righteousness died, to what extent would it serve? Becaw him get the pleasure of wickedness and die and the righteous suffer all the agonies and him die, it won't profit, 'caw it naw make him too strong to perish.

"So me say, I should just get up and just walk like everybody. When I try to get up, I just stand up like on an elevator and feel myself go right up and I reach the ceiling. When I look 'pon the ceiling I realize I gon to the ceiling and true me stop, like you walk to the gate and you stop at will. And when I look down I can see my father and I can see my body beside my father and my father friend. Me realize now, this is strange. Me start to think, if this is death, I wouldn't like to die. When I look at me hand, there was smoke, white smoke; I see my finger dem, everything naked, testicles, everything . . . and I think if this is death, I wouldn't like death. As much as I feel pain and I feel agonies, I would rather go through that night, rather go through everything. So it come where it is a lesson to me."

He broke off his narrative to call his wife.

"Jean? Jean!" But she was inside the house and did not hear him. It was a reminder of his dependent state.

"Well," he continued, "when me look, I don't see nobody at all and me say I try to go back where my father lie. And me cyan hear from this point. I just have to relax. And all at once I just feel like a force come across my body and just come right in. And I remember them say that if you're dead, you must feel, pinch yourself. So I sit down and pinch myself and when me pinch meself I say 'oohh!' I realize from that day I get a spiritual vibe. I realize what I experience is my death."

Jean comes in and Yabby asks her to bring something. A radio has been playing loudly by the side of the house where a man has been working by the minivan. Yabby has explained that his sister's daughter and her children live there in an outbuilding with him. He asks me if the radio is interfering with my tape recorder.

"I don't think so," I said.

Nevertheless he calls out to the man and asks him to turn down the radio.

"Very few musicians realize that we are on a mission," Yabby continued. "And what we are supposed to do is what we experience in this time. We are supposed to pass it on to the generation following. What we are supposed to be really recording is . . . the truth! Because if you notice, the songs that I've been recording are about my experience and spiritual life . . . which I benefit people by passing it on and they can pick it up in a song which we hand down to them, seen?"

"The interesting thing to me," I say, "is that you really didn't set out to be a musician per se, like these other folks did."

"If you hear the psalms, dem," Yabby went on, "you notice the title of the psalms . . . they were played by the chief musicians. That mean, they can hear music but they can't see it. Just like the works . . . you can hear the Word but you can't see it . . . the sound, like when you hear the sound? You feel it and you can't deny it. The Word, we hear it but we can't deny it. These sounds that we pass on, we must be very careful to know that it is the truth and the truth lasts forever.

"Most of these musicians nowadays invest money," Yabby went on, "money and pleasure, but the pleasure, it's like a work because, Jah know, when you have pleasure you have to get more pleasure to keep on living. But the works dem now, when we hear the Word we accept the life of the works and we speak of the experience of the Word so that we can benefit the generation following."

He expressed it another way to Steve Barrow.

"If you read Psalms 159 and Psalms 150," Yabby had noted, "it says 'we must praise Him in the dance.' Him say 'blow the trumpet in the new moon, the high sound Him cymbal, the stringed instrument, the tambourine, the singers.' Reggae music is the only spiritual music that has all of those things, flute, trumpet, and everything. Reggae music is the message of the world now, so that people can turn from them corruption and turn to righteousness, for Babylon shall go down!"[14]

We had been there nearly two hours and it seemed to me that Yabby was looking a bit tired. He had been talking almost continuously for the duration of our visit. I said that we should really be going. It had been more than a four-hour journey from Negril and we wanted to be well on our way before dusk.

"Remember, what you are experiencing now, you must live through it," Yabby said. "It is all for a reason. Guidance!"

With that we boarded the bus, eased up the narrow driveway and turned onto the country lane, waving goodbye to Yabby, who returned our wave from the porch. Jean walked beside the bus to the gate, waved us on our way with a smile, and closed the gate behind us.

Yabby's words rang in my ears as we pulled away: "Reggae music is the message of the world now, so that people can turn from them corruption and turn to righteousness, for Babylon shall go down."

This has been Yabby You's unwavering message for nearly forty years now. And so he continues to wait and watch with equanimity from his vantage point in the Jamaican countryside for the demise of a corrupt system. Miraculously, against long odds, his music has given people around the world the inspiration and faith to believe in the ultimate triumph of good over evil.

Nadia Gamal, photo by STAVRO, Beirut, Lebanon, "Arabesque" collection; courtesy of Phyllis Saretta

Nadia Gamal

The Oriental Dance Diva

He who knows the Dance knows God, and the ways in which Love
can kill. —Jelalhuddin Rumi[1]

It was a warm summer night in New York City in 1981; Town Hall
was packed to the gills and a buzz of anticipation rippled through the
crowd. For many in the audience, the evening's program was a once-in-
a-lifetime opportunity, one for which they had waited many years—a
chance to witness the first American performance by Nadia Gamal,
the greatest Oriental dancer in the Middle East. In the decades since
her emergence as a celebrated dancer in the early fifties, she had visited
the United States several times but had rejected all offers to perform.
She had doubted, with good reason, that there would be a proper presentation of her as a performer—and that there would be a proper
appreciation of her artistry, despite the many triumphs that had made
her both a star and a legend in the Middle East. She had danced at the
fabled Casino Opera in Cairo and starred in feature films as both a
dance performer and actress. She had been the first Oriental dancer to
appear at the prestigious Baalbeck Festival in Lebanon, the preeminent
cultural festival in the Middle East, and she had made triumphant
concert appearances in countries around the world. She had been the
palace dancer for the Shah of Iran and King Hussein of Jordan. Clearly
Nadia Gamal did not need America, and she was not one to compromise her principles in any case.

The problem was that Oriental dance, or *raks sharki* as it is known
in the Middle East, could only be understood by most Americans as
"belly dance," a term popularized in the United States by legendary
impresario Sol Bloom to promote North African and Middle Eastern

dancers at the Midway Plaisance of the 1893 Chicago World's Fair.[2] The Midway, largely because of the dancers, became a sensation.[3] Though the dancers were fully dressed in the folkloric garb of their native cultures, their movements were considered scandalous, given the Victorian mores of the nineteenth-century West. The hip movements and free-flowing arm movements employed by the dancers were sensational to people whose culture regarded any below-the-waist movement as improper; indeed, not so many years earlier the waltz had been considered to be scandalous. Respectable women wore corsets, which made any untoward movements virtually impossible. Attempts were made to ban the dancers, which, predictably, made them a tremendous attraction. Around the same time, an authentic dancer, possibly Egyptian, was performing in various American venues under the name Little Egypt. Some of the earliest films made by Thomas Edison were of "belly dancers." The term "hootchy-cootchy" was employed by the Midway barkers and became associated with the dancers. When burlesque exploded in popularity, hootchy-cootchy dancers—mostly American dancers with little or no knowledge of Middle Eastern dancing—were prime attractions.

A strange conflation of several factors led to the establishment by Americans and Europeans of something called "belly dance," which had only vague and largely distorted connections with the reality of dancers in the Middle East. Burlesque dancers appropriated the style of hootchy-cootchy dancers for their own purposes; Oscar Wilde created a sensation with his play *Salome*, initiating the concept of the "dance of the seven veils," which was amplified by Richard Strauss opera of the same name, despite the fact that dancers in the Middle East did not use veils at the time. Exotic fantasies of harems, dancing girls, and concubines were perpetrated by the European Orientalist painters despite the fact that *harem* was simply a word for the forbidden (to men) women's quarters of a Middle Eastern household, more likely to be populated by a man's mother-in-law, aunts, and female children than concubines or dancing girls. Only the very affluent could afford multiple wives and/or mistresses, and life in a typical harem was quite mundane compared to the fevered depictions of the European Orientalist painters and writers. Eighteenth- and nineteenth-century European travelers contributed to the distortions with their sensationalized descriptions of street dancers in Cairo and other large cities. These women were entertainers who, along with jugglers, acrobats, storytellers, and musicians, made a living by performing in the streets. Their costume was an enhanced version of everyday clothing of the area's women and did not resemble at all the harem outfit of Orientalist fantasy—though they commonly wore necklaces of coins and their bare arms and unveiled faces were provocative enough in locales where no respectable woman would expose any of her flesh in public. Their hip, chest, and arm movements—derived from folkloric dance styles common to the region—seemed to be wildly sensual and free to Westerners whose women never moved in such a way. These travelers' accounts of street dancers fed the belly dance myth (*danse du ventre*, the French called it) and before long Western travelers arrived in Egypt and North Africa eager to see the famed dancers.

The influx of Westerners (fostered by colonial domination of North Africa and the Middle East) created a market for belly dancers, and some local dancers began to conform to Western tastes. Places of entertainment featuring dancers sprang up, especially in port towns. Foreigners often pressed the dancers to strip or dance nude; most refused but some did, albeit usually privately and with distaste. The final step in the enshrinement of belly dance came from Hollywood, when early films propagated the "harem belly dancer" look. Ironically, when the Egyptian film industry took off (becoming the main source of feature films for the Arab world), musical scenes featuring dancers became common, their costumes evolving in the direction of the Hollywood creation and the style of dancing becoming less confined spatially as dancers accommodated European ideas of entertainment.

The Western fantasy conception of Middle Eastern dancers became a familiar and to some degree accepted feature of the Middle Eastern entertainment landscape, even as it obscured authentic Middle Eastern traditions. In Islamic cultures there had long been an ambivalent attitude toward dancers and musicians; the most conservative Muslims proscribe any sort of dancing or music, but a large proportion of the Muslim population has traditionally embraced dance and music as a part of any festive occasion. However, even those who enjoy dancing and music often look down on female entertainers as less than respectable.

All of this lay behind Nadia Gamal's reluctance to perform in the United States. For her it had been a constant battle to assert her preferred style of dance as not only respectable but as a serious art form. "Belly dance is not a correct term," she often said, "since most of the movements do not involve that part of the body." As a serious student of dance, her first instinct was to dismiss the term as objectively inaccurate. She and other Oriental dancers constantly found themselves caught between the hypersexual fantasies of Westerners on the one hand and the condemnation of the rigid moralists of the Middle East on the other.

It is an interesting fact that even a debased version of an art form can carry some essence of its genius and power—especially for the uninitiated. I first encountered Oriental dance in Istanbul, the gateway to the Orient, in 1971. Istanbul's streets were filled by jostling throngs and the modal melodies of Turkish music; the muezzin's cry echoed over the city five times a day. The domes, arches, and curving walls of Islamic architecture presented an alternate physical reality, a variation from the straight lines and right angles of European architecture. The sounds of the language and the music slid around and between the reference tones of the Western scale; the rhythms were irregular pulsations that spilled across the rigid limits of Western meter. A different aspect of the cosmos predominated there.

I cannot recall the name or exact location of the disreputable nightclub where I first saw Oriental dance, but the scene was electrifying. A drummer beat out insidious syncopations on the *dumbeg*, a small hourglass-shaped drum. A bouzouki player and electric organist played sinuous melodies. A clarinetist wailed keening cascades of notes. The dancers danced in turn, one after another, clad in beaded bras and belts, their wrists and arms encircled by gleaming bangles, as swaths of diaphanous material swirled around their hips and legs. Their costumes exemplified the standard Hollywood fantasy of a belly dancer that foreign and even many Middle Eastern audiences had come to expect in a cabaret or nightclub. Inauthentic though it may be, this style of costume is remarkably well-suited to the dramatic element of the dance: it is flattering to all body types, simultaneously concealing and revealing, shifting with the rhythms of the music, highlighting one feature or another as the dancer moves. The dancers shimmied and convulsed, arched their bodies, circled their arms snakelike in the air, whirling and declaiming in symbiosis with the music. They flashed smiles, looking coquettish one moment, haughty the next, and boldly inviting in still another. The confluence of melody, rhythm, and movement was entrancing, conveying an array of elemental emotions.

The dancers were not exceptional, but even the least skillful ones at one moment or another did something noteworthy—a particularly precise hip vibration, an especially dramatic spin or back bend. Each dancer's dance was an expression of her personality, so even mediocre technique did not diminish the impact of the dancer's spirit. It was individual expression, reminiscent of the Delta bluesmen in the way that the dancers took relatively simple phrases or movements and wove them together into highly personal, dramatic vignettes. Like the blues, this dance was a vehicle for storytelling, relating tales of human experience.

The dancers' movements were rooted in an ancient repertoire of body language, not all of it familiar to Westerners. Many of the movements spoke directly to the subconscious, presenting imagery from the collective unconscious, archetypal movements from a source lost in time: hands flung skyward in joyous abandon; head tossed to and fro in the anguish of love lost; a spirited prance of celebration; a hip-sway of invitation. These dancers through their dance connected with some prehistoric woman—an Ur-dancer who invented the movements as a dramatization of the most fundamental emotions and experiences.

In succeeding months I saw variations of this dance in a Tehran cabaret, on a side street in Herat, Afghanistan, and on television in Baghdad. Each dancer had something to offer but all seemed lacking in one respect or another. Some had devastating technique but a commonplace spirit; others radiated an irrepressible and irresistible spirit but lacked technique; still others had skill and personality but were unable to build an emotionally resonant narrative with their dancing. I longed to find the dancer who could put it all together—who had a virtuoso's command of the entire arsenal of movements, who could play off the music like a great musician, and whose spirit tapped into and conveyed the most fundamental emotions. In short, I was looking for an incarnation of the Ur-dancer.

A year or so later I found myself walking on Atlantic Avenue in

Brooklyn in the company of Ibrahim "Bobby" Farrah, a Lebanese-American who was perhaps America's foremost expert on Middle Eastern dance. Bobby, a dancer, choreographer, and teacher, was taking me to Rashid's Records, a record store at 191 Atlantic Avenue devoted to Middle Eastern music of all types. The stretch of Atlantic Avenue running from Henry Street to Court Street was the heart of New York's largest Arab community at that time. As we walked, he gave me historical perspective on Oriental dance.

"It combines the spirituality of the East with the Western idea of movement through space," he noted.

It was then that I first heard of Nadia Gamal.

"Nadia Gamal is the greatest cabaret Oriental dancer in the Middle East," Bobby remarked. "She expresses pure spirituality with her arm movements but then those hips start to move and she pulls you right into the earth!" He went on to extol her extraordinary technique, her dramatic flair, and the sheer power of her dancing. He had seen her perform in Lebanon and filmed her a couple of years earlier.

At Rashid's, Bobby flipped through LPs to find some good examples of Middle Eastern dance music for me. Then he pulled out an LP with a photo of a dancer dominating the cover and slid it across the rack toward me.

"This is Nadia Gamal," he said.

I stared at the woman on the cover. Against a blue background Nadia stood caught in mid-flight, her hands thrown skyward and her head tilted back in abandon, her long brown hair cascading down her back and front. She was wearing the classic cabaret belly dancer costume—heavy beaded bra, a beaded belt from which the flowing swaths of orange gauze alternated with panels of glittering orange-gold satin that would sway with each twist of her hips. If a dancer wanted to perform in nightclubs, some variation of this costume was required. As with most dancers in Egypt, a fine black mesh overlay the expanses of pale flesh between her bra and skirt, and her bra and neck—the result of a government decree. The mesh really did not conceal anything, so it functioned purely as a pro forma statement of modesty. She was wearing gold high-heel shoes and, even though she had been captured in a standing pose, it was a dynamic stance. One shoulder was thrust slightly forward in mid-shimmy, and the front panel of her skirt betrayed the motion of her hips by swaying off to her right. Her left knee was slightly bent. She smiled, her eyes half-closed in ecstasy, the moment of a dancer's triumph as she transcends the limits of earthly reality. It was an expression of ultimate joy. Looking at that photograph I had an instant intuition that Nadia Gamal was the contemporary incarnation of the Ur-dancer I was seeking.

Because she had never performed in the States, Nadia Gamal was a semi-mythical figure to aficionados of the dance in the United States, a fabled figure whose exploits were spoken of but never witnessed. Ironically, though an icon of Arab culture, she was not Arab. Her given name was Maria Kariadis. Her father was Greek and her mother Italian but she was born in Alexandria, Egypt, in 1937. She grew up in a show business milieu: her mother had a theatrical act and performed at the fabled Casino Opera in Cairo, a groundbreaking venue that presented elegant, extravagant, sophisticated cabaret entertainment for an affluent audience. As a young girl Nadia performed European folk dances as part of her mother's act. A significant component of the Casino Opera shows were Oriental dancers; these shows had been a key catalyst for theatrical presentation of Oriental dance. It was at Casino Opera that European notions of choreography and dance posture were mingled with Arab dance styles and the dancers' costumes evolved from traditional garb to the Hollywood version. The female proprietor of the Casino Opera, the redoubtable Badia Massabny, a Lebanese entrepreneur, also operated a school at the Casino and was responsible for training the most famous dancers in the Arab world.

In short, Nadia was born into the epicenter of Oriental dance in the Middle East. She was fascinated with dance, in particular Oriental dance, from an early age. Her father decreed that she could learn the dance if she pursued it in the proper way, through formal study and training. For years Nadia studied ballet, modern dance, piano, jazz, tap dancing, and more. She showed a high level of dedication and discipline from an early age. However her parents forbade her to perform in the Oriental style, due to her youth.

One day, when fourteen-year-old Nadia was on tour with her mother in Lebanon, one of the Oriental dancers in the show became ill and was unable to perform. Nadia demonstrated that she could perform in that style, and was allowed onstage to take the place of the ill dancer.

Nadia electrified the audience, and after that there was no stopping her. Soon she was appearing in Egyptian films, both as a dancer and an actress, which had the effect of rapidly spreading her fame, since Egyptian films were shown all over the Arab world. Her dynamic style and charisma set her apart from the other well-known dancers of the time.

In the 1956 black and white feature film *Zennuba*, for instance, nineteen-year-old Nadia dances in an Egyptian café as the Lebanese singing star Sabah sings the title song. Nadia's hair is shorter—a little less than shoulder length—and wavier than it would be at the height of her fame; she has the look of an ingénue. She wears a typical belly dance costume with striped bra and belt and a long, gauzy skirt. She weaves her dance among and around the people sitting at tables. It is an earthy Egyptian crowd of all ages; a young boy stares wide-eyed at her and a bearded old man holding a staff stands up and sings a line of the song. The people nod and smile; it is very much a communal entertainment. Nadia's dance is not unconventional but she dances with tremendous energy, moving quickly across the floor, utilizing all the open space in wide arcs. Now and then she executes a tight, precise, effortless spin. There is an astonishing lightness to her dancing; she moves like a bird flitting from tree branch to tree branch and smiles radiantly. Every move flows easily into the next and her offhand command and explosive energy is dazzling.

Touring the world, Nadia performed in Europe, the Far East, Latin America, even Canada, but never in the United States. She was more than simply a great performer, a star of the dance. She spoke, read and wrote seven languages, and became a dance scholar, researching the origins of the dance she loved. Her invitation to perform at the Baalbeck Festival in 1968 was recognition that Nadia had transcended the low status normally accorded female dancers in the Middle East and was presenting Oriental dance at such a high level that she had proved it could be respectable art worthy of the same regard accorded any other art.

In 1978 and again in 1981, Bobby Farrah arranged to bring Nadia to New York to give master-class workshops for dancers, at a time when American interest in belly dance had grown beyond the faddish attention of sophisticates who flocked to the Greek nightclubs on Eighth

Avenue in Manhattan in the late sixties and early seventies. Increasing numbers of women, many with extensive dance backgrounds, had become captivated by Oriental dance and were beginning to study authentic Middle Eastern dance in earnest. Many female dancers found that Oriental dance spoke to them in some fundamental way that no other dance style did. One musician on the scene noted the phenomenon succinctly: "Every woman I know who does this dance says it has deep meaning for her." Word of mouth proclaimed Nadia Gamal as the dancer who had most deeply accessed the potential of Oriental dance.

Unsurprisingly, a buzz of anticipation rippled through the Middle Eastern dance community when the news of the formidable Nadia Gamal's visit spread. When the great day arrived, the dance rehearsal studio in lower Manhattan was crowded with dancers, many of them Bobby Farrah's students but also many others eager to learn from the fabled Nadia Gamal. Besides the women crowding the open floor, a number of people sat on risers in the rear of the room. Bobby Farrah introduced her with eloquence and affection.

Nadia made her entrance, striding out majestically to the applause of the hundred or so dancers gathered in the studio. Some of them had worn belly-dance skirts or even full costumes while others wore leotards. Nadia wore a black leotard, with a belt of silver coins and a black sash hanging from her side. Silver high heel shoes completed her no-frills attire. Her long dark brown hair hung sleekly down to just below her shoulders. She had come to work.

She faced the expectant group ranged in front of her and immediately dashed the expectations of those who expected to indulge in mystique.

"If you are wearing a skirt," she announced in heavily accented but clear English, "I ask you to take it away or move to the side. For one reason, if you wear the skirt I cannot easily see behind you. And second thing, I cannot see properly what you do with the legs. If you can afford to take the skirt away, I can give you more remarks about what you do good and what you do bad."

She then began to demonstrate her first move—a shimmy—in different modes. Her movements were effortless and precise.

"Never do this," she said, demonstrating a broad, lazy, shimmy. "Because you get tired, you lose balance and . . . it looks ugly!"

Someone put a record on the record player and the haunting sound of a flute *taksim* (an improvised flute solo) pierced the hush.

Nadia stood facing the class.

"With one hand first . . ." she said, as she floated one arm serpent-like in the air. "And now the other one . . ." and she fluttered both arms in perfect, beautiful undulations like ripples on a pond. It was a seemingly simple movement yet no dancer in the room could duplicate her effortless mastery.

"Okay!" she said, her mouth a severe line as she clapped her hands together decisively, walked over to the record player and started the record again. The assembled dancers attempted to duplicate her movement. Then she stopped the record.

"All together, please!" she said, kneeling as she spoke and sitting back on her haunches. "Sit on your *poupou*!"

The music started up again. Nadia called out the cues for different movements with sharp exclamations as the music played, then she shut it off.

"The movement you are doing, we call it undulation. That is my way of dancing . . . undulation! You can see what I am doing with my body." She demonstrated, undulating as she stepped forward and back. "And the movements of the hands . . . no more than this high!" she said, holding her hands at shoulder height and demonstrating the whole sequence of moves she wanted the class to try.

"Okay?"

The class burst into spontaneous applause because of the quality of the movements she had just demonstrated. Her movements were sword-thrusts—quick, precise, and forceful.

"Okay!" she clapped her hands together sharply. "We do it once again because beautiful hands is very hard!" She dabbed the perspiration from her upper lip with a green silk handkerchief. "Get up and *then* work with your hands.

"Now, then, music! Usually sometimes we have the rhythm to give the body a rhythm." She snapped her fingers and clicked her heels on the floor in unison to demonstrate. "But where there is a melody, the violin goes 'hing, ungh, hing ungh' [she mimed playing a violin] and you go with the melody, the way he plays." Nadia undulated slowly up and down to an accordion solo, bouncing as it became more staccato.

"Okay, I want *this* from you!" She shook her hips in rapid-fire movement. The class murmured skeptically as she demonstrated the variations of the movements.

"Yes! Close your hands . . . push! . . . push! . . . push! . . . Can you feel it? It's better, no? The body is controlled by your hands. We have muscles here [she ran one hand along the fingers of the other hand] and we have feeling in our fingers. Perhaps you don't realize that. So don't keep your fingers like this (she held her fingers up clawlike) . . . it makes your body . . . tense! I will explain because you don't have an idea of how to control your body. Feet is just to try to give . . . how you say . . . support! If they are slipping, you cannot stand. But the movement is controlled by the hands . . . that gives you the movement."

She smiled as she demonstrated how a hand motion could flow into her body and stimulate a movement. Suddenly an abstract concept had become concrete reality.

"Now we go back to work! This time I will tell you nothing! Just dance!"

A few hours later, Nadia concluded the workshop. The assembled dancers broke into applause again. All concerned knew they had been in the presence of a master.

The analogy between blues and Oriental dance seemed especially relevant in the workshop. The individual stock blues phrases are relatively simple and have been played by endless thousands of musicians. But when you see one of the great bluesmen play those same strings of notes, it is like seeing them played for the first time. There is depth, power, and crackling energy in his playing. The same notes played by multitudes become monumental in his hands. It is all about phrasing.

So it was with Nadia Gamal. The shimmies and arm undulations and knee bends done by thousands of "belly dancers" were transformed by her into thunderclaps and lightning flashes, small explosions of energy and emotion. The workshop was a tantalizing glimpse of Nadia Gamal's charisma and power.

Bobby Farrah seized the opportunity of her presence to film an interview with her speaking about the dance. For the interview, Bobby and Nadia sat formally side by side, facing the camera on an overstuffed sofa against a backdrop of pillows embroidered with Berber designs. Bobby wore a gray striped *djellaba*, open at the throat and chest. Nadia sat formally, very erect on the couch, wearing a pale pink caftan with a jeweled silver Bedouin pendant hanging from her neck, her legs crossed and her hands clasped primly on her knee. Although her posture was formal, it was not stiff. Her body effortlessly assumed a statuelike pose, her swanlike neck suggesting elegance. Silver barrettes gleamed on each side of her long, dark hair, which was draped over her left shoulder and down her chest. Her plucked eyebrows were slender, dark arches over large brown eyes that were highlighted with turquoise eye shadow. A patina of rouge glowed on each porcelain cheek; her complexion was ivory with olive undertones. Her long, narrow nose bisected her perfect oval countenance, and her mouth was small, precise, and lipsticked. She looked serious, almost severe. At times a tinge of melancholy seemed to hover in her face, but now and then she smiled suddenly, like the sun breaking unexpectedly through storm clouds.

"When I went to Lebanon in 1971," Bobby began, "everyone told me I had to see you . . . 'you must see Nadia!' they said." Nadia's expression changed only slightly when he said this, becoming somewhat diffident, as if to distance herself from the compliment.

"Oriental dance is one of the most expressive dances," she began pedantically, perhaps to take the conversation out of the personal realm. "It is an expression dance. We express everything we know and feel. Originally it was in big palaces for kings and pashas . . . there were also many folk dances, village dances, primitive dances. Then there was Oriental dance onstage in theaters and nightclubs. It is not a sex dance! It is one of the oldest dances in the world and I think you have to be proud of it and make it beautiful."

"Nadia is the only Oriental dancer to do 'floorwork' in the Middle East," Bobby interjected, as if to lead her into more personal ground. Floorwork involves a series of dramatic movements executed by the dancer while literally reclining on the floor, often to a *taksim* (solo instrumental improvisation). With floorwork there is always the potential for the dancer to appear to be overly sexual in her presentation, if she does not execute properly. Thus, in the Middle East it was frowned upon.

"Bobby . . ." Nadia began, then smiled sheepishly. "Usually when I come to America I call him Bobby but when in Beirut I call him Ibrahim."

She chuckled and dipped her head in mirth.

"Bobby, I am not the only one because I learned it from someone else. But others may not know how to do it properly. Oriental dance is something very delicate. You can be very class or very vulgar. They won't allow vulgar in my country. I can do it because they never told me I can't!"

As she said this, she smiled proudly, even mischievously, knowingly. Clearly she was in a class by herself.

"Traditional dancers were storytellers," Bobby said. "It is the story of your life."

Nadia nodded somberly in agreement as he spoke.

"It's very ancient," she said. Her big brown eyes stared reflectively into space, focused on a far-off vision as she spoke. Her research had led her to trace the origin of the dance to the ancient Phoenicians, for whom it was an integral part of certain rituals.

"At one time this dance was done when a woman was sacrificed. Then, when Islamic [peoples] went to make war, then the men came back from war, the women served them food and drink and danced for them to make them happy . . . it's very old."

Her eyes widened and she moved her head from side to side, as if in wonder.

"It gives hope," she added contemplatively. "It's worth fighting for."

Now she was smiling easily. She was relaxing, opening up, animated by her love for the dance and the joy it gave her, as well as her determination to express its importance. It had been a long battle for respectability, given common Middle Eastern attitudes that in some places regarded dancers as little better than prostitutes. Ironically, female entertainers were in many ways the freest women in the Middle East, but they paid a price for that freedom.

"La Meri said 'you must have good technique so the body does not get in the way of the soul!' Oriental dance is for woman. Men dance folk dances, village dances. [In Oriental dance] a woman expresses herself about love, the feeling and . . . [she smiled demurely without finishing the thought].

"Wherever I went in Lebanon, dance was part of every event," Bobby noted. One of the consistently acceptable occasions for Oriental dancers in the Middle East had been at weddings, though often for the female guests only. Nadia nodded as he spoke, smiling as a flower blooms. As she spoke of dancing at a wedding, her gaze softened and the echo of wedding joy played on her face. But then she reverted to a more formal, instructional mode. For her, imparting knowledge about the dance was imperative—her life's mission.

"There is a difference between nightclub and stage," she said. "In the clubs you have many people around and you have to give them something to feel good and not to suffer. But stage is a big difference for Oriental dance. You can make a story . . . like 1001 Nights. A slave begging for forgiveness, for example. It is an expression dance. [For this reason] working with your own musicians is very important . . . using tape, I am against this!"

That last statement she delivered sharply. She frequently expressed herself absolutely and definitively. One of Nadia's greatest talents was her extraordinary musical sense. Not only did she have great sensitivity to nuances in the music being played for her dance performances but she demonstrated a great ability to translate those nuances into her dance.

"It is one of the oldest dances in the world. To prove it, we must study!"

She raised her hand for emphasis and her impeccably polished pink nails gleamed in the light. Dedication, discipline, and study were recurring themes with Nadia. Her conception of true artistry involved the necessity of being a perpetual student.

"I didn't yet achieve what I want," she mused. "I have so much more to learn!"

Here she smiled self-effacingly, at the same time trying to suppress the smile in order to maintain a solemn mien. She was modest, even humble about her skill. When asked by an interviewer for Arabesque magazine how she would rate herself as a dancer on a scale of 1 to 10, she said, "I would give myself the number 3."[4]

In her reminiscence "I Remember Nadia," the celebrated dancer Suhaila Salimpour recounted meeting Nadia at the workshop when she was a young girl. After the workshop, she had managed to run backstage and into Nadia's dressing room before Nadia reached it. Seeing the wide-eyed young girl in her dressing room, Nadia had said she could stay. As she removed her make-up, Nadia spoke to the young, would-be dancer.

"How old are you?"

"Fourteen," Suhaila answered. "But I first saw you when I was nine in the movie my uncle Bobby has of you."

"Do you know why I dance the way I do?" Nadia asked her. "Because I have suffered! I have gone through divorce, death, a lot of heartache . . . that's the art. You can show anyone a step, but not a soul. Always remember the music!"[5]

Nadia was a passionate woman whose determination and stubbornness were a product of love. She gave herself wholly and absolutely to the dance. She was a classic "all or nothing" personality. When she came to New York for the workshop, she stayed with dancer, teacher, and scholar Phyllis Saretta, known professionally in the dance world as Phaedra. Nadia was in an agitated mood. She was at odds with her husband at the time, a sheik who was a member of the royal family of Saudi Arabia. He had sent her a diamond ring as a peace offering; she expressed her displeasure by flushing it down the toilet. For such a woman, how would it be possible to perform in the United States when conditions were not right? During one of her visits, the Lebanese civil war had broken out. It was so upsetting to her that any thought of performing was unthinkable. On another occasion Bobby took her to the best Middle Eastern nightclubs in New York. Nadia had reacted with disdain. "If I came to these clubs it would take me thirty seconds to walk out," she had said.[6] The New York clubs reminded her of the waterfront dives in Egypt—places of ill repute. Years passed without Nadia performing in the States, even as her legendary status grew.

So it was no surprise that when the night of the Town Hall concert arrived, the theater was packed with an audience of Arab-Americans, especially many Lebanese, aficionados of Middle Eastern dance and culture, as well as dancers and musicians. Bobby's Near Eastern Dance Ensemble performed several numbers, very much in a cultural mode, their costumes evoking different Arab and Bedouin traditional dress. They were backed by an aggregation of some of New York's finest Middle Eastern musicians, sitting in a line of chairs onstage. Among them were oud/violinist player Simon Shaheen, percussionist Hanna

Mirhige, and other stalwarts of the Middle Eastern musical community. Anticipation for the special guest of the evening, Nadia Gamal, was building, however.

At long last Nadia was announced, and the musicians launched into a rollicking groove. The music intensified; still she did not appear. In Oriental dance, the entrance of the dancer is a statement in itself. Suddenly she strode majestically out onto the broad Town Hall stage and executed a triumphant spin. She faced the audience, threw her arms skyward, and flipped her hip toward the audience, like a proclamation, uttering a preemptory cry. The forceful precision of that simple movement generated a shock wave that seemed to throw the audience back in their seats. She was wearing silver high-heeled shoes, gold paneled skirt, and a veil draped around her neck and down her back, like a stole. Shimmying, turning this way and that, advancing and retreating, she suddenly whipped her head forward and back repeatedly amidst dramatic thrusts of hands and shoulders, her arms swirling in the air.

Abruptly she gestured, stopping the music, and began to remonstrate with the oud player. She picked up a wooden cane with a curved handle, a signature prop used in a particular traditional dance, and strode haughtily back and forth across the stage, waggling her hips reprovingly. The violin played a *taksim,* an impressionistic improvisation, and Nadia replicated the rising and falling melody with circular hip motions. Then she slammed the end of the cane down on the stage as a signal for the *taksim* to end. The orchestra kicked in and she twirled the cane in the air, then balanced it on her head as she moved forward and back, shimmying her shoulders all the while. Grabbing the cane off her head, she whacked it on the stage to punctuate the rhythm. Coquettish flips of her hips dissolved into rapid vibrations. She tossed the cane away dismissively, as though rejecting an unwelcome suitor, and posed statuelike for many seconds. Then she suddenly jabbed her finger at the orchestra and they began playing in earnest, increasing the tempo. The audience spontaneously began to clap to the rhythm, caught up by the rising energy of the music and the force generated by Nadia's movements; Nadia began to prance, shaking her hips first slowly, then more rapidly, teasing the audience with an explosion to come. Her movements were controlling the rhythm, sweeping the musicians and the audience into her vortex. As she vibrated, she lowered herself to the floor and rose up again. She looked down, raised her hands, and sped up her hip vibration, smiling delightedly as if observing someone else dancing. Her dance was now a joyous celebration of life itself. Nadia sashayed over to Hanna Mirhige on percussion and smacked her hands together, demanding more energy, more tempo. The orchestra sped up and she whirled into a climax. The audience jumped up clapping and cheering. She strode offstage as the band continued playing. But she was not finished.

Moments later Nadia re-appeared, wearing a black *djellaba* slit up the sides to her hips, carrying a large circular basket on her head as she strode forward in her high heels. She enacted a tableau—"the flower seller"—telling the story of a young girl selling flowers in the marketplace. With the basket balanced on her head she shimmied back and forth with unspeakable grace, her long dark hair trailing after her. Then she stood on one foot and revolved, maintaining the shimmy, the basket of flowers perched on her head all the while. Taking the basket off her head with both hands, she brought it down in front of her, proffering it, a picture of girlish innocence. She set the basket down in front of her, ululated a trilling high note, and jumped into an exuberant frenzy of joyous, skipping steps, playing finger cymbals as she moved. It was a village girl's dance of liberation.

The organ began playing a *taksim* and Nadia gathered up the flowers from the basket, tossing them into the audience and smiling a smile of benediction. Then she uttered an explosive expostulation: "heeh!" and the crowd erupted into rhythmic clapping as Nadia picked up the rhythm with an insistent hip-shake. Playfully, she mimed a fortune teller prophesying, then began clapping her hands together exuberantly, exhorting the crowd. She interrupted the rhythm, teasing the audience with abbreviated hip motions, stopping and starting, smiling mischievously, gesturing invitingly to the audience. She gestured with her hands as though asking for money, portraying a beggar, and stuffing imaginary bills into her belt. Abruptly she spun around and began a final volcanic eruption of hand and hip motions, bringing her performance to a shuddering climax as the crowd exploded again with shouts and wild applause. Nadia smiled radiantly and extended her hand to the musicians, inviting the audience to salute them.

Nadia's performance at Town Hall presented Oriental dance as a dance of life, a vehicle to enact human dramas and express elemental passions: life and love; suffering and death; longing and loss; birth and rebirth. Above all it was a manifestation of the essential universal life force and the miracle of creation.

Nadia and other Oriental dancers fought so hard to counteract the image of their dance as a dance of sexual stimulation that they often downplayed the natural expression of sensuality that was an aspect of the dance. Of course, this sensuality was only one aspect of the dance, not its raison d'etre. Nadia herself had said that, insofar as woman is the physical embodiment of the creation of new life, it is a preeminently female dance—a female body animated by a female spirit transmitting elemental life rhythms. Certainly one narrative danced by Oriental dancers is a narrative of seduction, along with narratives of longing, passion, despair, and love in its purest form. But all of these narratives are animated by a fundamental life force, amplified by the rhythms of the music. Very few dancers have been able to dance that life force as well as Nadia Gamal nor portray various narratives with as much dramatic force. The astonishing impact of her dancing that night at Town Hall, her passion and radiant spirit, made an indelible impression on all who witnessed it. And then she was gone, never to return.

A hallmark of Nadia's dancing was her ability to imbue a pivotal moment of her dance with maximum dramatic force through a single movement. Dancer and professor Andrea Deagon recalled seeing a 1984 broadcast of Nadia Gamal performance on Beirut television in which Nadia portrayed a bride who, on the eve of her wedding, was possessed by a demon, exorcised it, and returned to normal life. "You could see the very moment in which the demon took possession in her expression and body language," she wrote. "It was very effective drama."[7]

Nadia's dramatic ability was evidence that she was an accomplished actress as well as dancer; she blended the two abilities in her art. Often there was a moment in her dance when a movement or gesture by Nadia had profound impact; time seems momentarily to stop at these moments, and you are captured by an image of great portent. In the 1984 broadcast she incorporated movements from the *zar* dance, a folkloric dance in which the dancer attains a trance through which she rids herself of an evil spirit. It was a telling example of Nadia's ability to draw on the entire range of Middle Eastern dances in order attain the highest level of expressiveness.

As the years passed, the mental images of Nadia's dancing that night began to take on a dreamlike quality. More and more the memory seemed only a teasing hint of the fiery spirit and spectacular energy of her dancing. What would be the effect in a more intimate venue? However, in 1990 the news came that Nadia had died from pneumonia while in the hospital for treatment of cancer, at the relatively young age of fifty-three. She had continued to dance until the end and had brought to fruition her long-standing dream of starting a dance school.

Beyond the memories of those who saw her perform, very little evidence of her greatness has been preserved. The one full Nadia Gamal performance available on video was filmed in a Beirut nightclub late in her career, around 1986. Titled *The Legend*, it presents a vibrant performance in the round; but the camera work is often distracting, and it captures her primarily in the mode of entertainer. Bobby Farrah released one of the film clips he had shot of her in Lebanon in a collection titled *Rare Glimpses*, which also includes rare footage Thomas Edison shot of the dancer Fatima in 1896. Nadia's segment features an Oriental dance routine with casually spectacular technique (although with more formal, theatrical choreography). Also available on video is a feature film, *Mawwal*, starring Sabah and Nadia, who dances in a short theatrical dance scene, as well as playing a role in the film. None of these recorded performances captures the intensity of her appearance at Town Hall.

In 2006 I happened to see a review of the *Rare Glimpses* video and noted that it was obtainable from Phyllis Saretta, whose name I remembered from the masthead of *Arabesque* magazine (and from her work with Bobby's troupe). Phyllis had been Bobby's longtime collaborator as well as life partner, and was custodian of his vast collection of manuscripts, films, photographs, and recordings after his death in 1998. When I contacted her she told me of some unreleased film clips of Nadia dancing, shot at the same time as the footage included in the *Rare Glimpses* video. When I explained my interest in Nadia, she graciously granted my request to see it. I arranged for a viewing at a video production company in Manhattan that could properly handle such rare material. They set us up in a viewing lounge with a monitor and two large sofas. As I cued up the footage Bobby had shot of Nadia over thirty years earlier, I wondered how many people had ever seen the footage. I thought of the thousands who would have given a lot to see it. And I wondered whether any of the performances would reveal a new side of Nadia's artistry.

"She does three dances," Phyllis said. "One is Bedouin, one is *baladi* [traditional rural] style, and the last one is an Oriental dance."

The screen suddenly filled with the image of Nadia standing with her back to the camera. She gazes coquettishly over her shoulder. She wears a long indigo and black *djellaba*-like garment, slit up the sides to the hips—a theatrical version of a Bedouin woman's dress. Nadia never felt it necessary or appropriate to present an exactly authentic costume of Bedouin or any other ethnic group; her stage costumes drew on authentic cultural elements but adapted them to theatrical purpose. She turns her head rapidly from front to back.

I noted that she was dancing barefoot; in the Middle East it was most common for Oriental dancers to dance in high-heeled shoes. Nadia was well-known for dancing in heels, which she felt imparted a felicitous posture for Oriental dance.

"Hey, she's dancing barefoot!" I exclaimed.

"No, Nadia never danced barefoot," Phyllis said. "She said it was because she didn't want her audience to see her dirty feet. But I think it really was because she was short!"

When her feet become visible again in the video, it is clear that her feet indeed are bare.

"Omigod! You're right!" Phyllis exclaimed, peering closer at the monitor screen. "I never noticed that before!"

It was a revelation that the Grande Dame of Oriental dance, whose standards and proscriptions were well-known, on this one occasion at least broke her own rule. Perhaps she had made an exception for this privately made film, at least for the segment in which she was depicting a Bedouin woman. In any case, her dancing in this segment, though expert, is less dramatic than usual, no doubt in keeping with the reality of how a Bedouin woman would dance.

In the next segment Nadia appears in folkloric costume with a scarf in her hair; jewels are sewn into the scarf, and she wears a belt with large, coinlike jewelry. Her dancing in this segment is playful, even saucy, as if representing a village girl's delight in her newly blooming womanhood. She whips her hair back and forth and acts out the village girl's story.

In the final segment, Nadia appears in typical Oriental dance costume. When she begins to dance it is not with the contained energy of the Bedouin woman or the gay dance of the village girl, nor even with the celebratory attitude of a wedding dancer. It is the dance of the Oriental dancer, the dance for returned warriors, the dance for emirs and pashas, the ancient storytelling dance of the Ur-dancer.

The segment opens with Nadia standing in shadow, silhouetted against a pale pink background. She wears a dark green sequined cabaret costume with bands of pink, a paneled skirt with panels in front and back and her legs exposed almost to her hips. The broad belt of the skirt glitters with rows of silver and pink tassels. She wears a heavily sequined bra with a bunch of pink and silver tassels hanging like a bouquet down the middle of her chest. A heavy silver chain and brooch is draped from her neck down to her navel. A veil loops around her neck and hangs down her back on both sides, framing her long dark hair streaming down the middle of her back. Fine black mesh, nearly invisible, variegates her pale torso. Silver bracelets adorn her upper arms. Black high-heeled shoes complete her costume.

Nadia stands statuelike against the pale dawn of the backdrop, a petite, slender vision of alabaster. Dramatically she grabs the veil and raises her arms, spreading it like angel wings, as one ready to ascend to heaven. Abruptly she explodes into a rapid hip-shimmy, spinning and turning from side to side, smiling invitingly as though offering something she knows her unseen audience will like. She executes a rapid yet extended whirl; she is announcing herself. But then she turns serious, looking straight at her audience and throwing her head to the side with an anguished expression—the look of someone whose passion has gone unfulfilled.

The musicians play a *taksim*, a plaintive fiddle and slow *dumbeg* beats accented with a pizzicato cello. Nadia twists her body in arcs of longing. She twitches and shivers as though caught in the throes of uncontrollable passion. Then her expression hardens, her eyes narrow, and her mouth compresses assertively—as though making ready to show her audience something, to make them feel her passion. She arches and twists in a little drama of aching need. All of a sudden she jumps up into a rapid shimmy, and just as suddenly breaks it off. Slowly, she arches back, into an impossibly deep backbend, until her hair touches the floor. As she does so she crosses her arms across her chest, a gesture of modesty. She stares at her audience, her head upside-down, as she holds the deep back bend.

Abruptly, yet with astonishing grace, she falls to the floor, collapsing in a heap on her back, her legs bent double beneath her and her hair spread halo-like on the floor. She moves her arms in a supplicating manner, inviting, seducing, hugging herself, her eyes half closed as she surrenders to desire— one of those profound movements Nadia employed for maximum dramatic effect.

The *dumbeg* kicks into a rapid drumbeat, and she begins to rise, slow undulations morphing into rapid pelvic and hip vibrations. She rises gracefully and stretches toward the sky, breaking into a rambunctious hip-shake that she then ratchets down to slow, precise shimmies. She arches her eyebrows and holds her head high, confidently, even haughtily, a queen of dance who knows she has her audience in her thrall. Then she smiles saucily, cutting her eyes coquettishly as she undulates to the rhythm, slowly building up the momentum. She spins and falls to the floor, her hands describing mysterious intertwined circles. She jumps into a Turkish step of farewell; she spins and throws her head back and her hands to the sky in a final posture of triumph.

Nadia's Oriental dance was mesmerizing and powerful. She was by turns a temptress, a lover, a wife, a mother, and ultimately the physical embodiment of female power. It is hard to imagine anyone taking his or her eyes off Nadia in full flight. The amazing thing was that the torrent of physical expression had been choreographed. Nadia did not believe in spontaneous improvisation. Her dancing always unfolded in a logical progression. In spite of that, her dancing appeared entirely natural and vibrant. Its power seemed to be the power of an unfiltered outpouring of feeling. Like any great actress, she was able to inhabit, emotionally and spiritually, the narrative she danced, and the strength of her technique and the power of her execution made her dance come powerfully alive. She had tremendous focus and discipline; she disciplined herself to work within the structure of her choreography. Nadia choreographed everything because she was so passionately dedicated to perfection. Her commitment to Oriental dance was unconditional. She danced with the fierce passion of a possessive lover, in love with a pure vision of the dance itself. It was her riposte to those who would reduce and stereotype the dance to a dance of sexual stimulation.

I thought of Flaubert who, in the grip of an Orientalist fever in 1845, had traveled up the Nile to find the dancers exiled from Cairo by the king. There he found Kuchek Hanem, a fabled dancer with whom he dallied for months, mesmerized by her charms and her "Dance of the Bee." It is an open question whether he truly saw beyond the immediate gratification of his lust and a romanticized indulgence in exotica forbidden by his own culture. On one occasion he returned after having traveled for some time and found Kuchek Hanem away. Another dancer, a Nubian woman, declared to Flaubert: "Kuchek Hanem is not a dancer."[8] And she proceeded to demonstrate her superior dancing.

It is no longer possible to find the *ghawazee* gypsy dancers high up the Nile. Islamic fundamentalists effectively eliminated their livelihood by threatening violence against those who would employ dancers at weddings or other celebrations, but the dancers were disappearing even before that happened. In Cairo the number of dancers has dwindled, and the few remaining famous dancers often travel with bodyguards in light of the fundamentalist threat. Kuchek Hanem is long gone. Now Nadia Gamal is gone and another like her may never come again. She was formed in a time and place that has disappeared. She dances on in the dreams of those who saw her.

In the end, it may be Flaubert, wrongheaded though he may have been, whose words best convey the impact created by the likes of Nadia Gamal. It is the dialogue Flaubert created for his version of the Queen of Sheba, words one can easily imagine Nadia Gamal uttering: "I am not a woman. I am the world!"[9]

Notes

Nina Simone: The High Priestess of Soul

1. "Little Girl Blue." *Nina Simone Live at Montreux*, DVD (2005; New York, NY; Eagle Eye Media).

2. Gene Taylor. "Why? (The King Of Love Is Dead)." 1968, EMI Grove Park Music and Ninandy Music, all rights controlled by EMI Grove Park Music (publishing) and Alfred Publishing (print). All rights reserved. Used by permission from Alfred Publishing Co., Inc.

3. *Ibid.*

4. Nina Simone with Stephen Cleary. *The Autobiography of Nina Simone* (Cambridge, MA: Da Capo Press, 1993), 89.

5. Nina Simone. "Mississippi Goddam." WB Music c/o Warner Chappell, all rights controlled by WB Music (publishing) and Alfred Publishing (print). All rights reserved. Used by permission.

6. Simone with Cleary, 90.

7. Stanley Wise interview. *The Legend*, DVD, directed by Frank Lords (Quantum Leap, 1999).

8. Simone with Cleary, 90.

9. *Ibid.*, 24.

10. *Ibid.*, 24.

11. *Ibid.*, 26.

12. An untitled poem written by Nina Simone at age twelve, originally published on the back of the LP jacket of her album *Here Comes the Sun* (RCA). Reprinted by permission of the Nina Simone estate.

13. *Ibid.*, 31.

14. Prologue. *The Legend*, DVD.

15. Simone with Cleary, 41.

16. *Ibid.*, 42–43.

17. Vladimir Sokhaloff interview. *The Legend*, DVD.

18. Simone with Cleary, 42–43.

19. *Ibid.*, 50.

20. "Return Home." *Nina Simone at Town Hall*, CD (EMI 7243 4 73215 2 8), 2005.

21. Simone with Cleary, 93.

22. Backstage. *The Legend.* DVD.

23. *Ibid.*

24. *Ibid.*

25. Simone with Cleary, 41.

26. Art D'Lugoff interview. *The Legend,* DVD.

27. Sylvia Hampton with David Nathan, *Nina Simone: Break It Down and All Hand Out* (London: Sanctuary, 2004), 126–27.

28. *Ibid.,* 11.

29. Nostalgia. *The Legend,* DVD.

30. Homecoming. *Ibid.*

31. Simone with Cleary, 175–76.

32. Epilogue. *The Legend,* DVD.

33. God, God, God. *Live At Ronnie Scott's,* DVD, directed by Stephen Cleary and Rod Lemkin (1985, London, Waldham Films).

Sun Ra: Composer from Saturn

1. "My Mystery Is Endless." *Sun Ra: A Joyful Noise,* DVD, directed by Robert Mugge, (1989, New York, Winstar Home Entertainment).

2. "Mythocracy." *Ibid.*

3. Marshall Allen interview. *Brother from Another Planet,* directed by Don Letts (BBC4 broadcast, Oct. 28, 2005).

4. Untitled poem from the back cover of *The Heliocentric Worlds of Sun Ra Vol. 2* (ESP Disk LP-107, 1966).

5. John F. Szwed. *Space Is The Place: The Life And Times Of Sun Ra"* (New York: Pantheon, 1997), 25.

6. *Ibid.,* 219.

7. *Ibid.,* 218.

8. June Tyson is reported on a number of occasions to have stated that when she was performing with Sun Ra she was an angel or celestial being; for instance, see Mike Walsh, "Sun Ra: Stranger from Outer Space," http://www.missioncreep.com/html.

9. Sun Ra. "Astro-Black." Published by Enterplanetary Koncepts.

10. Tam Fiofori. "Sun Ra's Space Odyssey." *Down Beat* 14 May 1970: 16.

11. Michael Ray interview. *Brother from Another Planet.*

12. Szwed, 7.

13. Michael Ray interview. *Brother from Another Planet.*

14. Szwed, 7.

15. "Mythocracy." *Sun Ra: A Joyful Noise.*

16. Sun Ra et al. "An Interview with Sun Ra" (1990, Slought Foundation Online

Content, www.slought.org). Interview conducted by Francis Davis in Philadelphia at Sun Ra's house, January 19, 1990.

17. Yahya Abdul Majid. *Brother from Another Planet.*

18. "Sun Ra Interviewed." *Sun Ra: Life at the Palomino*, DVD, Transparency, 2005.

19. Sun Ra et al. "An Interview with Sun Ra."

20. Szwed, 373.

Fela Anikulapo-Kuti: The Afrobeat Rebel

1. Carlos Moore. *Fela Fela: This Bitch of a Life* (London: Allison and Busby, 1982), 55–59.

2. Fela Anikulapo-Kuti. "Trouble Sleep Yanga Wake Am." Published by Cherry River Music and EMI Music.

3. Moore, 135.

4. Rikki Stein. "A Remembrance." *The Observer* 12 Aug. 2007: 66.

Bob Marley: The Reggae Shaman

1. Bob Marley. "Concrete Jungle." Published by Spirit Music Group. Print rights administered by Hal Leonard Music.

2. Bob Marley. "Small Axe." Published by Spirit Music Group. Print rights administered by Hal Leonard Music.

3. Timothy White. *Catch a Fire: The Life of Bob Marley* (New York: Henry Holt, 1983), 64.

4. *Ibid.*

5. Stephen Davis. *Bob Marley* (London: Arthur Baker, 1983), 162.

6. Noted Marley expert Roger Steffens gave me this estimate based on numerous accounts he had heard from people who were present.

7. Bob Marley. "Trench Town Rock." Published by Spirit Music Group. Print rights administered by Hal Leonard Music.

8. Vincent Ford and Rita Marley. "Crazy Baldhead." Published by Spirit Music Group. Print rights administered by Hal Leonard Music.

9. Bob Marley. "War." Published by Spirit Music Group. Print rights administered by Hal Leonard Music.

10. Bob Marley. "Exodus." Published by Spirit Music Group. Print rights administered by Hal Leonard Music.

11. Bob Marley. "Redemption Song." Published by Spirit Music Group. Print rights administered by Hal Leonard Music.

Augustus Pablo: Composer of Dreams

1. Lol Bell-Brown. *Augustus Pablo: Original Rocker* (Oxford, UK: Trax on Wax, 2001), 2.

2. *Ibid.*, 60.

3. *Ibid.*, 62.

4. Telephone interview with Robbie Shakespeare.

5. Pablo interviewed by David Dorrell. "BPM at the Dub Club," directed by Andrew Nichols (1993, Granada Television, A Music Box Production).

6. Telephone interview with Robbie Shakespeare.

7. Interview with Joan Higgins.

8. *Ibid.*

9. *Ibid.*

10. Robert Palmer. "Ringing Changes on Jamaica Reggae." *New York Times* 26 Apr. 1981: 21.

11. Jim Miller. "Master of the Melodica." *Newsweek* 19 Oct., 1981: 94.

12. Augustus Pablo. Liner notes for *Earth's Rightful Ruler*, CD (Message/Shanachie Entertainment, PBL 1005, 1983).

13. Interview with Joan Higgins.

14. Augustus Pablo. *Blowing with the Wind*, CD (Shanachie SH 43076, 1990).

15. Telephone interview with Neil Fraser a/k/a the Mad Professor.

The Neville Brothers: First Family of Groove

1. Jabo Starks interview by Jim Payne. Posted at www.funkystuff.com/starksinterview/htm. Jabo Starks, one of the key drummers for James Brown, stated that he "got a lot of stuff" from New Orleans drummers and called Clyde Stubblefield, another important James Brown drummer, "closer to a New Orleans drummer than anything else." A third James Brown drummer, Clayton Fillyau, states that it was New Orleans artist Huey "Piano" Smith and the Clowns who created funk.

2. Joseph Modeliste, Arthur Neville, Leo Nocentelli, George Porter. "Hey Pocky A-Way." Published by Bug Music/Bugaloo Music/Cabbage Alley Music.

3. Art, Aaron, Charles, and Cyril Neville, and David Ritz. *The Brothers Neville* (Cambridge, MA: Da Capo, 2000), 108.

4. Bunny Matthews. "Art Neville" (interview). *Wavelength* Feb. 2003: 30.

5. Jerry Karp. "Cyril Neville." *Wavelength* May 1986: 30.

6. *The Brothers Neville*, 18.

7. *Ibid.*, 16.

8. *Ibid.*, 11.

9. Matthews. "Art Neville," 44.

10. "Cyril Neville Talks About Big Chief Jolly." Video clip, Culture Exchange

Project/Living Folklore Project. 2004. www.culturecollective.org. Posted on YouTube.

11. John Sinclair. "The Nevilles Come Home." *Wavelength* May 1989: 47.

Yabby You: The Jesus Dread

1. DJ Nouns, Pady, Slim Jah. "Yabby You Live in 2005." Translation from the original French review posted at articles.dubroom.org/233/htm. Review of Yabby You's performance at the JASound Festival in Bagnols Keze, France, August 6, 2005. Originally posted at www.riddimkilla.com.

2. *Ibid.*

3. *Ibid.*

4. Author unknown; it may be King Sounds. Taken from the liner notes of Vivian Jackson, *Deliver Me from My Enemies*, LP (Vivian Jackson, 1977).

5. Vivian Jackson. "Deliver Me from My Enemies." Vivian Jackson Music/Westbury Music.

6. Vivian Jackson. "Conquering Lion." Vivian Jackson Music/Westbury Music.

7. Vivian Jackson. "Anti-Christ." Vivian Jackson Music/Westbury Music.

8. Steve Barrow. Liner notes from Yabby You, *Deliver Me from My Enemies*, CD (Blood & Fire, 2006).

9. Vivian Jackson. "Fire Dey A Mus Mus Tail." Vivian Jackson Music/Westbury Music.

10. Vivian Jackson. "Sat Up on the Gully Bank." Vivian Jackson Music/Westbury Music.

11. Steve Barrow. Liner notes from Yabby You, *Jesus Dread (1972–1977)*, CD (Blood & Fire, 1997).

12. Robert Christgau. *Christgau's Record Guide: The 80's* (New York: Pantheon, 1990).

13. Vivian Jackson. "Give Thanks and Praise." Vivian Jackson Music/Westbury Music.

14. Steve Barrow. Liner notes from Yabby You, *King Tubby's Prophecy of Dub*, CD (Blood & Fire, 1995).

Nadia Gamal: The Oriental Dance Diva

1. A number of secondary sources attribute this quotation to Rumi, but I have not been able confirm it with a primary source.

2. Donna Carlton. *Looking For Little Egypt* (Bloomington, IN: IDD, 1994), ix–x, 16–17.

3. *Ibid*, 15.

4. Glenna Batson. "Nadia Gamal: Interview with the Artist." *Arabesque* vol. 11, no. 2: 9.

5. *Ibid.*, 12.

6. Suhaila Salimpour. "I Remember Nadia." www.therealsuhaila.com/articles.

7. Andrea Deagon. "Dancing the Eternal Image: Visual and Narrative Archetypes." people.uncw.edu/deagona/raqs/articles.htm.

8. Gustave Flaubert. *Flaubert In Egypt.* Translated by Francis Steegmuller (New York: Penguin, 1972), 154.

9. Gustave Flaubert. *The Temptation of Saint Anthony* (New York: Grosset & Dunlap, n.d.), 42.

Bibliography

Books

Barrow, Steve, and Peter Dalton. *The Rough Guide To Reggae.* London: Rough Guides, 2001.

Bell-Brown, Lol. *Augustus Pablo: Original Rocker.* Oxford, UK: Trax on Wax, 2001.

Carlton, Donna, *Looking For Little Egypt,* (Bloomington, IND, IDD Books, 1994).

Christgau, Robert. *Christgau's Record Guide: The 80's.* New York: Pantheon, 1990.

Corbett, John, ed. *The Wisdom of Sun Ra.* Chicago: Whitewalls, 2006.

Davis, Stephen. *Bob Marley.* London: Arthur Baker, 1983.

Flaubert, Gustave. *Flaubert in Egypt.* New York: Penguin, 1996.

Flaubert, Gustave. *The Temptation of St. Anthony.* New York: Grosset and Dunlap, no date.

Garland, Phyl. *The Sound of Soul.* (New York: Pocket Books, 1971.

Hampton, Sylvia, with David Nathan. *Nina Simone: Break Down and Let It All Hang Out.* London: Sanctuary, 2004.

Marley, Rita, with Hettie Jones. *No Woman No Cry: My Life with Bob Marley.* New York: Hyperion, 2004.

Moore, Carlos *Fela Fela: This Bitch of a Life.* London: Allison and Busby, 1982.

Neville, Art, Aaron, Charles, and Cyril, and David Ritz. *The Brothers Neville.* Cambridge, MA: Da Capo, 2000.

Nieuwkierk, Karin. *A Trade Like Any Other: Singers and Dancers in Egypt.* Austin: University of Texas Press, 1995.

Schoonmaker, Trevor, ed. *Black President: The Art and Legacy of Fela Anikulapo-Kuti.* New York: Palgrave Macmillan, 2003.

Simone, Nina, with Stephen Cleary. *The Autobiography of Nina Simone.* Cambridge, MA: Da Capo, 1993.

Steffens, Roger, with Leroy Pierce. *Bob Marley and the Wailers: The Definitive Discography.* Cambridge, MA: Rounder Books, 2005.

Ra, Sun. *Collected Works Vol. 1: Immersion Equation.* Chandler, AZ: Phaelos, 2005.

Szwed, John F. *Space Is the Place: The Life and Times of Sun Ra.* New York: Pantheon, 1997.

Taylor, Arthur *Notes and Tones: Musician to Musician Interviews*. Cambridge, MA: Da Capo, 1993.

Taylor, Don. *Marley and Me*. New York: Barricade, 1995.

Veal, Michael. *Fela: The Life and Times of an African Musical Icon*. Philadelphia: Temple University Press, 2000.

White, Timothy. *Catch a Fire: The Life of Bob Marley—The Definitive Edition*. New York: Henry Holt, 1998.

Periodicals

Antar, Elias. "La Danse du Ventre." *Saudi Aramco World* Sept./Oct. 1971.

Batson, Glenna. "Nadia Gamal: Interview with the Artist I." *Arabesque* vol. 1, no. 5.

Batson, Glenna. "Nadia Gamal: Interview with the Artist II." *Arabesque* vol. 1, no. 6.

Batson, Glenna. "Nadia Gamal: Interview with the Artist III." *Arabesque* vol. 2, no. 1.

Batson, Glenna. "Nadia Gamal: Interview with the Artist IV." *Arabesque* vol. 2, no. 2.

Bodley, Ivan. "Orchid in the Storm." *Wavelength* Apr. 1986.

Brock, Jeremy. "The Indians." *Wavelength* Mar. 1981.

"The Brothers Keep the Faith." *Wavelength* Sept. 1990.

Fry, Macon. "Aaron Neville." *Wavelength* May 1985.

Gayle, Carl. "De Baldhead Bridge Is Burning Down." *Black Music* Dec. 1997.

Grass, Randall. "Heartbeat Dub Straight Ahead." *Village Voice* 17–23 Dec. 1980.

Grass, Randall. "Fela Anikulapo-Kuti: Art of the Afrobeat Rebel." *Drama Review* Spring 1986.

Grass, Randall. "Fela Anikulapo-Kuti, Still Suffering." *Reggae and African Beat* Dec. 1984.

Grass, Randall. "Fela Freed." *Spin* July 1986.

Grass, Randall. "Fela: Rebel on Ice." *Spin* May 1985.

Grass, Randall. "Fela: Return of the Afrobeat Rebel." *Musician* Oct. 1983.

Gunn, Barbara. "The Neville Brothers." *Wavelength* May 1981.

Karp, Jeremy. "Cyril Neville." *Wavelength* May 1986.

Kaslow, Andy, and Bunny Matthews. "The Indians." *Wavelength* Feb. 1981.

Katz, David. "Yabby You: The Prophet Speaks." *The Beat* vol. 14, no. 2 (1995).

Matthews, Bunny. "Art Neville." *Offbeat* Feb. 2007.

Matthews, Bunny. "The Metric System." *Wavelength* April 1989.

Miller, Jim. "Master of the Melodica." *Newsweek* 19 Oct. 1981.

Palmer, Robert. "Ringing Changes on Jamaican Reggae." *New York Times* 26 Apr. 1981.

Samuels, Shephard H. "Aaron Neville." *Wavelength* July 1981.

Scheiner, Matt. "Yabby You's Not Forgotten." *Global Rhythm* Mar. 2007.

Sinclair, John. "The Nevilles Come Home." *Wavelength* May 1989.

Stein, Rikki. "A Remembrance." *Observer* 12 Aug. 1997.

Stein, Rikki. "Black President." *Straight No Chaser* no. 43 (Autumn 1997).

Thomas, J. C. "Sun Ra's Space Probe." *Down Beat* 13 June 1968.

Townley, Ray. "Behold my house of light is said to be a house of darkness." *Down Beat* 10 May 1973.

Liner Notes

Barrow, Steve. *Deliver Me from My Enemies* (Blood & Fire BAFCD 051), 2006.

Barrow, Steve. *Jesus Dread* (Blood & Fire BAFCD 021), 1997.

Barrow, Steve. *King Tubby's Prophecy of Dub* (Blood & Fire BAFCD 007), 1994.

Davis, Francis. *Jazz in Silhouette* (Evidence ECD 20012-2), 1991.

DiLiberto, John. *Lanquidity* (Evidence ECD 22220), 2000.

DiLiberto, John. *Sound Sun Pleasure* (Evidence ECD 22014-2), 1991.

Grass, Randall. *Beware Dub* (ROIR RE 188), 1994.

Hawke, Harry. *El Rockers* (Pressure Sounds 29), 2000.

Litweiler, John. *Sun Ra Visits Planet Earth/Interstellar Low Ways* (Evidence ECD 22039-2), 1992.

Nathan, David. *Live At Town Hall* (EMI 7243 4 725 15 28), 2004.

Sounds, King. *Deliver Me from My Enemies* (Vivian Jackson LP), 1977.

Szwed, John F. *The Magic City* (Evidence ECD 22069), 1992.

Szwed, John F. *The Singles* (Evidence ECD 22164-2), 1996.

Internet Sources

Campbell, Robert L., with additions by divers hands. "Sun Ra Discography: LPs, CDs, issued cassettes, and singles." www.dpo.uab.edu~moudey/discintr.htm.

"Charles Neville" Digital interviews. Ross Gita Communication, 2003. www.digitalinterviews.com/digitalinterviews/views/neville.shtml.

Christiansen, Thor. "Swept Away: Cyril Neville Still Angry in Katrina Aftermath." Originally published by the *Dallas Morning News*. www.cubanow.net.

Deagon, Andrea. "Dancing the Eternal Image: Visual and Narrative Archetypes." people.uncw.edu/deagona/raqs/articles.

DJ Nouns, Pady, and Slim Jah. "Yabby You Live in Concert." articles.dubroom.org/233.htm.

Dorrell, David, interviewer. "BPM at the Dub Club." Early 1990s. www.youtube.com/watch?v=F9YoO6YARR8.

Endo, Toshiyo. "Discography of Fela Anikulapo-Kuti (Oct. 15, 1938–Aug. 2, 1997)." //biochem.chem.nagoya-u.ac.jp~endo/EAfela.html.

Neville, Cyril. "Cyril Neville Talks about Big Chief Jolly." Video. Cultural Exchange Project/ Living Folklore Project. August 2004. www.culturecollective.org.

Nupie, Roger. "Dr. Nina Simone: Official Discography." www.ninasimone.com/discography/htm.

"Rockers' Sounds 'Cross Town." Originally published in *New Musical Express*, 1986. www.uncarved.org/dub/pablo/html.

Salimpour, Suhaila. "I Remember Nadia." www.therealsuhaila.com/articles.

Sun Ra, et al. "An Interview with Sun Ra." Interview by Francis Davis in Philadelphia. Slought Foundation Online Content. 1990. www.slought.org.

Videos

Farrah, Ibrahim. Unreleased videotape interview of Nadia Gamal, circa 1981.

Ibrahim Farrah Presents the Nadia Gamal Dance Workshop. Dir. Ibrahim Farrah. Hollywood Music Center, 2007.

The Legend. Dir. Frank Lord. DVD, Quantum Leap, 1999.

The Magic Sun. Dir. Phill Niblock. Music Video Distributors, 2005.

Music Is the Weapon. Dir. Jean-Jacques Flora and Stephane Tchaigadjieff. Universal, 2003.

Nina Simone: Live at Montreux 1976. Dir. Raymond Jaussi. DVD, Eagle Eye Media, [YEAR].

Nina Simone: Live at Ronnie Scott's. Dir. Steve Cleary. DVD Waldham Films, 1985.

Sun Ra: A Joyful Noise. Dir. Robert Mugge. Winstar Home Entertainment, 1989.

Sun Ra Arkestra: Live at the Palomino. Transparency, [YEAR].

Sun Ra: Cry of Jazz. Dir. Edward Bland. Quantum Leap, 2004.

Sun Ra: Space Is the Place Dir. John Coney. Plexifilm, 2003.

Audio Recordings

Ra, Sun. *The Creator of the Universe*. Transparency 0301, 2008.

Interviews

Anikulapo-Kuti, Fela. Telephone interview. May 1986.

Fraser, Neil. Telephone interview. 2007.

Higgins, Joan. Negril, Jamaica. May 2007.

Jackson, Vivian. Vere, Clarendon, Jamaica. May 2007.

Marley, Bob. Philadelphia. November 1979.

Neville, Aaron. Philadelphia. Fall 1983.

Neville, Art. New Orleans. May 1983.

Neville, Charles. New Orleans. May 1983.
Neville, Cyril. New Orleans. May 1983.
Pablo, Augustus. Philadelphia. December 1985.
Ra, Sun. Philadelphia. 1979.
Saretta, Phyllis. New York. 2007 and 2008.
Steffens, Roger. Telephone interview. April 2008.

Selected Discography

Some of the artists discussed in this book have vast catalogues; others' are surprisingly meager, given their importance. For artists with limited catalogues, I have listed virtually everything that is readily available by them. For those with huge catalogues, I have selected releases that I feel convey the essence of the artist and that illuminate different facets of their artistry.

Nina Simone

There is very little that Nina Simone recorded that is not worth hearing. She was such a powerful and creative performer that even her lesser performances, usually a result of working with lesser material, have interesting or expressive elements.

Somewhat overlooked these days is *Little Girl Blue* (Fuel CD 302 061 544 21), her stupendous, jazzy 1958 debut. This reissued version includes a few contemporaneous bonus tracks not on the original version. Highlights include her original versions of "I Loves You Porgy," "Love Me or Leave Me," "Don't Smoke in Bed," and "My Baby Just Cares for Me," all signature songs. From 1959 through 1992 she was astonishingly prolific, on three successive labels: Colpix, Phillips, and RCA. The cream of these three eras can be found on three superlative anthologies: *Anthology: The Colpix Years* (Rhino R2 725 67), which features a lot of great live material (five of her ten Colpix albums were live recordings); *Four Women: The Phillips Recordings* (Verve 440 065 021 2), a four-disc set including all of her recordings for the label during the years 1964 through 1967—arguably her peak period—with such classics as "Mississippi Goddam," "I Put a Spell on You," "See Line Woman," and "Four Women"; and *The Essential Nina Simone* (RCA 07863 66307 2), which delivers many of the highlights of her more pop-oriented tenure at RCA, including "To Be Young Gifted and Black," the sexy "I Want a Little Sugar in My Bowl," the great blues "In the Dark," and "Ain't Got No/I Got Life," from the musical *Hair*.

Unlike many artists, Nina Simone in live performance equaled, and often surpassed, her studio recordings. Her spontaneity, emotive ability, and charged relationship with her audiences frequently led to magic moments. *Nina Simone Live at Town Hall* (EMI 7243 4 73215 2 8) documents her 1959 breakthrough concert in

New York City. It is highlighted by her interpretations of such traditional material as "Black Is the Color of My True Love's Hair" and "Cotton-Eyed Joe," as well as Billie Holiday's "Fine and Mellow." *Live at the Village Gate* (Collectibles Col-CD 5438) captures her in a more intimate setting with a stunning, hypnotic performance of "House of the Rising Sun," cut before the Animals' hit version and around the same time as Bob Dylan's version on his debut album. Another standout is her version of the African song "Zumbi."

A studio album worth seeking out is *Nuff Said* (Sony/BMG 82876, import), a mixture of live recordings and studio cuts. It includes the electrifying "Why? (The King of Love Is Dead)" as well as the excellent "Backlash Blues," "Ain't Got No/I Got Life," and "Sundays in Savannah." The often underrated 1978 album *Baltimore* (Legacy/Epic ZK 57906) finds her in perhaps the glossiest setting of her career; but the material, including her tart reading of the title track (a Randy Newman composition), is choice.

Finally, an extraordinary box set, *To Be Free* (Sony Legacy 711009), attempts to give a comprehensive overview of Nina's career in the course of three audio CDs, one DVD, and an extensive booklet with rare photos and commentary. The CDs feature a high proportion of great live recordings, including eight previously unreleased tracks, but it is the DVD, which includes a previously unreleased 1970 documentary highlighted by great performance footage, that makes this a "must have" for Nina fans.

Fela Anikulapo-Kuti

During his 1970s peak, Fela was churning out up to four albums a year, though most featured only two long (up to twenty minutes) cuts. His recording career can be sorted into three periods: his pre-Afrobeat and early Afrobeat period from 1964–72, where his recordings tended to be shorter, since they often were released as singles; his classic period from 1972–80, when his Afrobeat was most powerfully propulsive, with tracks running ten to twenty minutes; and his Egypt '80 period, which ran from 1981 to the end of his life and generally featured a slower, more meditative style on even longer recordings. Most of his catalogue has been handily reissued on a series of "two-fers," which combine two albums' worth of music, sometimes with bonus tracks.

You can hear the pre-Afrobeat Fela on *Koola Lobitos 1964–1968/The Los Angeles Sessions 1969* (Wrasse 054), which presents Fela's jazz/highlife experiments with his first band, Koola Lobitos, and then the nascent Afrobeat he recorded with his band during their 1969 sojourn in the States, both of mainly historical interest. *Live with Ginger Baker* (Wrasse 055) captures him in 1971, at the peak of his early phase, showing his James Brown influence effectively on "Black Man's Cry." *Roforofo Fight/Fela Singles* features some of his most distinctive early work, including "Roforofo Fight,"

"Go Slow," and "Trouble Sleep Yanga Wake Am." *Open and Close/Afrodesia* (Wrasse 044) collects some of his most accessible early work, including the hits "Don't Gag Me" and "Chop and Quench"; Tony Allen's drumming on "Open and Close" is stupendous. *Gentleman/Confusion* (Wrasse 069) is essential; "Gentleman" is a masterpiece of straightforward Afrobeat power.

Zombie (Wrasse 048), one of his most celebrated recordings, which was banned in Nigeria on its 1976 release, epitomizes Fela's classic period of powerful grooves and hard-hitting social commentary. *Shuffering and Shmiling/No Agreement* (Wrasse 072) juxtaposes one of his most complex compositions in "Shuffering and Shmiling" with perhaps his most straightforward funk recording in "No Agreement."

The Egypt '80 sound reached another kind of peak in 1989 with the release of two albums, collected on *Beasts of No Nation/Overtake Don Overtake Overtake* (Wrasse 052). On CD, each of these moody, slow-building tracks clocks in at around thirty minutes each!

There are literally dozens of great Fela albums and in his entire discography only a few, such as *Teacher Don't Teach Me Nonsense* and *I Go Shout Plenty*, are relatively dull and best avoided.

Sun Ra

Sun Ra's music is infinite. Proof of this is found in the more than one hundred albums he released during his lifetime, which includes a staggering variety of music, but also in the fact that Sun Ra albums continue to surface years after his passing. This is a result of both the extreme rarity of some of albums released during his lifetime as well as Sun Ra's habit of recording relentlessly, not only in studios but also at live performances, at rehearsals, and even in hotels. It is an impossible task to convey the essence of Sun Ra in ten albums or less, so this selection is bound to be arbitrary, given the extreme diversity of his work. This list includes some acknowledged classics as well as some examples of the diverse directions he pursued.

Supersonic Jazz (Evidence ECD 22015-2), recorded in 1956, is an early high point that captures the Arkestra delivering the sound of a hard-bop big band stretching toward uncharted rhythmic and harmonic arenas. *The Magic City* (Evidence ECD 22069), recorded in 1965, is widely considered one of Sun Ra's masterpieces. The sprawling title composition, which is symphonic, even programmatic in feel even though it lacks clear thematic structure, relates more to composers such as Stravinsky, Webern, and Schoenberg than to jazz. *The Heliocentric Worlds of Sun Ra Volume One and Volume Two* (ESP Disk 4026), originally issued as two separate albums in 1965 and 1966, respectively, have been issued together, though this double-CD version may be out of print now. The two albums, available as single CDs (ESP Disk 114 and 117, respectively), operate in a similar realm to *The Magic City* but are even more abstract and challenging. *Atlantis* (Evidence ECD 22067-2) offers several short, quirky, rhythmic, small-group recordings, emphasizing electric keyboards, that are unlike anything else in Sun Ra's catalog. On the other hand, *Space Is the Place* (Impulse IMPD-249), from 1972, is dominated by the hypnotic twenty-plus-minute African-inflected groove of the title track with the chanted title phrase. *Lanquidity* (Evidence 22220-2), from 1978, has been misleadingly characterized as Sun Ra's disco or funk album; nonetheless it is fairly groove-oriented, highly accessible and enjoyable.

One of the best ways to appreciate Sun Ra's utter uniqueness is to listen to one of his few solo piano recordings. *Monorails And Satellites* (Evidence ECD 20013-2) delivers a selection of eight original compositions while *Solo Piano Recital: Teatro La Fenice Venizia* (Golden Years of New Y 21, import), recorded in Italy, tackles such standards as "St. Louis Blues" and "Take The A Train," as well as originals. Other dimensions of Sun Ra can be seen on *The Singles* (Evidence CD 22164-2), which collects Sun Ra's productions of doowop, blues, and R&B artists of varying but often interesting quality, plus a number of Arkestra recordings spanning twenty-odd years. *Strange Strings* (Atavistic Records ALP 263) is the infamous circa 1966–67 recording on which Sun Ra had his musicians utilize newly-bought instruments from Asia, Africa, and the Middle East, which they did not know how to play, with surprisingly good results. The CD also includes "Squeaking Door," which is—you guessed it!—Sun Ra playing a squeaking door! The recently released *Creator of the Universe* (Transparency 0301), a two-disc set, presents a lecture he gave at the University of California at Berkeley in 1971 on one disc and a contemporaneous live performance from San Francisco on the other.

Bob Marley

Bob Marley, whose recording career stretched from 1962 to his death in 1981, is another highly prolific artist. Virtually everything, with the exception of some demos and crossover experiments, is worth hearing. Every one of the ten albums released by Island Records during his lifetime, with the exception of the live double album *Babylon by Bus* (Island 314 548 900) (which does not hit the heights of an earlier live recording from the London Lyceum), is superlative. Only the posthumous Island album *Confrontation* (Island 314 548 903-2), which Bob did not live to complete, falls below that standard, although it contains such gems as "Buffalo Soldier."

The best of his earliest recordings with the original Wailers, including their first Jamaican hits in the ska era (made from 1964–66 for Coxsone Dodd's Studio One label), are nicely anthologized in *Bob Marley and the Wailers: One Love* (Heartbeat HB 111/112). Some of the best of the Wailers' transitional period from 1966–72—the rock steady and early reggae years—can be found on *The Complete Wailers 1967–1972 Part I* (JAD CD 1062), with such lesser-known highlights as the nearly a capella "Selassie Is the Chapel," "Black Progress," and "Nice Time," as well as some of their

Leslie Kong–produced hits. Many Wailers fans point to their two Lee Perry–produced collections *African Herbsman* (Trojan CD 803 99) and *Soul Rebels,* reissued as *Rasta Revolution* (Trojan CD 0676 90201 2), from 1971 and 1972 respectively, as their greatest work. The combination of Perry's rhythms and musical sense with the Wailers' matchless harmony singing and some of their greatest material is hard to beat. *African Herbsman* is the earthier of the two, with such key tracks as "Small Axe," "Trench Town Rock," "400 Years," "Kaya," and "Duppy Conqueror," many of which would be rerecorded in succeeding years. *Rasta Revolution* has a spacey, often haunting atmosphere, especially on such hypnotic numbers as "Try Me," "Cornerstone," "Rebels Hop," and "Soul Rebel."

Catch a Fire (The Deluxe Edition) (Island 3124548 635 2) is the Wailers' 1973 international debut, presented here in two versions, the original but previously unreleased Jamaican recording and the internationally released version with overdubs of guitar and keyboard by rock musicians (which, oddly enough, do not detract). More than any other album, *Catch a Fire* captures the original Wailers as a band. *Natty Dread* (Island 314 548 895 2) marks the transition from the original Wailers to Bob Marley with the I-Three backing vocalists. *Natty Dread* is perhaps the most relentlessly political of Bob Marley's albums, with such songs as "Dem Belly Full," "Three O' Clock Road Block," and "Revolution," and the band has become a well-tuned machine. *Live* (Tuff Gong 314 548 896 2) captures the transcendent concert at the Lyceum in London that announced a new international superstar. Drawing mainly on material from *Natty Dread* and *Burning,* it offers the definitive version of "No Woman No Cry." *Exodus (The Deluxe Edition)* (Island 314 586 408 2) is a collection that brings together spiritual and romantic threads of Bob's music in sublime style with the unstoppable title track and such tuneful crossover hits as "Three Little Birds" and "Is This Love." This edition includes a second disc of cuts from a 1977 Rainbow Theater concert plus contemporaneous Lee Perry–produced 12" singles "Punky Reggae Party" and "Keep on Moving." *Survival* (Island 314 548 901), released in 1979, is another very political album, but politics has never sounded so catchy on such songs as "Zimbabwe," "Survival," and "So Much Trouble in the World."

In general, the studio albums Bob Marley made for Island are so strong that it is pointless to buy compilations of this period. An exception is the four-CD box set *Songs of Freedom* (Island 314 512 280 2), which stretches from "Judge Not," Bob's very first recording, through "Redemption Song," one of his last great recordings. In between are many excellent rare Jamaican singles, such as "Hypocrites," "Jah Live," "Screwface," "Craven Choke Puppy," and "Smile Jamaica."

Augustus Pablo

Augustus Pablo is an artist whose recordings have often been fleetingly available or available only in limited quantities through grassroots outlets. Only a handful of his albums have been relatively continuously available during the past twenty-five years.

This Is Augustus Pablo (Heartbeat CDHBEA 34), his first album, features one of his early hits, "Pablo in Dub," as well as "Dub Organizer," a key composition. It does not, unfortunately, have his first big hit, "Java." *Original Rockers* (Greensleeves GREW 8) offers a great selection of his seminal early productions, including the immortal "Cassava Piece," "Up Warieka Hill," and "Rockers Dub." *King Tubby Meets Rockers Uptown (The Deluxe Edition)* (Shanachie SH 45059) presents this preeminent dub classic along with four extra related tracks drawn from rare singles. *East of the River Nile (The Deluxe Edition)* (Shanachie SH 45051) is Pablo's finest instrumental, as opposed to dub, album; this edition includes six rare related tracks, including the original version of the title track. *King David's Melody (The Deluxe Edition)* (Shanachie SH 45064) may be Pablo's second greatest instrumental album, offered here with four bonus tracks. *Blowing with the Wind* (Greensleeves GREW 149), released in 1990, is Pablo's finest late-period album, an interesting mix of acoustic instruments, unique textures, and digital rhythms. *El Rockers* (Pressure Sounds PSCD 29) is a fascinating collection of mostly rare singles related to the tracks on *King Tubby Meets Rockers Uptown* and *Original Rockers*; many are the full instrumental versions of dubs on *Rockers Uptown* or else different versions of cuts from these albums.

Quite a number of compilations of Pablo's productions, including his productions of singers and deejays, are intermittently available. *The Rockers Story: The Mystic World of Augustus Pablo* (Shanachie SH 45068, box set) is this author's attempt to give a comprehensive, multidimensional overview of Pablo's artistry as composer, producer, instrumentalist, and artist: four CDs cover the breadth of his career, including his productions of singers; a DVD presents rare performance video of Pablo.

The Neville Brothers

The problem for the Neville Brothers, as one of the world's greatest live bands, has always been the difficulty of capturing their magic in the recording studio. As a result, their discography is extremely patchy. Their second album, *Fiyo on the Bayou* (A&M CD 4866 DX1564), from 1981, is enjoyable—with solid versions of the title track (a Meters tune), "Brother John," and "Iko Iko"—but something about the production seems freeze-dried. They finally got it right in 1989 on the Daniel Lanois–produced *Yellow Moon* (A&M CD 5240), which balances such standout originals as "My Blood," "Yellow Moon," and "Sister Rosa" with luminous covers of "With God on My Side" and "A Change Is Gonna Come," all tied together with Lanois' subtle electronica. *Brother's Keeper* (A&M 75021 53212 2), the followup, has a similar feel and includes the standout "Brother Jake." The remainder of their nineties output is hit-and-miss, but 2004's *Walking in the Shadows of Life* (Back Porch/EMI 72435

70989 22) is one of their most funk-oriented outings and, but for the claustrophobic production and overuse of programmed drums, could have been a triumph.

Not surprisingly, some of their best recordings are live. *Nevillization: Live at Tipitina's Vol. 1* and *Vol. 2* (Spindletop—out of print) was originally issued as two separate albums, each recorded in 1982 at Tipitina's. They capture the omnidirectional excitement of their sets at the absolute peak of their Tipitina's sojourn. The original albums have been reissued in various forms; some of them, such as *Live at Tip's* (Rhino), lack some of the tracks from the original two albums. The best bet is try to find the original two volumes, which are sometimes available on the Internet. *The Wild Tchoupitoulas* (Mango 162 539 2) is the Nevilles' collaboration with their uncle, Big Chief Jolly, and his Mardi Gras Indian gang, along with the Meters. It is a stone classic, as it takes such traditional Indian tunes as "Meet Me Boys on the Battlefront" and "Big Chief Got a Golden Crown," along with Cyril Neville's magnificent "Brother John," and fleshes them out with true harmony choruses, rather than chants, and Caribbean-inflected rhythm tracks.

Though most Neville Brothers compilations are unsatisfying, *Treacherous: A History of the Neville Brothers* is useful, as the first disc includes early singles by Art and Aaron. Included also are the three best tracks from the group's spotty eponymous debut album as well as the great "Hate Fear Envy and Jealousy" from *Nevillization Vol. I*. Much of Aaron Neville's recent solo career has been beautifully sung, homogenized adult pop, but his gospel albums are worth checking out. A special treat, if you can find it, is *Orchid in the Storm* (Hyena 9306), a beautiful set of fifties harmony-group and pop ballads led by Aaron's heavenly singing over very spare backing.

Yabby You

Yabby You should be as well known internationally as roots reggae icons Culture and Burning Spear but, because he rarely toured and most of his recordings have been only intermittently available, he remains obscure. Unfortunately, it seems unlikely that this situation will change, because Blood and Fire, the UK reggae reissue label that has done much to keep his recordings in the public eye during the past decade, may have gone out of business—and thus their titles listed here will go out of print. *Jesus Dread* (Blood & Fire BA FACD 021) is indispensable, a two-CD set that presents the entire *Conquering Lion* album, Yabby's debut and a seminal roots reggae work, plus rare deejay and dub versions of its tracks, along with most of his second album, *Walls of Jerusalem,* and a number of rare singles from that time period. *Deliver Me from My Enemies* (Blood & Fire BAFCD 051) is a beautifully recorded, accessible reggae classic; this edition includes several rare singles. *Fleeing from the City* (Shanachie 43026) is Yabby You's splendid 1983 "comeback" album, recorded after several years of inactivity. Though out of print, copies can be found on the Internet.

Prophecy of Dub (Blood & Fire BAFCD 007) features the immortal King Tubby's powerful dub versions of tracks from *Conquering Lion* and is one of Tubby's best dub sets. The rare *Beware Dub* (ROIR RE 188), currently out of print, is one the most satisfying dub albums ever made, as it features atmospheric dubs of a variety of Yabby You productions. *Dub It to the Top* (Blood & Fire BAFCD 038) is another highly enjoyable selection of dubs of Yabby's productions of both instrumental and vocal artists, notably Michael Prophet. *Yabby You Meets Mad Professor and Black Steel in Ariwa Studio* (Ariwa ARICD 083) is a 1993 recording, Yabby's most recent album release. Though patchy, it has enjoyable moments.

Nadia Gamal

Given Nadia Gamal's stature in the Middle East as a famous dancer and film actress, it is hard to believe that there is so little visual record of her forty years of perform-ing. Unfortunately, most of what is commercially available offers only a glimpse of her prodigious talent and charisma. Some of the films in which she performed as a dancer may be available on DVD in the Middle East, but I have only occasionally seen one, *Mawwal* (for this, try www.aramovies.com). A couple of clips from her early Egyptian films may be found by using the "search" function on the YouTube home page (www.youtube.com).

The best commercially available performance by Nadia is found on the DVD *Ibrahim Farrah Presents Rare Glimpses Vol. 1: Dances from the Middle East* (Phyllis Saretta) which is a one-hour compilation of rare Middle Eastern dance clips, high-lighted by an excellent, though somewhat theatrical, Oriental dance performance by Nadia Gamal, shot in a studio in Lebanon in 1971 by Bobby Farrah. A second, more powerful Oriental dance performance by Nadia was shot by him at the same time, as well as Bedouin and balady dance sequences; the only way to see these is to go to the Jerome Robbins Dance Division of the New York Public Library, located at Lin-coln Center. *Rare Glimpses*, is available only from Phyllis Saretta (Phaedra@phaedra-dance.com). It also contains the first known film footage of an Oriental dancer, shot in 1897 by Thomas Edison, as well as great footage of Bedouin gypsies in Lebanon and an authentic guedra (trance dance) from Morocco. A second volume is planned, which reportedly will include one more clip of Nadia Gamal.

Nadia Gamal: The Legend (Hollywood Music Center DVD 8800) presents the only full -length cabaret performance of Nadia Gamal on video. Shot in the late Eighties in a Beirut nightclub, Nadia is accompanied by her long-time percussionist, Setrak Sarkissian, as well as an orchestra. While it is a good performance, due to the setting and camera work, its ultimate impact is more entertaining than transcen-dent. Ibrahim Farrah Presents Nadia Gamal Dance Workshop (Hollywood Music Center HMC-DVD 9565) presents ninety minutes of the dance workshop Nadia gave in New York at Bobby Farrah's behest in 1981. This will be of interest mainly to dancers.